CYRANO DE BERGERAC
AND THE
POLEMICS OF MODERNITY

❧

CYRANO DE BERGERAC
AND THE
POLEMICS OF MODERNITY

❧

Erica Harth

❧

Columbia University Press
New York and London
1970

This study, prepared under the Graduate Faculties of Columbia University, was selected by a committee of those faculties to receive one of the Clarke F. Ansley awards given annually by Columbia University Press.

Erica Harth is Assistant Professor, French literature, at Columbia University.

PQ
1793
H3

ACKNOWLEDGMENTS

I would like to express my appreciation to all those whose help made this book possible. To my teacher and sponsor of the original dissertation project, Professor Otis E. Fellows, I extend my warmest thanks for the many pleasurable hours of thought-provoking discussion, invaluable guidance, and advice, which he offered me with unfailing patience. I am extremely grateful to Professor Nathan Edelman for his indispensable criticisms and suggestions, the great amount of time and care he took with the text, and his kind encouragement. The scrupulous readings of Professor Donald M. Frame, Professor Lawton P. G. Peckham, and Professor Joseph F. Bauke were of considerable help to me in preparation of the manuscript. Special thanks are due to Professor Marjorie Hope Nicolson, whose works have provided me with a rich source of material and ideas. I am very thankful for the assistance lent to me by Professor Pierre Horn in the preparation of the translations of quoted material. I am indebted to Professor James A. Coulter and Professor Seth L. Schein for their help with certain classical references.

02727

ACKNOWLEDGMENTS

Mrs. Edna B. White's excellent advice and moral support were of much value to me in writing the book. I am particularly grateful to Mr. Alan Scribner for his perspicacious reading of the text and his constructive criticisms.

At the Columbia University Press, I am very appreciative of the cooperation of Mr. Harry Segessman and Miss Naomi Aschner. Miss Aschner's conscientious work on the manuscript greatly facilitated its publication.

I wish to thank the following publishers for permission to quote selections from their publications: Stanford University Press, *The Complete Essays of Montaigne,* translated by Donald M. Frame; Harvard University Press, *The Great Chain of Being,* by Arthur O. Lovejoy; The Clarendon Press (Oxford), Lucretius, *On the Nature of Things,* translated by Cyril Bailey; The Trustees of The Smith College, "The Defense of Galileo of Thomas Campanella," translated and edited by Grant McColley, in *Smith College Studies in History,* Vol. XXII.

Erica Harth

New York, New York
October 1969

❧

CONTENTS

꧁꧂

INTRODUCTION

When the "new authors" were to be summoned forth for questioning in Gabriel Guéret's *Guerre des autheurs anciens et modernes* (1671), it was Cyrano de Bergerac who was called first.[1] Thus was Cyrano judged, by a man roughly his contemporary, to be a fitting head of the "moderns." Although critical perspective on the battle figuring in the title of Guéret's work has been greatly altered by the events of the nearly three hundred years since its publication, it is still justifiable to consider Cyrano de Bergerac one of the first of the "moderns."

Cyrano's death in 1655 preceded by some years the most dramatic scenes in the Quarrel between the Ancients and the Moderns. Charles Perrault did not begin his impassioned public defense of the Moderns until 1687 with the publication of his *Siècle de Louis le Grand*, followed by the *Parallèle des Anciens et des Modernes* (1688–1696). Fontenelle's decisive *Digression sur les anciens et les modernes* did not appear until 1688. The dispute over Homer between Madame Dacier and Houdard de La Motte erupted only at the end of the seventeenth century, and Swift did not complete his *Battle of the Books* until 1704.

Although the formal Quarrel is remembered chiefly as a brilliant spate of literary thrusts and parries, its broader implications must not be forgotten. They have been explored by Hippolyte Rigault and Hubert Gillot,[2] whose works make it apparent that not only the belles-lettres, but also profound philosophical questions, were at stake in the Quarrel. The underlying issues, ultimately more significant than the literary garb in which they were clothed, had been sources of discomfiture for a long time. With the crystallization of these issues by the Copernican revolution and the new astronomy, the crucial intellectual phase which provided the prelude to the Quarrel was initiated. Cyrano's works traversed this period. They are among the most illustrative of its temper and of what it heralded for succeeding generations.

In the fundamental conflict of the Quarrel between the principles of authority and progress, authority was represented not only by the masters of classical antiquity but also by scholasticism and the Judaeo-Christian religious heritage.[3] Francis Bacon's Idols were not to remain intact for long. Ready targets for the iconoclasm of the eighteenth-century *philosophes*, they had already been considerably dented by the seventeenth-century *libertins*. But caution was the rule in the age of Richelieu, Mazarin, and Louis XIV, and the *libertins* were not in reality as free as their name would imply. Such open expression of revolt against established religion and authority as characterizes the works of the *philosophes* was not advisable in Cyrano's time. In 1624 the *parlement* of Paris had condemned several professors' opinions contradicting Aristotelian doctrine and had prohibited the further teaching of ideas not in conformity with the ancient, approved authors.[4] The history of Galileo's difficulties with the papal office in Rome had clearly demonstrated with what reception new ideas were to be met by the Church. Consequently, the *libertins érudits*, such as Gassendi or La Mothe Le Vayer, withdrew from open combat behind the cloak of ficeism. Idol-breaking was left to the less prominent and more daring few, such as Cyrano.

The definitive elaboration of the Moderns' viewpoint, in the form of a theory of human progress, was not made until 1688, with the appearance of Fontenelle's *Digression sur les anciens et les modernes*.[5] But a prerequisite to the formulation of this doctrine, as John Bury points out, was the undermining of the role of Providence, a concept displaced in fact by the idea of progress.[6] It was Providence, Bury observes, that came under the most insistent attack by the seventeenth-century sceptics.[7] Cyrano carried this attack one vital step further. As a solution to the emergent conflict between scientific inquiry and established religion, he endeavored to remove religious considerations completely. Only by the repudiation of religious or intellectual idols, as both Francis Bacon and Descartes realized, could the way be opened to rational investigation of what William James has termed the "stubborn and irreducible facts."[8]

Idol-breaking, then, was a necessary preliminary stage in the development of the modern scientific method. In the seventeenth-century reaction against dogmatism, as Gillot has remarked, it became associated with the sceptical principle of universal doubt.[9] But the Moderns were not content with scepticism as a final philosophical stand. The *philosophes* required an outlook unfettered by metaphysics and yet relieved of the epistemological barrier that scepticism inevitably places in the path of its followers. Such an outlook is ideally found in the relativism which permeates Cyrano's works. A modified form of scepticism, it retains an iconoclastic spirit while providing the flexibility and freedom necessary to scientific examination.

As the modern scientific method is predicated on the rejection of dogmatism, so the acceptance of the idea of progress, the ultimate victory of the Moderns, is contingent upon an understanding of the value of science.[10] The diffusion of recent scientific discoveries and theories is effectively accomplished by works of popularization, a genre favored by the *philosophes*. Few of these works appeared in the seventeenth century, an age in which ponderable compendia with the generic title *Physique* abounded. Gassendi's voluminous *Syntagma philosophicum* hardly lent itself to perusal by the average layman. Cyrano's *Autre Monde*[11] is one of the first examples of scientific popularization. As Otis Fellows has noted,[12] Cyrano was not a man of science, nor was he even particularly learned. But his work served the invaluable purpose of presenting in fanciful and eminently readable form scientific and philosophical ideas of the day. Cyrano stood almost alone in his time in his acceptance of the Copernican system and of Epicurean materialism refined of the religious overtones brought to it by Gassendi. His work reveals what was in the intellectual air of the mid-seventeenth century in France and, by contrast with the works of his contemporaries, what was deliberately prevented from coming out into the open. The *Autre Monde* may thus be perceived as a gauge both of the current philosophical mood and of its author's "modernity."[13]

The various flying machines, the whimsical apparatus of Cyrano's voyages, illustrate the utilitarian spirit of the *Autre Monde*, a spirit which, according to Richard Jones, is manifested by "the craze for inventions and . . . the enthusiastic promulgation of projects."[14] The *Autre Monde* is stamped with the optimistic belief that such inventions as are described therein, although not necessarily intended as serious suggestions, yet could conceivably bring benefit to mankind.

Those distinctive features of Cyrano's work underlined by Fellows—intellectual libertinism, satirical treatment of man and society, scientific precocity[15]—coincide with the attitudes signaled by Jones as characteristic of the Moderns' criticism of traditional philosophy: (1) the "spirit of adventure," (2) the recognition of the "need of an unbiased and critical mind and freedom of thought and discussion," (3) the utilitarian standard.[16]

The adventuresome spirit of the interplanetary traveler whose wanderings lead him also into new intellectual realms, his relentless assault on tradition and authority, his delight in novel gadgets designed for man's edification—these traits of the author of the *Autre Monde* mark him as one of the earliest crusading Moderns. Breaking what Abraham Cowley called the "scarecrow deity" of authority ("To the Royal Society") has had far-reaching results, glimpses of which are easily discernible in Cyrano's writings. The relativism advocated by him, together with the scientific and epistemological theories he espoused, were to be the main contributions of the "moderns" to modernity as we conceive of it today.

BIOGRAPHICAL NOTE

On the life of Cyrano de Bergerac, the authoritative work of Frédéric Lachèvre,[17] based on an examination of original documents, has largely superseded other accounts,[18] including even the still very usable thesis by Pierre Brun.[19] Georges Mongrédien's recent study[20] adds nothing significant to the biographical information given by Lachèvre. The present review of the major facts of Cyrano's life accordingly follows Lachèvre.

Cyrano was born in 1619 Savinien de Cyrano, the fourth son of Abel de Cyrano and Espérance Bellanger, in the family's house in Paris on the rue des Deux-Portes, today known as the rue Dussoubs. The family moved shortly after Cyrano's birth to the rue des Vieux-Augustins and then left Paris in 1622 for the château of Mauvières, one of two properties[21] which Abel de Cyrano had inherited from his father, Savinien I de Cyrano. At Mauvières, Cyrano's education was entrusted to a country priest under whose tutelage was also Cyrano's future friend and apologist, Henry LeBret.

Cyrano's studies were continued at the Collège de Beauvais, on the rue Saint-Jean-de-Beauvais in Paris. Its principal since 1615 was Jean Grangier, a professor of rhetoric at the Collège d'Harcourt, of Latin oratory at the Collège de France, and undoubtedly the model for the bombastic pedant Granger in Cyrano's comedy *Le Pédant joué*.

At about the time Cyrano was finishing his studies, his father sold the properties of Mauvières and Bergerac (July 1636) and moved back to Paris to a house on the rue Saint-Jacques. Cyrano did not remain in Paris but joined the *Compagnie des Gardes*, under the command of a Monsieur de Carbon de Casteljaloux and composed almost entirely of Gascon gentlemen. If Cyrano's legendary reputation as a flamboyant swordsman has any basis in fact, it would have been during this period that he acquired dueling skill. Wounded at Mouzon in 1639 and again, in the throat, at the siege of Arras in 1640, Cyrano retired from military service to pursue an intellectual career.

Upon his return to Paris, Cyrano seems to have been associated in some way with the Collège de Lisieux. Gassendi arrived at Luillier's house in 1641 to tutor the latter's bastard son Chapelle. It is very difficult to determine exactly, and is a matter of scholarly debate, what Cyrano's relations were with Gassendi and the circle of *libertins*, both *érudits* and not, to whom he was to become a philosophical guru. There is no reason to suppose that Cyrano actually took lessons with Gassendi, or that he personally knew Molière, an alleged member of the group, whose *Fourberies de Scapin* owe such an obvious debt to the *Pédant joué*. But Gassendi's influence on Cyrano is incontestable, warranting the assumption that if Cyrano was not in fact his pupil, he at least came into indirect contact with his ideas through others who frequented him.

In 1645 Cyrano became afflicted with an unspecified disease which Lachèvre proposes was syphilis. Whatever it was, a graphic description of the ills he must have suffered is offered by Cyrano in his poem "La Maladie" (I, xliii–xlv). It was during this time, in 1645 or 1646, and not while he was a student at the Collège de Beauvais, as had been thought previously, that Cyrano composed his *Pédant joué*.[22] Upon completion of this comedy, Cyrano began work on the *Autre Monde*,[23] now and then writing various letters, including, after the outbreak of the Fronde, eight *mazarinades*.

Toward the end of 1652, Cyrano began a period of service to the duc d'Arpajon, to whom he dedicated his tragedy *La Mort d'Agrippine* and his *Oeuvres diverses*, both published in 1654. The play was performed around the end of 1653 or the beginning of 1654, probably at the Hôtel de Bourgogne. Widely judged a succès de scandale, it undoubtedly survived for only a few performances. The *Oeuvres diverses* contained Cyrano's letters (most of which were written between 1647 and 1650) and his *Pédant joué*.

In 1654 Cyrano was struck by a falling beam, initiating a long illness that was to terminate in his death fourteen months later on the 28th of July 1655. Was he the victim of an accident or some clever Jesuit skulduggery? The point has been heatedly and futilely debated by numerous scholars. Lachèvre does not even attribute his death to this mishap, but to the effects of the syphilis he had supposedly contracted earlier; however, this is nothing more than a gratuitous assumption on his part.

❦

Cyrano's pious friend LeBret had an expurgated edition of the *Estats et empires de la lune* published in 1657 under the title *Histoire comique*.[24] Until the rediscovery of the original manuscripts in the late nineteenth century, this was the only version of the *Estats de la lune* available to the general public. In Lachèvre's definitive edition of Cyrano's voyages, the text of the *Estats de la lune* is based on the two manuscript versions of Paris and Munich,[25] with the 1657 text corresponding to the manuscript variants given in the footnotes. No manuscript of the *Estats et empires du soleil* has survived. This voyage was first published in 1662 by Charles de Sercy, along with several letters, the *Entretiens pointus,* and the *Fragment de physique,* under the title *Nouvelles Oeuvres.*

1

❧

MIRACLE:
THE ATTACK

The consistent denunciation of miracles by Cyrano is one of the most original aspects of his work. A close examination of his method of assault will provide an understanding of his thinking on such basic issues as religion, sorcery, and superstition. Textual analysis of his treatment of miracles and a discussion of his contemporaries' ideas on them will reveal that Cyrano's position was distinctive.

Cyrano's attack on miracles, whether in his *Autre Monde*, his letters, or his two plays, is presented in a satirical or ironic fashion. This does not mean that his works are in themselves satires, but merely that the genre of each permits a satirical or, as in the case of *La Mort d'Agrippine*, an ironic treatment of the subject. The two voyages of the *Autre Monde* are a good example. Classified by William Eddy as extraterrestrial fantastic voyages (subdivisions of what he terms the "Philosophic voyage").[1] their form is fluid enough to include many satirical passages.[2]

Because the voyages are not strict formal satires, it is difficult to establish a consistent picture of that character whom Alvin

MIRACLE: THE ATTACK

Kernan chooses to call the satirist.[3] In the *Estats et empires de la lune,* for example, the character, Cyrano, changes drastically from the scene in the *paradis terrestre* at the beginning to the closing scenes in which he is engaged in a long colloquy with the *fils de l'hôte.* In the first scene Cyrano expresses such irreligious opinions that the saintly Hélie forbids him to eat the fruit of the *Arbre de Sçavoir* and indeed taxes him with atheism (I, 31). In the closing scenes Cyrano is the upholder of religion and morality and is shocked at the unconventional views of his host (I, 90 ff.).[4] The two contrasting attitudes presented in each scene are, of course, satiric devices, similar to the ones in Pascal's *Provinciales.* The underdog is pitted against the respectable fellow as a means of satirizing the generally accepted views of the latter. It is to be assumed that both the character Cyrano of the *paradis terrestre* scene and the *fils de l'hôte* are at once "satirists" and *porte-parole* for the ideas of the author Cyrano.

Cyrano's account of terrestrial paradise, suppressed in the 1657 printed edition of his moon voyage, departs radically from that of the Bible. The serpent, in a Rabelaisian episode, is transformed into a phallic symbol (I, 28). The fruit of the Tree of Knowledge produces not wisdom but ignorance—unless you are fortunate enough to bite through the thick outer skin (I, 29). Adam, according to Elijah, who serves as Cyrano's guide in paradise, after having been expelled from paradise, was made by God to eat the skin of this fruit so that he would not find his way back.

Il fut, depuis ce temps-là, plus de quinze ans à radotter et oublia tellement touttes choses que ny luy ny ses descendans jusques à Moyse ne se souvinrent seulement pas de la Création. (I, 29)

After this time he was to spend more than fifteen years babbling, and so completely did he forget everything that until the time of Moses neither he nor his descendants remembered even so much as the Creation.

It is to be noted that, due to the fruit's power, neither Adam nor his descendants remembered the Creation, suggesting that there elapsed a considerable period of time in which generations of men were ignorant of the Creation, a fancy which casts some doubt as to the veracity of the events in Genesis.

Elijah recounts to Cyrano his marvelous experience prompted by his consumption of a piece of the fruit which happened to lack the brain-numbing skin.

Il me sembla qu'un nombre infiny de petits yeux se plongèrent dans ma teste et je sçeus le moyen de parler au Seigneur. Quand depuis j'ay faict réflexion sur cet enlèvement miraculeux je me suis bien imaginé que je n'aurois pas pu vaincre par les vertus occultes d'un simple corps naturel la vigilance du Séraphin que Dieu a ordonné pour la garde de ce Paradis. Mais parce qu'il se plaist à se servir de causes secondes, je creus qu'il m'avoit inspiré ce moyen pour y entrer, comme il voulut se servir des costes d'Adam pour luy faire une femme, quoy qu'il peust la former de terre aussy bien que luy. (I, 29)

It seemed to me that an infinite number of tiny eyes plunged into my head and that I discovered the means of speaking to the Lord When afterwards I reflected on this miraculous translation, I thought that I would not have been able to overcome by the occult virtues of a simple natural body the vigilance of the Seraph which God ordered to guard this Paradise. But because it pleases him to use secondary causes, I believed that he had inspired me with this means of entering, as he chose to use Adam's ribs to make him a wife, even though he could have formed her of clay just as easily as he did Adam.

Instead of simply accepting his "enlèvement" as a miracle, Elijah reflects upon it, and this attitude is adopted in a similar passage by the character Cyrano. After he eats of the fruit, he finds that although the terrestrial paradise has vanished, he still remembers everything. But he finds a natural explanation for this "miracle."

MIRACLE: THE ATTACK

Quand depuis j'ai faict réflexion sur ce miracle, je me suis figuré que cette escorce ne m'avoit pas tout à fait abruti à cause que mes dents la traversèrent et se sentirent un peu du jus de dedans, dont l'énergie avoit bien dissipé les malignitez de la pelure. (I, 32)

When afterwards I reflected on this miracle, I fancied that the skin had not entirely stupefied me, because my teeth had bitten through it and had tasted some of the juice within, whose power had dissipated the malignities of the rind.

Although both Elijah and Cyrano refuse to accept a miracle without questioning, their meditations upon it differ. Elijah decides that he would not have been able to enter paradise alone, by natural or mortal means,[5] so God gave him supernatural or divine means. God also could have left the formation of Eve to natural means; he could have formed her of clay instead of creating her miraculously from Adam's rib. Why did he choose the latter way? Elijah's answer is that he prefers to use "causes secondes" or miraculous means. Therefore, Elijah, while careful to ponder and analyze the miraculous, concludes by accepting it as the effect of God's will.

Cyrano, on the other hand, reflecting on the mysterious disappearance of paradise and his equally mysterious remembrance of it, does not have recourse to God in his explanation. He could easily have said that although God banished him forever from that holy place, he yet wished him to retain a memory of it. Instead, he ascribes the preservation of his wits to a natural cause. It is Cyrano's attitude and not Elijah's which will be adopted throughout the *Autre Monde*. The rational, human explanation of miracles is found consistently in Cyrano's works.

The climax of the *paradis terrestre* scene occurs at the moment when Elijah, about to describe one of the *"assomptions"* (to the paradise in the moon) that he had mentioned to Cyrano, begins by: "Sçachés donc que Dieu. . . ." (Know then that

God. . . .) As if waiting for the word "God" as a cue, Cyrano interrupts with a humorous and totally irreverent account of the assumption of Saint John the Evangelist. His blasphemous speech moves Elijah to exile him forthwith from paradise (I, 31).

Biblical miracles are mocked throughout the *paradis terrestre* scene. There is a satirical reference to Jacob's Ladder and a parody of the story of the Flood (I, 24, 25–26), perhaps reflecting a popular belief that paradise must have been located on the moon because the floodwaters would then not have been able to reach the just inhabiting it.[6]

The satirical attack on miracles in the *paradis terrestre* scene is linked to an attack on revealed religion. Not only are the miracles of Genesis parodied, but also a doctrine as essential to the Judaeo-Christian heritage as that of Creation is questioned. Elijah accepts God's will to produce "causes secondes" as sufficient explanation of miracles, but the character Cyrano does not. And if his will does not produce miracles, which then indeed are no longer miracles at all, a serious doubt must be placed on revealed religion.

Luciano Erba, who views the *Autre Monde* as an allegorical, mystical, and magical work, finds that its most sublime episode is the *paradis terrestre* scene, which he likens to Dante's *Paradiso*.[7] Erba thus eliminates any consideration whatsoever of the satirical elements. An interpretation of this scene which similarly removes from it not only all satirical, but also all intellectual, elements is found in Edward W. Lanius's recent study.[8] The humor in the *paradis terrestre* scene, however, especially in Cyrano's version of the serpent and of the "assumptions," would be difficult to overlook. It is obvious that if the scene is satirical, it is the events of Genesis which are being satirized. Richard Aldington acknowledges Cyrano's parody of the Bible and sees in these passages the influence of the burlesque school.[9]

MIRACLE: THE ATTACK

Miracles are again put to a test in the dialogue with the *fils de l'hôte*. This time the assault on the miraculous includes a criticism of man's credulity. Cyrano has bestowed a left-handed compliment on his host's misguided intelligence: "C'est un aussy grand miracle de trouver un fort esprit comme le vostre, ensevely de sommeil que de voir du feu sans action" (I, 91). (It is just as great a miracle to find a sharp mind like yours buried in slumber as to see an inactive fire.) The host chides him for his use of the word "miracle."

Mais . . . ne déférés-vous jamais vostre bouche aussy bien que vostre raison de ces termes fabuleux de miracles? Sçachés que ces noms-là diffament le nom de Philosophe. Comme le Sage ne veoit rien au Monde qu'il ne conçoive ou qu'il ne juge pouvoir être conceu, il doibt abominer touttes ces expressions de miracles, de prodiges, d'événemens contre Nature qu'ont inventés les stupides pour excuser les foiblesses de leur entendement. (I, 91)

But . . . do you not ever banish from your lips as well as from your reason these fabulous terms of miracles? Learn that such words disgrace the name of Philosopher. Since the Sage sees nothing in the World that he does not understand or that he does not judge capable of being understood, he must abominate all these expressions—miracles, prodigies, phenomena contrary to Nature—that the ignorant have invented to excuse the weaknesses of their minds.

The philosopher-host's objection to the use of the term "miracle" is that it is an insult to human intelligence, which is self-sufficient and at least potentially capable of understanding anything without having recourse to supernatural explanations. This affirmation of the power of human reason, reminiscent of Descartes, is again found in a famous passage from the letter "Contre les sorciers": "La raison seule est ma reine, à qui je donne volontairement les mains" (II, 212). (Reason alone is my queen, to whom I voluntarily swear allegiance.) In Cyrano's world, according to John Spink, "everything can be conceived and can exist; nothing is impossible."[10] Cyrano's attitude toward human reason contrasts sharply with the fideism of most of his scholarly contemporaries, including that of his supposed teacher, Gassendi.[11]

Cyrano protests that he has seen miraculous cures with his own eyes, to which his host replies that they are caused by "la force de l'imagination" (the force of imagination) (I, 92). A sick man is not cured by prayers but by his desire to get well: "N'est-il pas bien plus vraysemblable que sa fantaisie, excitée par les violens desirs de la santé, a faict cette opération?" (I, 93). (Is it not much more likely that his imagination, stimulated by his violent desires for health, effected this task?) Imagination would here seem to include the will to recover, and in the *Estats du soleil, imagination* and *volonté* are used almost synonymously. It is, for instance, Cyrano's strong desire ("cette ardeur de ma volonté" [I, 135] [the ardor of my will]) which finally enables him to land on the sun. He describes also the influence of the imagination in attaining his goal: "Je roidis avec plus d'attention que jamais toutes les facultez de mon âme pour les attacher d'imagination à ce qui m'attiroit" (I, 135). (With more care than ever I stiffened all the faculties of my soul so as to attach them in imagination to what was pulling me.) The association of will and imagination in this context underscores the human effort in producing effects that some may presume to be miracles. It reflects Cyrano's confidence in the powers of man to do what is commonly attributed to God's omnipotence.

The most striking effect of the imagination is to be found in the scene of the *Estats du soleil* in which the sun-creatures willfully undergo several metamorphoses. The "Homme-Esprit" of the sun explains to Cyrano the role of imagination in the metamorphoses, which he might unknowingly assume to be miraculous.

MIRACLE: THE ATTACK

Mais écoute, et je te découvriray comment toutes ces métamorphoses qui te semblent autant de miracles ne sont rien que de purs effets naturels. Il faut que tu sçaches qu'estant nés habitans de la partie claire de ce grand Monde où le principe de la matière est d'estre en action, nous devons avoir l'imagination beaucoup plus active que ceux des régions opaques, et la substance du corps aussi beaucoup plus déliée. Or cela supposé, il est infaillible que nostre imagination ne rencontrant aucun obstacle dans la matière qui nous compose, elle l'arrange comme elle veut, et, devenuë maistresse de toute notre masse, elle la fait passer, en remuant toutes ses particules, dans l'ordre nécessaire à constituer en grand cette chose qu'elle avoit formée en petit. (I, 145)

But listen, and I will reveal to you how all of these metamorphoses which seem to you so many miracles are nothing but simple natural effects. You should know that being natives of the light part of this great World, where the principle of matter is to be in action, we necessarily have a much more active imagination than the inhabitants of the opaque regions, and also a much more loosely packed bodily substance. Now with this supposition it is certain that our imagination, encountering no obstacle in the matter of which we are composed, arranges this matter as it wishes, and, having become mistress of our entire mass, the imagination rearranges it, by moving all of its particles, into the order necessary to constitute on a large scale what it had formed on a small one.

Although the metamorphoses will eventually be seen as much more complex than simply effects of the will or imagination, Cyrano is here emphasizing their natural, rather than supernatural, cause. The "Homme-Esprit" replaces miracles by the power of imagination to rearrange matter. It is undoubtedly the doctors of theology to whom Cyrano is referring when he says that, owing to the explanation of the sun-creature, he was able to rid himself of certain widely accepted notions propounded by them: "Je me désabusay d'un grand nombre d'opinions mal prouvées, dont nos

Docteurs aheurtez préviennent l'entendement des foibles" (I, 145). (I was undeceived concerning a great number of poorly proved opinions with which our obstinate Doctors prejudice the intellects of the weak.) The "opinions" are evidently those supporting belief in divinely inspired miracles. Cyrano would substitute natural, materialistic, and human reasons for these opinions, which he considers merely the prejudices of the weakminded: "Je conceus . . . que cette imagination pouvoit produire sans miracle tous les miracles qu'elle venoit de faire" (I, 146). (I understood . . . that the imagination could produce without a miracle all the miracles which it had just effected.)

The theory of imagination as one of the explanations of miracles is outlined by Pomponazzi in his *De Incantationibus*. Henri Busson cites the passages from the *Autre Monde* just discussed as uses by Cyrano of Pomponazzi's theory.[12] In the passage on imagination in the *Estats du soleil*, Cyrano mentions several examples of well-known marvels having imagination as their cause. Busson sees the influence of Montaigne's essay on imagination here,[13] and Montaigne, who brings up the question of miracles not infrequently in the *Essais*, may well have served as an inspiration to Cyrano. The latter's works contain many echoes of Montaigne's judgment of miraculous effects: "Il me semble qu'on est pardonnable de mescroire une merveille, autant au moins qu'on peut en destourner et elider la verification par voie non merveilleuse." (It seems to me that we may be pardoned for disbelieving a marvel, at least as long as we can turn aside and avoid the supernatural explanation by nonmarvelous means.)[14] Montaigne, who, according to Busson, definitely does use the *De Incantationibus,* may therefore have been the source through which Pomponazzi's ideas filtered through to Cyrano, especially since by the beginning of the seventeenth century Pomponazzi's book itself was hard to find and rarely read.[15]

MIRACLE: THE ATTACK

One passage in particular in the *Estats du soleil* resembles a passage on the power of imagination in the *De Incantationibus*. When Cyrano meets Campanella he is mystified by the fact that the old philosopher can read his mind and asks him what "demon" could have given him the information. Campanella explains that there was no demon at all; the power of the imagination, based on a materialistic logic, alone accounts for the seemingly marvelous trick.

Afin de connoistre vostre intérieur, j'arrangeay toutes les parties de mon corps dans un ordre semblable au vostre; car estant de toutes parts situé comme vous, j'excite en moy par cette disposition de matière, la mesme pensée que produit en vous cette mesme disposition de matière. (I, 178)

In order to know your interior, I arranged all the particles of my body in an order similar to yours; for having a structure like your own in all parts, I provoke in myself by this arrangement of matter the same thought that is produced in you by the same arrangement of matter.

Pomponazzi attributes the influence of one person's imagination on other people to the force exerted by the "agent" which is sufficient to produce effects on one's own "passive" nature as well as similar ones on the passive nature of others. The materialistic concept of thought found in Cyrano is not, however, developed here. The active is transmitted to the passive by a sort of vapor, whereas in Cyrano the influence is made possible by the arrangement of matter alone.

Bien que ce soit par les espèces dans l'âme, par les passions en nous et dans les corps où on les trouve que se produisent ces effets extraordinaires [de l'imagination], rien n'empêche que des effets semblables soient extériorisés dans le corps d'autrui. L'hypothèse se prouve parce qu'il évident que le passif a les mêmes dispositions chez les autres qu'en nous et parfois de meilleures, et que l'agent a une puissance suffisante pour cela: les effets peuvent donc se produire chez autrui (Platon étant disposé comme Socrate, l'agent émettant une sorte de vapeur de mêmes propriétés pour l'extérieur que pour l'intérieur, les mêmes effets se produisent chez Platon *ad extra* que chez Socrate *ad intra*).[16]

Although it is by the species in the soul, by the passions in us and in the bodies where they are found that these extraordinary effects [of the imagination] are produced, nothing prevents similar effects from being exteriorized in the bodies of others. The hypothesis is proved, because it is evident that the passive has the same arrangements in others as in us, and sometimes better ones, and the agent has sufficient power for the externalization. The effects can therefore be produced in others (Plato being arranged like Socrates, the agent emitting a sort of vapor of the same properties for the exterior as for the interior, the same effects are produced in Plato *ad extra* as in Socrates *ad intra*).

A more fundamental similarity between Pomponazzi and Cyrano is to be found in one of the three reasons listed by the former for not attributing miraculous-seeming cures and other marvels to the work of demons:

Les causes naturelles nous suffisent pour expliquer ces phenomènes et il n'y a aucune raison nécessitante de les attribuer aux démons: il est donc vain d'y recourir. Il est ridicule en effet et tout à fait extravagant d'abandonner ce qui se voit, ce qui se prouve par raison naturelle pour chercher l'invisible et l'invraisemblable.[17]

Natural causes suffice to explain these phenomena, and there is no overriding reason to attribute them to demons: it is therefore futile to have recourse to them. It is in fact ridiculous and completely foolish to abandon that which can be seen and proven by natural reason to seek the invisible and the implausible.

MIRACLE: THE ATTACK

For Pomponazzi as well as for Cyrano natural causes should be sought as the source of miracles. But Pomponazzi's "natural" causes include ones not accepted by Cyrano, such as occult powers and astrological influence.[18] For Cyrano all the causes are natural or human, which means that miracles as such do not exist.

The implications of Cyrano's satirical presentation of miracles are far-reaching. In his treatment of doctrine of Creation, for instance, Cyrano goes considerably beyond mere parody. The *fils de l'hôte* expounds his ideas on the controversial problem of the origin of the world, one of paramount importance for thinkers and theologians of Cyrano's time. He begins his argument by denying Creation and ends it by denying God, in a significant progression of ideas. His primary objection to Creation is the Aristotelian *ex nihilo nihil*. In giving alternative explanations of the world's beginning, he arrives at the conclusion that God need have played no part at all.

Car dites-moy, en vérité, a-t-on jamais conceu comment de Rien il se peut faire Quelque chose? Hélas! entre Rien et un Atome seulement, il y a des disproportions tellement infinies que la cervelle la plus aigüe n'y sçauroit pénétrer. Il fauldra donc pour eschapper à ce labirinthe inexplicable que vous admettiés une Matière Eternelle avec Dieu, et alors il ne sera plus besoing d'admettre un Dieu, puisque le Monde aura peu estre sans luy. (I, 75–76)

For tell me, in truth, has anyone ever understood how from Nothing Something could be created? Alas! between Nothing and one single Atom there are such infinite disproportions that the keenest brain could not penetrate them. In order, then, to extricate yourself from this inexplicable labyrinth, you will have to admit a Matter coeternal with God, and then you will no longer need to admit a God, since the World could exist without him.

Lachèvre notes with well-placed surprise (I, 75, n. 1) Brun's comment on this passage that Cyrano avoided atheism by making matter coeternal with God. Brun's error would have been understandable had he been using LeBret's 1657 printed edition in which the last part of the quotation was omitted, but since he was using the manuscript of the Bibliothèque Nationale it is difficult to see why he chose to ignore what Weber has called the "passage de l'averroïsme à l'athéisme dans la pensée de Cyrano"[19] (transition from Averroism to atheism in Cyrano's thought) in the last clause. It is an essential transition. As a result, Cyrano dispenses entirely with Averroist solutions to the question of Creation and all compromises between Mosaic Creation and the Aristotelian concept of the eternity of the world.[20] In the opinion of the *fils de l'hôte*, once matter coeternal with God is admitted, God becomes superfluous because matter can arrange itself, and in a long passage following this one he shows how it does just that (I, 76–82). Busson remarks that Cyrano absolutely refuses to explain the origin of the world by Creation and will explain it only by natural (atomistic) causes.[21]

Running like a motif throughout the conversation with the *fils de l'hôte* is the humorous attempt of Cyrano to convert him. The consistently irreligious replies of the lunarian constitute a kind of "Profession de foi d'un libertin." His faith is not in religious doctrine and miracles, which he vehemently refutes, but in reason and common sense. Along with Creation he will reject the ideas of the soul's immortality and of resurrection, replacing them with totally materialistic explanations. He ridicules the paradoxical notion of the incorporeal soul of man leaving the body at death while the animal's corporeal soul dies with the body. And if the human soul needs the five senses to function perfectly in life, how can it function perfectly after death, when it is deprived of all of them (I, 93–94)?

Cyrano correctly deduces from the foregoing statements by the *fils de l'hôte* that the idea of resurrection is only a "chimère." The young philosopher calls it a "Peau-d'Asne" (fairy tale) and proceeds to attack it by his fable of a Christian eating a Mohammedan. What will happen to offspring of the Christian, made up of the substance of the Mohammedan, at the resurrection? Will the Mohammedan recover his body? But in that case the young Christian will not have one. If he, however, recovers his, the Mohammedan in turn will be deprived of his. God could of course create a new body for the Mohammedan, but in that case he would no longer be the same individual, since Christian doctrine affirms a man to be the unity of his body and soul. God's only recourse would be to damn and save the same man for all eternity (I, 94–95).

The outlandish dilemma posed by the *fils de l'hôte* to illustrate what he considers to be the absurdity of the resurrection is indisputably the result of materialistic thinking. Having negated the spirituality and immortality of the soul by having it be dependent on the senses, he discusses resurrection chiefly as a bodily phenomenon, which he demonstrates to be logically impossible. The materialistic account renders meaningless such ideas as damnation and salvation. The distinction between sinner and saint (he conveniently uses as examples a Mohammedan and a Christian to dramatize the differences—and the lack thereof) becomes blurred when a man is seen as no more than his material substance, composed of other material substances entirely indifferent as to moral attributes.

Cyrano had previously in the *Estats de la lune* alluded to the idea of resurrection in a materialistic fashion. The *démon de Socrate*, after a short absence, reappears to the captive Cyrano in the form of a youth. Cyrano, knowing him only as an old man, does not recognize him. The demon tells him how he was able to effect the change by resurrecting a young cadaver.

Sans estre apperçu, je m'inspiré dedans [dans le corps] par un souffle. Mon vieil cadavre tomba aussi tost à la renverse; moy, dans ce jeune, je me levé. On cria miracle, et moy, sans araisoner personne, je recourus promptement chez vostre basteleur où je vous ay pris. (I, 40)

Without being perceived, I insufflated myself inside [the body]. My old corpse immediately fell back, and I rose up in this young body. Everyone shouted "miracle," and I, without enlightening anyone, ran promptly to your mountebank, where I fetched you.

Although this resurrection may be part of the "marvelous" baggage of a fantastic voyage, Cyrano calls our attention to the fact that it is not miraculous, as the uninformed public would believe.[22] In the context of all the adventures on the moon, the young man's revivification is a marvel, but one for which a rational account can be given. The "miracle" can be reasoned out. Busson clarifies this passage by informing us that according to both Théophile Raynaud and the *Naudeana,* a certain professor of medicine at Montpellier named Saporta (d. 1605), son of Antoine who was a fellow student of Rabelais, made a public speech denying the miracle of the resurrection. The *Naudeana* goes on to mention a book in Latin by a doctor in which a rational explanation is offered for miracles of resurrection. Raynaud also states that Saporta was punished by death for his blasphemy.[23] The passage in Cyrano, according to Busson, reflects these events.[24]

Man's immortal soul is constantly the butt of mockery for the misanthropic birds in the "Histoire des Oiseaux." Busson lists five passages in the *Autre Monde* in which the soul's spirituality and immortality are denied, four of which are found in the "Histoire des Oiseaux.[25] The refusal on the part of the superior birds to grant immortality to man's soul is here part of a general debunking of man. Immortality is more directly attacked in a passage in *La Mort d'Agrippine,* also mentioned by Busson.[26]

It is, as Busson remarks, a passage stoical in tone. Agrippina depicts to Sejanus in graphically lurid terms the death awaiting him as punishment for his treason. Sejanus counters with calm denials of the soul's immortality and therefore of any reason to fear death: "De ma mortalité je suis fort convaincu; / He! bien, je dois mourir, parce que j'ay vescu" (II, 149). (Of my mortality I am convinced;/Ah well, I must die, because I have lived.) Agrippina nevertheless attempts to overwhelm him with fear in describing to him the horrors of the last moments. She concludes: "Voilà de ton destin le terme espo vantable" (This will be the frightful end of your destiny), to which Sejanus replies: "Puisqu'il en est le terme, il n'a rien d'effroyable. / La mort rend insensible à ses propres horreurs" (II, 149). (Since it is the end, it holds nothing to fear. / Death renders us indifferent to its horrors.) Death is a state of complete nonexistence: "Estois-je malheureux, lors que je n'estois pas? / Une heure après la mort, nostre âme évanouie / Sera ce qu'elle estoit une heure avant la vie" (II, 150). (Was I unhappy when I existed not? / One hour after death, our vanished soul / Will be what it was an hour before life.)

The entire passage, with its emphasis on the soul's mortality and consequently on the nothingness of death, is especially reminiscent of Lucretius,[27] a major source for Cyrano. The pronouncements of Sejanus on death, however, reveal not only the stoical spirit of the De Rerum Natura, but also an irreverence, if not atheism, which bear Cyrano's own stamp. This is particularly evident in Act II, scene iv, in which Sejanus denies the power of the gods. His dialogue with Terentius is almost comic in tone and indeed seems misplaced in a tragedy. The very frivolity of Sejanus's replies may have been a dramatic device used by Cyrano to show just how little the gods meant to the Roman reprobate. It may also have been due to the absence of classical restraint in separating genres, which was perhaps responsible for the equally misplaced monologue on death and immortality by Granger at the end of Le Pédant joué. Whatever the reason, Sejanus gives an amusing reply to Terentius's somber warning to fear the gods. Terentius admonishes: "Respecte et crains des Dieux l'effroyable tonnerre!" (Respect and fear from the Gods their dreadful thunderbolts!) Sejanus replies:

> Il ne tombe jamais en Hyver sur la terre.
> J'ay six mois pour le moins à me moquer des Dieux
> En suitte je feray ma paix avec les Cieux. (II, 120)

> They never fall on the earth in winter.
> I have at least six months to mock the Gods
> After which I will make my peace with Heaven.

Terentius again enjoins him to believe in the gods: "Qui les craint, ne craint rien." (Whoever fears them fears nothing.) Sejanus replies with an ironic play on Terentius's words, that the gods are to be counted as mere creations of man, and if they have any usefulness at all it is but to help maintain political order:

Ces beaux riens qu'on adore, et sans sçavoir pourquoy,
Ces altérez du sang des bestes qu'on assomme,
Ces Dieux que l'homme a faicts, et qui n'ont poinct faict l'homme,
Des plus fermes Estats ce fantasque soustien,
Va, va Térentius, qui les craint, ne craint rien. (II, 120)[28]

These fine nothings which we adore, without knowing why,
These beings thirsting after the blood of beasts which we fell,
These Gods which man has made, and which have not made man,
Of the strongest States a whimsical support,
Now, now Terentius, whoever fears them fears nothing.

Busson sees a strain of Machiavellianism, typical of the *libertins,* in Cyrano's works, and as an example he cites the following from Cyrano's satirical letter, the "Apothéose d'un ecclesiastique bouffon": "J'avoue que pour la manutention des Estats, il y a beaucoup de choses vraies qu'il faut que le peuple ignore, beaucoup de fausses que nécessairement il faut qu'il croie."[29] (I will admit that for the administration of States, there are many

~§ 25

true things of which it is necessary that the people remain ignorant, many false things which they must of necessity believe.)
Another example of Machiavellianism can be seen in the above-
quoted speech of Sejanus. His statement that religion can serve
to support a well-ordered society is not an attempt by Cyrano to
defend religion but a cold-blooded rational effort to find some
use for it, and in the letter quoted by Busson, Cyrano goes on to
say: "Mais nostre religion n'est pas establie sur cette maxime" (II,
167). (But our religion is not based on this principle.) He thereby indicates that this is what he, Cyrano, finds of practical value
in religion, but not religion's own account of its raison d'être
(although in Cyrano's eyes perhaps it should be).

Terentius, in the scene from *La Mort d'Agrippine,* tries in
vain to refute Sejanus's blasphemies with the traditional argument
of the harmony of the world as proof of God's existence: "Mais
s'il n'en estoit point! [des dieux] cette Machine ronde . . ." (II,
120) (But if there were none [Gods], this round Machine . . .),
but Sejanus cuts him off with his final answer: "Ouy, mais s'il en
estoit, serois-je encor au monde?" (II, 120). (Yes, but if there
were would I still be on this earth?)

Spink points out that Cyrano uses the same argument in his
letter "Contre le pédant" to prove the existence of God.[30] He notes
other inconsistencies which do not, however, modify his appraisal
of Cyrano as having "an eminently sane and courageous mind."[31]
Cyrano's argument in "Contre le pédant" seems to be mainly a
rhetorical device used in his murderous denunciation of the Jesuit.
The entire letter consists of an accumulation of insulting ex-
aggerations, not unlike those found in the *Pédant joué,* which
produce a comical impression. The passage in *La Mort d'Agrippine* should be taken more seriously.

Henry Lancaster quotes Cyrano's contemporaries Tallement
des Réaux, La Monnoye, and Guéret to demonstrate that their
reaction to the *Mort d'Agrippine* was generally shock at its im-

piety.[32] And, indeed, Gabriel Guéret, in his *Guerre des autheurs anciens et modernes* (1671) has Balzac allude thus to the reception of Cyrano's play:

Je ne parle point des impiétez qui vous sont si naturelles, et qui se rencontrent à chaque page, c'est le principal caractère de toutes vos pieces, et vous sçavez bien aussi que c'est ce qui fit deffendre vôtre [*sic*] Agrippine, qui sans trente ou quarante Vers qui blessent les bonnes Moeurs auroit diverti longtemps le Public, et tiendroit encore sa place sur le Théâtre.[33]

I will not speak of the impieties which come so naturally to you, and which are found on every page; this is the chief characteristic of all your works, and you know very well that it is what caused the censorship of your *Agrippina*, which, minus thirty or forty Lines offending good Manners, would have entertained the Public for a long time, and would still rank high in the Theatre.

La Monnoye relates in the *Menagiana* that there were shouts of protest at Cyrano's atheism from the audience when Sejanus said, "Frappons, voila l'Hostie."[34] (Let us strike, here is the *Hostie*.) The indignation may have been ill-founded, since Cyrano, perhaps employing a wily double-entendre, does use "hostie" in the sense of "victim," as Lancaster has pointed out.[35] But the audiences could perfectly well have been shocked at other passages in the play, such as the dialogue of Sejanus and Terentius on the gods. However, Lancaster feels that their reaction even to other passages was not justifiable, because Cyrano did not necessarily share the opinions expressed by Sejanus. Spink acknowledges this possibility, but ultimately rejects it.[36] Lancaster considers that since Sejanus is portrayed as a villain, his ideas could not coincide with Cyrano's.[37] Busson evidently does not agree when he comments that Cyrano was exceptional for his time in expressing the materialism found in *La Mort d'Agrippine*.[38]

The notion that Sejanus was meant by Cyrano to be a villain

of whom he disapproved is worth examining. There are several curious aspects of the play bearing on this question. Although the title is *La Mort d'Agrippine*, Agrippina herself does not die in the play. The subject of the play would seem rather to be death in general, and more specifically "la mort qu'a voulue Agrippine" (the death wanted by Agrippina). It will be remembered that she desired the death of either Sejanus or Tiberius (II, 106–107). But she constantly derides the weaknesses of Tiberius,[39] and in Act IV, scene ii, she even tells him that he is a victim not worthy of her wrath. Drawing out a dagger which she disdainfully throws at the emperor's feet, she says to him: "Mais vis en seurté, la Veufve d'un Alcide/Rougiroit de combattre un Monstre si timide" (II, 136). (But you may live in safety; the Widow of a Heracles/ Would blush to do combat with so timid a Monster.) However, if Tiberius's death is not worthy of her, Sejanus's is. At the end of the scene quoted above, in which Agrippina is unsuccessful in her attempt to humble Sejanus before his death, she finds herself concluding that he is to be admired for his conduct at his last hour:

> Je te rends grâce, ô Rome!
> D'avoir d'un si grand coeur partagé ce grand Homme;
> Car je suis seure, au moins, d'avoir vengé le sort
> Du grand Germanicus par une grande mort. (II, 150)[40]

> I render thanks unto you, O Rome!
> To have bestowed such a great heart on this great Man;
> For I am at least certain of having avenged the fate
> Of the great Germanicus with a great death.

No main character in *La Mort d'Agrippine* can really be considered likable, with the possible exception of Agrippina, who is depicted as a little too bloodthirsty for the taste of most spectators. Livia is an adulteress, the murderer of her husband and brother;

Tiberius has already turned into the cruel tyrant remembered by history, and each protagonist is plotting against the next. It would therefore seem unlikely that Sejanus was singled out to be the villain, for a villain must, after all, be contrasted with goodness, and one would have to conduct a careful search to find it in this play.[41] Sejanus shows, if anything, a courage and nobility in the face of death, recognized by Agrippina, which give him more stature than the other characters. Cyrano evidently did not intend to disparage what Sejanus represents, but rather to write a play about death and about what Cyrano himself considered a great and noble death. This is not to say that Sejanus becomes a hero,[42] but if evil has its banality so has it its originality. Viewed as a nonconformist, an evil one perhaps, but with the courage of his convictions, Sejanus is not truly villainous. It is highly probable that Cyrano did not wish to dissociate himself from the ideas expressed by his protagonist, but that he was in agreement with them.

It is precisely the expression of atheistic ideas by a character of whom the author does not disapprove that distinguishes this mid-seventeenth-century tragedy from others of the time. Lancaster has stated that Cyrano's play and Jean Magnon's *Séjanus* are identical in theme.[43] While certain aspects of the plots may be similar, the central character of each, Sejanus, retains an individual identity. Magnon's Sejanus is a real villain. He is ruthlessly ambitious, cruel, and a consummate Tartuffe in tragic guise.[44] Cyrano's Sejanus is obviously ambitious too, but he is mainly characterized by his atheistic stoicism. There is no hint in Magnon's play of irreligion on the part of Sejanus, although we might of course assume that a man so wicked could not possibly be religious. The most blasphemous lines in the play are pronounced by Sejanus to defend himself before Tiberius:

> Que le Ciel à vos pieds m'abisme d'un tonnerre
> Ou que vif devant vous, m'engloutisse la terre,
> Ou que je sois, mon Prince, éloigné de vos yeux;
> Serment bien plus sacré, que celui de nos Dieux.[45]

> Let Heaven strike me down at your feet with a thunderbolt
> Or let the earth swallow me up alive in front of you,
> Or let me, my Prince, be removed from your eyes;
> An oath much more sacred than that of our Gods.

Sejanus emits no stoical reflections upon death in this play. In contrast to the defiant fortitude with which Cyrano's Sejanus goes forth to meet his doom, Magnon's protagonist stabs himself.[46] Although Cyrano undoubtedly knew and used Tacitus, the historian's description of Sejanus seems a more fitting one for Magnon's character than for Cyrano's:

He had a body which could endure hardships, and a daring spirit. He was one who screened himself, while attacking others; he was as cringing as he was imperious; before the world he affected humility; in his heart he lusted after supremacy, for the sake of which he was sometimes lavish and luxurious, but oftener energetic and watchful, qualities quite as mischievous when hypocritically assumed for the attainment of sovereignty.[47]

Among sources for *La Mort d'Agrippine*, Brun lists *La Mort de Sénèque* by Tristan l'Hermite, to whom Cyrano pays homage in the *Estats de la lune* (I, 35–36). Here again the similarities are but superficial. Tristan's play is imbued with Christian feeling, and Seneca, while expressing stoical ideas similar to those of Cyrano's Sejanus, is a totally different figure from the crafty conspirator in *La Mort d'Agrippine*. Seneca is the embodiment of virtue, and there are definite suggestions that if he is not already a convert to Christianity, he soon will be.[48] There is no trace of the impious iconoclast Sejanus exulting in his defiance of law and tradition.

Sejanus's stoicism is not at all religious in tone; it represents the rational materialistic attitude of a mortal who accepts death as the end of both physical and psychical life. Spink's judgment of Cyrano's stand on religion applies especially to *La Mort d'Agrippine*: "Cyrano was as non-pagan as he was non-Christian. There is no trace of religious feeling in his work at all."[49]

Although it would appear that in Cyrano's "Lettre contre les sorciers" the object of the attack is witchcraft and all supposed miraculous events resulting from superstition, in reality the questions of superstition and religion are treated in conjunction with each other, and the attack is much more subtle and acrid than it would seem at first. At the outset of the letter Cyrano openly states his position against sorcery.

Non, je ne croy point de Sorciers, encore que plusieurs grands personnages n'ayent pas esté de mon advis, et je ne deffère à l'authorité de personne, si elle n'est accompagnée de raison, ou si elle ne vient de Dieu, Dieu qui tout seul doit estre cru de ce qu'il dit, à cause qu'il le dit. (II, 212)

No, I do not believe in Witches at all, even though several august personages have not shared my opinion, and I bow to the authority of no one, if it is not accompanied by reason, or if it does not come from God, God whose words alone must be believed, because it is he who utters them.

It is noteworthy that even in his opening statement Cyrano links the ideas of witchcraft and religion by modifying his rationalistic view of superstitious beliefs with a statement of faith in God. This could be construed as the type of fideistic device used by La Mothe Le Vayer or any of the *libertins érudits* often to mask what could be considered a dangerous scepticism.[50] It is more likely, however, that Cyrano makes but a feeble attempt to disguise his hypocrisy, and even goes so far, within this same letter, as to undermine his own statements of faith by extending his attack on sorcery to the province of religion.

Lachèvre appends a note to the passage just quoted (II, 212, n. 1) in which he asks us to compare it to a passage in the *Estats de la lune.* Cyrano replies to the blasphemies of the *fils de l'hôte* with an affirmation of God's omniscience: "Je n'ay rien à respondre . . . à vos arguments sophistiques contre la resurrection, tant y a que Dieu l'a dit, Dieu qui ne peut mentir." (I have nothing to reply . . . to your sophistic arguments against resurrection, since God announced it—God, who does not lie.)

Lachèvre's comparison might be valid were it not for the reply of the *fils de l'hôte*: "N'allez pas si viste, me réplicqua-t-il, vous en estes desja à 'Dieu l'a dit'; il fault prouver auparavant qu'il y ait un Dieu, car pour moy je vous le nie tout à plat" (I, 95). (Not so quickly, he replied, you have already arrived at "God has said so"; first you have to prove that there is a God, because for my part, I flatly deny it.) It is not the character Cyrano, with his statement of faith practically identical to the one found in "Contre les sorciers," who has the last word, but the *fils de l'hôte,* whose even more irreligious reply to what has been called Cyrano's "pari" (I, 95–96)[51] immediately following the above interchange ends their philosophical discussion on a note of scepticism so profound that the blasphemous *fils de l'hôte* is carried off by the devil (I, 95–96).

In offering reasons why he does not believe in witches Cyrano uses criteria for arriving at the truth about them similar to those of Gabriel Naudé in his *Apologie pour tous les grands personnages qui ont esté faussement soupçonnez de magie* (1625). René Pintard lists two ways used by Naudé to prove that great men accused of magic did not practice it: (1) explaining an apparently inexplicable fact by finding analogous situations in natural occurrences (the "scientific" method), and (2) denying any validity to the facts in question by demonstrating the unreliability of the witnesses (the "historical" method).[52] Cyrano uses the scientific method in his explanations of the witches' sabbath and of possessed persons (II, 215). He avails himself of the historical method when he expresses his doubt as to the truth of witnesses' testimony (II, 213).

After clarifying his position on the matter of the existence of witches, Cyrano discusses a much-debated historical problem of miracles described by Busson. If pagan miracles, not readily accepted by the Church, can be explained by natural causes, then the following problem arises: to be consistent, one must either hold all pagan miracles to be of supernatural origin or all Christian ones to be of natural origin.[53] Cyrano's treatment of this question is the first hint in the letter that something other than witchcraft is being attacked. He is well aware of the paradox, later to be explored in detail by Fontenelle, of ascribing natural causes to supposedly supernatural phenomena before Christ's advent and yet maintaining the existence of the supernatural after the Crucifixion. In a finely ironic passage he stresses the absurdity of this proposition. But in dealing with the historical problem of the supernatural, Cyrano does not discuss pagan miracles, except insofar as he employs the generic term "Oracles." He refers only to diabolical effects found in the Old Testament. The references to the Old Testament indicate that Cyrano, the noble prosecutor of superstition and sorcery, is stepping out of his role to point a sly finger at the Church. Yes, he asserts, I do believe in these miraculous events because the

Bible relates them. Yet his affirmation is seriously undermined by the tone of ridicule he injects in implying that it would put a great strain upon our credulity to accept the idea that all diabolical activity abruptly ceased at the advent of Christ.

Examinons donc, sans qu'il nous importe de choquer les opinions du vulgaire, s'il y a autrefois eu des démoniaques et s'il y en a aujourd'hui. Qu'il y en ait eu autrefois, je n'en doute point, puisque les Livres sacrez asseurent qu'une Chaldéenne, par art magique, envoya un Démon dans le cadavre du Prophète Samuel, et le fit parler; que David conjuroit avec sa harpe celuy dont Saül estoit obsédé et que nostre Sauveur Jésus-Christ chassa les Diables des corps de certains Hébreux et les envoya dans des corps de pourceaux. Mais nous sommes obligez de croire que l'Empire du Diable cessa quand Dieu vint au monde, que les Oracles furent estouffez, sous le berceau du Messie et que Satan perdit la parole en Bethléem, l'influence altérée de l'Estoille des trois Roys luy ayant sans doute causé la pépie. (II, 215–216)

Let us therefore examine, without caring if we shock the beliefs of the common people, if there were formerly any possessed men and if there are any today. That there were some formerly I do not doubt, since the Sacred Book assures us that a Chaldean woman sent a Demon into the corpse of the Prophet Samuel by magic arts, and made him speak; that David exorcised with his harp the demon with which Saul was obsessed, and that our Savior Jesus Christ chased the Devils from the bodies of certain Hebrews and sent them into the bodies of swine. But we are obliged to believe that the Reign of the Devil ceased when God came into the world, that Oracles were stifled by the cradle of the Messiah, and that Satan lost his speech in Bethlehem, the new influence of the Star of the three Kings having undoubtedly afflicted him with pip.

Luciano Erba has noted that Cyrano says we are *obliged* to believe in the cessation of the devil's reign, and not that he himself actually does.[54] This is an essential point which Erba mentions to demonstrate Cyrano's interest in the occult. It is evident, however, that in the context of a letter whose ostensible purpose is to attack superstitious belief, it would be inconsistent on Cyrano's part to make an about-face and suddenly declare that he believes the devil still holds sway.[55] It would appear likely that the ironic use of the word "obligez" suggests that the Church obliges us to believe no longer in pagan miracles but in its own, which is precisely the contradiction Cyrano cannot accept. In rejecting it he must leave the province of witchcraft and enter that of religion, in order to decry all miracles.

At the end of this passage he assimilates the occult with the religious in playfully endowing the star of Bethlehem with an astrological "influence" on Satan, causing him to be tongue-tied. The association of the religious and the occult is followed by a second statement of faith in which Cyrano says that he will continue to disbelieve in energumens until the Church commands him otherwise (II, 216). But the preceding passage leads one to question the sincerity of his statement. Can we suppose that a man so unprepared to accept the miracles of the Church will believe what it wants him to believe?

Cyrano continues his subtly wicked association of superstitious and religious belief when he challenges the devils to perform real miracles and not the sham which has failed to deceive him:

Si les Diables sont forcez, comme vous dites, de faire des miracles afin de nous illuminer, qu'ils en fassent de convaincants; qu'ils prennent les tours de Nostre-Dame de Paris, où il y a tant d'incrédules, et les portent sans fraction dans la çampagne Sainct-Denis danser une sarabande Espagnolle. Alors nous serons convaincus. (II, 217)[56]

If the Devils are forced, as you say, to perform miracles in order to enlighten us, let them perform convincing ones; let them take the towers of Notre-Dame de Paris, where there are so many unbelievers, and carry them without breakage to Saint-Denis to dance a Spanish saraband. Then will we be convinced.

This feat would be a real miracle, but of course such a thing has never happened, and will never happen, Cyrano implies, because real miracles do not exist. But in choosing a hypothetical "real" miracle, Cyrano seizes upon a religious symbol, the towers of Notre-Dame, and, not content to make use of them alone, places "incrédules" within their walls, thus emphasizing the element of doubt in religious matters which he wishes to convey by the very idea of such an impossible miracle.

In ridiculing the rites of excorcism Cyrano does not lose the opportunity to ridicule the rites and symbols of the Church, and so again makes obvious that his attack is not confined to witchcraft alone. The allegedly possessed person trembles at the touch of holy water; but is this water any more holy than the body into which the devil has entered? If he would suffer contact with flesh made in God's image, baptized and sanctified by holy oils, why would he recoil from water "sur laquelle on a simplement récité quelques prières" (over which a few prayers have been recited) (II, 217)? The water thus described no longer seems very holy, and Cyrano is questioning not only the existence of the devil but belief in the power of what is presumed to be sacrosanct. The questioning is extended to the cross, waved at the possessed in another attempt at exorcism. It is but a vain attempt, says Cyrano, because what after all is a cross but a length together with a width, which is found everywhere there is matter. If the energumen can see a length and a width anywhere, why present him with another (II, 218)? The target of the attack has been transferred from witches and the possessed to the object with which the devil is to be exorcised. The cross, like the holy water, is reduced from a religious symbol with miraculous power to a perfectly natural, everyday object having no special power at all to distinguish it from any other object.

The association of religious and magic rites in the "Lettre contre les sorciers" must be borne in mind when reading the last statement of faith at the end of the letter:

Ce n'est pas, comme je vous ay déjà dit, que je doute de la puissance du Créateur sur ses créatures; mais à moins d'estre convaincu par l'authorité de l'Église, à qui nous devons donner aveuglément les mains, je nommeray tous ces grands effets de magie, la gazette des sots ou le "Credo" de ceux qui ont trop de Foy. (II, 218)

It is not, as I have already told you, that I doubt the power of the Creator over his creatures; but unless I am convinced by the authority of the Church, to whom we must blindly swear loyalty, I will call all these great effects of magic the gazette of fools or the "Credo" of those who have too much Faith.

The use of the verb "devoir" here may be similar to that of the "obligez" previously discussed. Cyrano does not say that he himself possesses such blind loyalty, but only that one is obliged to have it. The religious terms "Credo" and "Foy" would again imply religious as well as superstitious belief.

Cyrano's purpose in writing this letter thus appears to be twofold. In attacking belief in witchcraft he takes a bold stand in the flamboyant period of the Loudun witches. Brun emphasizes his courage in publishing the letter, an opinion echoed by Mongrédien.[57] But his letter is preceded by such polemics against sorcery as Pomponazzi's De Incantationibus (1556), Vanini's De admirandis naturae arcanis (1616), and Naudé's Apologie pour les grands hommes accusés de magie (1625). Cyrano is much more daring in his cleverly implied criticism of divine miracles. One may justifiably wonder why the criticism in this letter is more veiled than in the Estats et empires de la *lune*, but it will be remembered that all the sections on miracles in the latter work were scrupulously deleted by LeBret from the first printed edition of 1657, and that even the expurgated version was published only after Cyrano's death. We do not know exactly when Cyrano wrote his "Lettre contre les sorciers," published in the *Oeuvres diverses* of 1654. Lachèvre believes that most of the letters date from the period 1647–1650 (I, xc), and since the *Estats de la lune* was finished at about the end of the year 1648 (I, 1), it is probable that Cyrano had at least already been working on the *Estats de la lune* when he wrote his "Lettre contre les sorciers." He may have wished to use a slightly more sober tone in a work destined for publication. In any event, the writer of the *Estats de la lune* and of the "Lettre contre les sorciers" obviously shared the same opinions, and if these are expressed in a more restrained way in the letter, it may be concluded that it was a matter of expediency.

In the *Estats du soleil* it is Cyrano himself who is accused of witchcraft, after the fictitious public has read his account of the moon voyage. His accusers ask permission of Colignac, Cyrano's friend and protector, to burn the dangerous author (I, 103). The accusers are none other than some august magistrates (I, 102)[58] who speak with the authority of the State, giving Cyrano the opportunity to scorn official recognition of sorcery: "Y a-t-il aucun Parlement qui se connaisse en sorciers comme le nostre?" (I, 102). (Is there any Parliament so knowledgeable in witches as ours?) On what basis do they accuse him? He has had suspicious communication with the moon and the *démon de Socrate.*

Comment! aveoir monté à la Lune, cela se peut-il sans entremise de. . . . Je n'oserois nommer la beste; car enfin, dites-moy, qu'alloit-il faire dans la Lune? (I, 102)[59]

—Belle demande . . . il alloit assister au sabat qui s'y tenoit possible
ce jour-la. Et, en effet, vous voyez qu'il eut accointance avec le
Démon de Socrate [sic]. Après cela, vous étonnez-vous que le Diable
l'ait, comme il dit, rapporté en ce monde? mais quoy qu'il en soit, . . .
je n'ay jamais veu de sorcier qui n'eust commerce avec la Lune.
(I, 102)

What! to have risen to the Moon, can that occur without the intervention of. . . . I dare not name the beast; for after all, tell me, whatever was he going to do in the Moon?

—A fine question . . . he was going to attend the sabbath which was
perhaps taking place that day. And, in effect, you see that he had
some acquaintance with Socrates's Demon. After that, are you surprised that the Devil brought him back to this world, as he says?
But whatever the case, . . . I have never seen a witch who did not
have some communication with the Moon.

The accusation is based on a misinterpretation, both of the
nature of Cyrano's dealings with the moon and of the démon de
Socrate. These misinterpretations may have been suggested to
Cyrano by Kepler's Dream, published in Latin in 1634, and
its attendant circumstances in which interesting parallels with
the Autre Monde may be seen.

Because of misinterpretations of the allegory in the Dream,
Kepler's mother was tried as a witch in 1621, and from 1621 to
1630 Kepler wrote 223 footnotes to the Dream in order to
explain the real meaning of the allegory.[60] Duracotus had been
thought to be Kepler, and Fiolxhilde his witch-mother. Fear of
witches was so widespread in Germany at this time that it was
no wonder his mother was subjected to the trial.[61] However, in
his notes Kepler reveals that Duracotus is meant to represent
Science and Fiolxhilde the Ignorance which gives birth to
Science.[62]

MIRACLE: THE ATTACK

The "Daemon" in Kepler's *Dream* was also misinterpreted. His explanation of its real meaning contains some striking similarities with Cyrano's *démon de Socrate*. Kepler's Daemon is from Levania, which is Hebrew for the moon.[63] Thinking that *daimon* came from the Greek *daiein*, "to know," Kepler used "Daemon" in the sense of "one who knows." His Daemon from Levania was therefore supposed to be a specialist on the moon. The capitalization of "Daemon" (note that it is capitalized in Cyrano also)[64] creates the possibility of the same misinterpretation as in the passage just quoted from the *Estats du soleil,* that is, "evil spirit" instead of the spirit of knowledge.[65] Lachèvre is of the opinion that Cyrano's demon, a commonplace of classical antiquity, was more immediately inspired by a character in *Le Page disgracié* of Tristan l'Hermite (I, 34, n. 1). This character is an alchemist not designated as a "démon" but only as a "Philosophe."[66] Any resemblance to Tristan is difficult to discern.

The confusion by the superstitious of natural science with supernatural, magical rites, described by Kepler in the beginning of his dream and elucidated by him in footnotes, occurs also in a humorous passage in the *Estats du soleil*. A group of villagers condemns a book of Descartes possessed by Cyrano as a sorcerer's manual, thus misreading Descartes in much the same way that Kepler had been misread.

Quand ils apperceurent tous les cercles par lesquels ce Philosophe a distingué le mouvement de chaque planète, tous, d'une voix, heurlèrent que c'estoit les cernes que je traçois pour appeler Belzébut. (I, 109)

When they saw all the circles by means of which this Philosopher described the movement of each planet, they all roared in one voice that I was tracing those circles to call forth Beelzebub.

The villagers are singing *Kyrie Eleison,* which reminds us of Cyrano's association of religious and superstitious belief. Their misinterpretation of Descartes's book as a handbook of magic may well be a suggestion of the beginnings of the conflict between science and religion.[67] The comparison of religion to superstition is more forcefully made in the "Histoire des Oiseaux" in the course of Cyrano's trial by the birds. The lawyer for Cyrano's adversary, wishing to prove Cyrano is a man, lists several reasons for this allegation. The final one is his love of "magic":

En ce qu'il lève en haut tous les matins ses yeux, son nez, et son large bec, colle ses mains ouvertes la pointe au Ciel, plat contre plat, et n'en fait qu'une attachée comme s'il s'ennuyoit d'en avoir deux libres; se casse les jambes par la moitié, en sorte qu'il tombe sur ses gigots; puis avec des paroles magiques qu'il bourdonne, j'ay pris garde que ses jambes rompuës se rattachent, et qu'il se relève aussi guay qu'auparavant. Or vous sçavez, Messieurs, que de tous les animaux il n'y a que l'Homme seul dont l'âme soit assez noire pour s'adonner à la Magie, et, par conséquent, celuy-ci est Homme. (I, 158)

In that he lifts up high every morning his eyes, his nose, and his large beak, sticks his open hands together, palm to palm, pointed towards Heaven, and makes of them one joined together, as if he were tired of having two free ones; snaps his legs in half, so that he falls on his hindlegs; then when he mutters magic words, I noticed that his broken legs become fastened together again, and that he gets up just as cheerful as before. Now you know, Gentlemen, that of all the animals Man alone has a soul black enough to devote himself to Magic, and, consequently, this one is a Man.

In a superfluous note, Lachèvre informs us that Cyrano is here describing the act of prayer (I, 158, n. 4). As in the "Lettre contre les sorciers," but much more bluntly, both religious and magic rites, treated as one, are ridiculed. Blind credulity, superstition, religious faith: these are the targets for Cyrano in his assault on the miraculous.

MIRACLE: THE ATTACK

❦

In attacking miracles, Cyrano was inevitably led to discussing the several problems—the existence of God, divine miracles, sorcery—with which we have seen him occupied. Busson specifies that Cyrano's position with respect to these issues, of primary philosophical significance in the sixteenth and seventeenth centuries, was one of the boldest of the time.

Cyrano est hanté des mêmes questions que nous avons relevées chez tous ses contemporains: Dieu, immortalité de l'âme, éternité du monde, miracles et démonologie. Sur tous ces chapitres il a pris le parti le plus irréligieux pour son temps.[68]

Cyrano is haunted by the same questions which we have pointed out in all of his contemporaries: God, the immortality of the soul, the eternity of the world, miracles, and demonology. On all of these issues he has taken the most irreligious stand for his time.

His attitude toward miracles is in fact one of those aspects of his work which distinguish it from his supposed sources and from the works of his contemporaries.

Lachèvre relates in somewhat picturesque detail Cyrano's discovery of Bishop Francis Godwin's *The Man in the Moone* in its French translation by Jean Baudoin (1648) (I, lxii, lxv). Brun includes Godwin's book among the sources for the *Autre Monde*;[69] Harold Lawton in his article on Baudoin's translation discusses its influence on Cyrano,[70] and Aldington in his first appendix lists Cyrano's borrowings from Godwin.[71] LeBret mentions Godwin's work in his preface to the *Estats de la lune*,[72] and Cyrano himself meets its hero, the Spaniard Domingo Gonzalès, on the moon and quips that he would not have used his machine to arrive there if he could have used the birds ("gansas") on which Gonzalès made his voyage.[73] Lachèvre correctly notes that in spite of the resemblances between the two works, the differences are profound.[74] The bishop's book has, of course, nothing scandalous about it, and is also less concerned with scientific questions than Cyrano's (I, lxv).

Godwin's work is Christian in inspiration, and so his lunar inhabitants are believers in Christ.[75] Godwin also expresses the hope, at the beginning of his tale, that it will not offend the Church, an appeal in which Grant McColley sees an allusion to the struggle beginning in the 1620s over the censorship of books.[76]

Before departing for the moon, Gonzalès, who has fled to the East Indies after killing one of his relatives in a duel, has an idyllic interlude on an island which he describes as a kind of terrestrial paradise.[77] This is but a Robinsonian episode, complete with a black slave in attendance, and contains none of the parody of the Old Testament found in Cyrano's *paradis terrestre* scene.

After leaving the moon on his gansas, Gonzalès lands in China, where he is accused of being a magician. Again, this passage bears no resemblance to the satire on sorcery and superstitious belief found in the opening of the *Estats du soleil* when the same accusation is leveled at Cyrano. Gonzalès, in fact, is ultimately acquitted of the charge, and finds life in China very pleasant. He could, however, have justifiably been taken for a magician since he did possess and use a magic stone (the "Ebelus") given him by the moon's supreme monarch Irdonozur, the properties of which enabled his body to become weightless or could add to the attractive powers of the earth.[78] Further evidence of Gonzalès's acquaintance with the supernatural is to be found in his flight to the moon during the course of which he is greatly disturbed by "the Illusions of Devills and wicked spirits" in the air.[79] This type of magic or of the supernatural is only an object of derision for Cyrano.

John Wilkins's stand on the miraculous in *The Discovery of a New World* (1638), also listed by Brun among the sources for the *Autre Monde*,[80] is closer to Cyrano's. On the question of the authority of the Bible, treated at length by Campanella in his *Defense of Galileo*, Bishop Wilkins is evasive. He attempts to deny its authority in the fields of science and philosophy: "The negative Authority of Scripture is not prevalent in those things which are not the Fundamentals of Religion.[81] . . . 'Tis beyond the scope of the Old Testament or the New, to discover anything unto us concerning the Secrets of Philosophy."[82] In thus shielding himself from attack by the Church, Wilkins is not necessarily expressing fideism. Rather he seems to be struggling to delimit the spheres of science and religion so as to give full independence to the former and yet maintain his faith. He takes a firm position on miracles. He argues for the natural as against the supernatural origins of comets, and in doing so inveighs against recourse to both authority and miracles as explanations of the unusual.

Others there are, who affirm these [the comets] to be some new created Stars, produced by an extraordinary Supernatural Power. I answer, True, indeed, 'tis possible they might be so, but however 'tis not likely they were so, since such Appearances may be solved some other way; wherefore to fly unto a Miracle for such things, were a great injury to Nature, and to derogate from her Skill; an Indignity much misbecoming a Man who professes himself to be a Philosopher. *Miraculum* (saith one) *est ignorantiae Asylum*; a Miracle often serves for the Receptacle of a lazy Ignorance; which any Industrious Spirit would be asham'd of; it being but an idle way to shift off the Labour of any further search. But here's the misery of it, we first tye our selves unto *Aristotle's* [sic] Principles, and then conclude that nothing could contradict them but a Miracle; whereas 'twould be much better for the Commonwealth of Learning, if we would ground our Principles rather upon the frequent Experiences of our own than the bare Authority of Others.[83]

Wilkins is here the spokesman for the rational man, rejecting divine and supernatural intervention in the sphere of science and seeking empirical truth. His speech is comparable to the impassioned reply of the *fils de l'hôte* to Cyrano's use of the word "miracle." It is chiefly in their outlooks on religion that Cyrano and Wilkins differ, but the gap is wide. Wilkins, even in setting aside the authority of the Bible and the supernatural in scientific matters, remains respectful, and he will ultimately rely on faith in the Providence of God.[84] The bishop is, of course, writing a philosophical "Discourse,"[85] whereas Cyrano's work is in general literary. It is Cyrano's use of satire and irony, elements absent in the *Discovery*, that renders his attack on miracles startling. The bishop Wilkins could hardly be charged with the impiety laid to Cyrano, and most of his other works deal with religious matters.[86]

Campanella, whose importance for Cyrano is attested to by his presence in the *Autre Monde*,[87] does not eliminate magic but rationalizes it in his *De Sensu rerum*. Magic for him is a scientific discipline, different from the positive sciences only in that the objects of its study are unknown to most men.[88] The role of astrology in his *Civitas solis* (1623) is extensive. In the utopia's temple there are two globes, representing the heavens and the earth, and with the depiction of the stars are written the names and influences of each.[89] The stars are consulted to find the propitious moment for reproduction of the species,[90] for agriculture,[91] and for other human concerns. The Solarians also have discovered a way to prolong and rejuvenate life, the mysterious nature of which Campanella does not disclose.[92]

Campanella's is a modified astrology; he attempted to render it "scientific" by eliminating from it all superstitious elements, such as false signs and predictions. The relations between the sidereal and terrestrial worlds were, he believed, a subject for scientific inquiry, but his knowledge was insufficient and he was impeded by the general penchant for unscientific astrological explanations typical of his time.[93] Léon Blanchet relates Campanella's treatment of astrology to a traditional attitude toward the miraculous beginning with Pomponazzi, characterized by the tendency to explain the supernatural in terms of the "natural," occult properties along with imagination being considered natural forces. It is when the influence of the stars, "attraction," and other occult phenomena are rejected as "natural" causes, that is, when "natural magic" ceases to command respect even as a quasi science, that the attack on miracles will begin to challenge religion directly. Explanation by occult causes is a step in the direction of complete rationalization of miracles, and the danger of this step did not go unnoticed.[94] Campanella defines the limits of astrology as a fideist would those of science, in his *Defense of Galileo*:

It is now established that . . . wisdom is a virtue and astrology a useful science. When Machiavellianism is exalted above divinity, and when man excludes God and considers his proper study an inquiry into what is above nature, human wisdom is properly condemned. Astrology is justly rebuked when, like that ancient astrology which raised itself above the Prophets in Babylon, it presumes to predict with certainty events not subject to prophecy, or when by conjecture as to future occurrences, it handicaps a sober analysis of affairs.[95]

Despite the ingenious attempts of Luciano Erba to detail all the cabalistic, mystical, occult elements in Cyrano's work,[96] it must be recognized that Cyrano does not anywhere suggest that he himself is a partisan of the occult, although he may perhaps use literary devices or ideas borrowed from this domain for his own purposes.[97] In the letter "Pour les sorciers," Agrippa[98] is presented in full astrological trappings:

A l'endroit du coeur estoit attachée sur sa robe une chauve-souris à demy-morte, et autour du col un carcan chargé de sept différentes pierres précieuses dont chacune portoit le caractère du planète [sic] qui la dominoit. (II, 208)

Around the area of the heart, a half-dead bat was attached to his robe, and around his neck was attached an iron collar adorned with seven different precious stones, each one of which bore the sign of the planet ruling it.

Astrology here seems to be included in sorcery as an object of Cyrano's mockery. Cyrano elsewhere does not give occult explanations of miracles. He tries to remove all mysterious or divine elements, and thus poses a far greater threat to religion than Campanella. The critical step in the evolution of the attitude towards miracles, rejection of occult causes, is taken by Cyrano.[99]

The relationship between Campanella's position on miracles and his religious beliefs is, however, a delicate question, understandable only in the light of his panpsychism. Divine miracles can be explained in natural terms (in terms, that is, of natural magic), but since for Campanella God is omnipresent, the supernatural explained by the natural always retains its divine quality. He can thus reconcile his rationalistic method with the belief in an immanent God.[100]

There are critics who have seen Cyrano as heir to the pantheism of Campanella and the Italian naturalistic philosophers.[101] Spink remarks that Cyrano applied the old Italian naturalism to the new cosmology and to materialism.[102] His work represents for Spink a combination of panpsychism with atomism.[103] The elements of panpsychism which Cyrano may have acquired from Campanella and the Italians have been so transformed in his materialistic thinking as to remove him considerably from their philosophical position on the question of the supernatural. For Campanella the supernatural, while explainable, does exist because God's immanence imprints all of nature with the divine. Cyrano would deny the existence of the supernatural as such, explaining it only in natural terms, and deriding belief in all things beyond the realm of the natural.

The Solarians in Campanella's utopia are a people Christian in spirit. On the sixth wall of the city, Jesus and the apostles occupy "the most dignified position" of the various gods and historical personages represented there.[104] The Solarians believe in the immortality of the soul[105] and in the creation of the world, although not necessarily the Biblical Creation.[106] One of the crimes punishable by death on the sun is a crime against God.[107]

Biblical miracles are not rejected by Campanella. In *The Defense of Galileo*, he interprets the miracles of Joshua and Hezekiah to fit in with the new cosmology. It was the earth and not the sun which ceased to move "and was turned back by a true miracle."[108] The sun ceased to move only according to appearances. Cyrano describes a similar "miracle" in the account of his first attempt to fly. Instead of reaching the moon, he falls to earth again and thinks, considering the time he left, that it should now be midnight, but he sees by the position of the sun that it is noon, and reflects thus:

Je vous laisse à penser combien je fus estonné; certes, je le fus de si bonne sorte que, ne sçachant à quoy attribuer ce miracle, j'eus l'insolence de m'imaginer qu'en faveur de ma hardiesse, Dieu avoit encore une fois recloué le Soleil aux Cieux afin d'esclairer une si généreuse entreprise. (I, 9)[109]

You can just imagine how astonished I was; so much so, to be sure, that not knowing to what to attribute this miracle, I had the insolence to imagine that as a reward for my audacity God had once again riveted the Sun to the Heavens, in order to give light to such a noble enterprise.

The occasion furnishes Cyrano with a chance to satirize both the old cosmology and the notion of an anthropocentric God who works miracles for man alone.

Campanella merely adjusts the cosmology in his discussion

of the miracle of Joshua, and goes on to comment on the nature of miracles in such a fashion as not to eliminate anthropocentrism: "Miracles are miracles to us, not to God, whom nothing amazes. They are created because of us, not because of God, and, as the Apostle says, because unbelievers are so many."[110] McColley observes that an acceptance of more empirical criteria of knowledge in Campanella's time and later did not necessarily mean rejection of the Bible's authority.[111] So Campanella, while defending the new cosmology, as does Cyrano, does not partake of the latter's derisive attitude toward Biblical miracles, and indeed asserts the authority of the Bible. In this he, and not Cyrano, is following the intellectual mainstream of his day.[112] Faith and the spirit of scientific inquiry, while often enmeshed in a delicately intricate balance in Campanella's work, can thus coexist for this thinker. If his allegiance was divided, as McColley believes,[113] part of it was still to the Church, and this allegiance is conspicuously absent in Cyrano.

Bacon's *New Atlantis* and Sir Thomas More's *Utopia*, both of which supposedly served as models for the author of the *Autre Monde*,[114] bear little resemblance to Cyrano's work in the matter of miracles.

The inhabitants of Bacon's isle of Bensalem profess a kind of Christian deism. They had been converted to Christianity by an extraordinary miracle which occurred about twenty years after the Ascension. A large pillar of light surmounted by a cross of light appeared to the island dwellers. A wise man interpreted it as a true divine miracle, and distinguished it from an effect of nature or an illusion, in the following homily:

Lord God of heaven and earth; thou hast vouchsafed of thy grace, to those of our order to know thy works of creation, and true secrets of them; and to discern (as far as apperaineth to the generations of men) between divine miracles, works of Nature, works of art and impostures, and illusions of all sorts. I do here acknowledge and testify before this people, that the thing we now see before our eyes, is thy finger, and a true miracle. And forasmuch as we learn in our books, that thou never workest miracles, but to a divine and excellent end (for the laws of Nature are thine own laws, and thou exceedest them not but upon great cause), we most humbly beseech thee to prosper this great sign, and to give us the interpretation and use of it in mercy; which thou dost in some part secretly promise, by sending it unto us.[115]

Although Salomon's House is really a temple of knowledge guided by the empirical principles of Bacon's experimentalism, his utopia, like Godwin's, remains a Christian one in which divine miracles can occur.

The same may be said of More's utopia. Astronomy, not astrology, is practiced there,[116] and superstitious beliefs are frowned upon. Divine miracles, however, are respected.

They [the Utopians] despise and laugh at auguries, and the other vain and superstitious ways of divination, so much observed among other nations; but have great reverence for such miracles as cannot flow from any of the powers of Nature, and look on them as effects and indications of the presence of the supreme Being, of which they say many instances have occurred among them; and that sometimes their public prayers . . . have been answered in a miraculous manner.[117]

The religion of the Utopians, some of whom were converted to Christianity after the arrival of Europeans,[118] seems to be a nonsectarian deism.[119] Its tenets, however, are Christian: the immortality of the soul, God's Providence, a system of rewards and punishments in the afterlife.[120] The author of the *Utopia* even offers a solution to the paradox of granting an immortal soul to man and a corporeal one to animals, a question which troubled thinkers from Montaigne to Descartes and on into the eighteenth century and is taken up by Cyrano in the *Estats de la lune*.[121] More's Utopians believe that the souls of beasts are immortal too, but of a lower order than man's.[122]

The religious freedom which John H. Randall, Jr., says was advocated by More[123] is severely limited. Men who do not believe in the soul's immortality, or in the other religious principles of the Utopians, are not only barred from public office and despised, but also are practically ostracized.

> Thus they [the believers among the Utopians] are far from looking on such men as fit for human society, or to be citizens of a well-ordered commonwealth; since a man of such principles must needs, as often as he dares do it, despise all their laws and customs: for there is no doubt to be made that a man who is afraid of nothing but the law, and apprehends nothing after death, will not scruple to break through all the laws of this country.[124]

More's description of the godless man could quite easily fit Cyrano's Sejanus. But the idea of Machiavellianism in More's passage occurs in a quite different context from the ones in which we find it in Cyrano. In More it justifies limiting religious freedom, since complete freedom could allow unbelievers to wreak havoc in the state without fear of punishment, a notion to be refuted later by Bayle. For Cyrano it is the only possible justification of religion, the others being valueless in his eyes. The Christian spirit permeating the utopia of More, as well as those of Bacon, Godwin, and Campanella, is not to be found in Cyrano's *Autre Monde* or in his other works. The very principles upheld by Thomas More are satirized by Cyrano.

The question of Cyrano's personal religious beliefs has been much debated. Did he 'convert" on his deathbed, as his friend LeBret would have us believe?[125] LeBret's gallant testimony is of course that of a friend so desirous of presenting posterity with a morally untainted Cyrano that he carefully extracted all offensive or potentially offensive passages from the *Estats de la lune* for the 1657 printed edition. Lachèvre, however, relies on LeBret's account, and asserts that Cyrano, in conformity with the other seventeenth-century *libertins*, died as a Christian (I, xcii). Brun is more sceptical as to the sincerity of this supposed conversion.[126] We will undoubtedly never know what actually happened on Cyrano's deathbed, nor is it of great consequence.

Did Cyrano's *libertinage* imply atheism? Was he simply a deist? On these issues, too, the critics are divided. Lachèvre, who makes no attempt to conceal his prejudices, obviously considers him to have been an utterly impious *libertin* until the moment of his conversion. Brun sees him as a *libertin*, but not as an atheist, basing his opinion largely on Cyrano's letter "Contre un Jésuite assassin et médisant."[127] He would have Cyrano believe in the Providence of a God whose ways are not necessarily known to man.[128] Busson shares this view. He maintains that nowhere in Cyrano's writings does he directly attack the existence of God,[129] an opinion which could definitely be questioned in the case of the dialogue with the *fils de l'hôte* in the *Estats de la lune*. The key word, at any rate, is "directly," since such attacks could very well be veiled, indeed had to be veiled in Cyrano's time.[130] The devices of satire and irony so frequently used by him naturally lend themselves to covert attack. According to Busson, Cyrano believed not in the God of the Bible but rather in the more impersonal God of the *Quatrains du déiste*, and his parodies of Biblical scenes in the *Estats de la lune* should be looked upon as those of a deist.[131] Jean-Jacques Bridenne also considers him a deist.[132]

For Antoine Adam he is an atheist whose views kept him on the outskirts of literary society.[133] Spink views him as an atheist who, in rejecting miracles and magic, rejected belief in any kind of divine or supernatural being.[134] Pintard is willing to admit he could have been an atheist.[135]

Charles Dassoucy, the onetime friend of Cyrano, distinguishes between deists and atheists in his *Pensées dans le Saint-Office de Rome*.[136] Contrary to Marin Mersenne's estimate that there were 50,000 atheists in Paris in the early seventeenth century,[137] Dassoucy states that there were very few, and that he never knew any. But he did know some "faux athées," who led morally reprehensible lives and, unlike true atheists, feared death.[138] He classifies Cyrano as a "faux athée," asserting that he died mad.[139] Dassoucy, whose sole aim at this point was to criticize Cyrano, is not to be taken too seriously. His description of atheists, moreover, loses any objective value when it is reasoned, as Dassoucy likely did, that the stronger his indictment of them, the more favorable would be his chances of release from prison.

Textual evidence weighs in favor of labeling Cyrano an atheist. The *Autre Monde* is unquestionably the work of an unbeliever, and we have seen that the *porte-parole* for Cyrano in the *Estats de la lune* are highly sacrilegious in outlook. *La Mort d'Agrippine* is clearly a vehicle for atheistic, materialistic ideas, and the final speech of the *Pédant joué* is an expression of similar attitudes. Professions of faith made elsewhere, such as in the "Lettre contre les sorciers" (II, 212) or the letter "Contre un Jésuite assassin et médisant" (II, 177) must be looked upon with scepticism if the tenor of Cyrano's major works is considered.

It is less important to categorize Cyrano as an atheist or a deist than to view him in relationship to the position of his contemporaries. Pintard lists three groups of *libertins*: (1) sincere Catholics led to questioning by the scientific and intellectual upheaval begun in the period of the Renaissance, (2) emancipated Protestants fired with a nonreligious philosophical zeal, and (3) "de vrais mécréants qu'a travaillés le levain des doctrines novatrices ou plus souvent, celui du vieil humanisme païen, et qui, achrétiens ou anti-chrétiens de coeur, s'adonnent sans remords sinon toujours sans prudence à cette ironie qui est leur revanche contre les contraintes qu'on leur impose"[140] (true infidels leavened with innovating doctrines, or more often with the old pagan humanism, and who, achristians or antichristians at heart, are addicted without compunction if not always without prudence to the irony which is their revenge against the shackles imposed upon them). Although Pintard does not mention Cyrano when he classifies certain *libertins* according to these groups, it is clear that he should be assigned to the third. In this group Pintard places Luillier, the father of Chapelle. The latter, whom Cyrano knew, perhaps served as the model for the *fils de l'hôte*.[141]

Cyrano was obviously not a sincere Catholic, and his satirical treatment of miracles proceeds from no liberal reforming spirit such as the one which Lucien Febvre says inspired the satirical scenes in Rabelais.[142] The tradition of undermining miracles goes back to Pomponazzi, and miracles are the great bête noire for the seventeenth-century *libertins*, but it was unusual to go a step beyond fideism and question the existence of God. Pintard underlines the difference between the prudent *libertins érudits* and the *mécréants* such as Cyrano, to whom they left the writing of more shocking, irreligious ideas.[143]

The conflict of reason and faith which Pintard sees as giving way to that of science and religion in Gassendi's time,[144] is reflected in Cyrano's insistence on a scientific, empirical outlook as opposed to a superstitious or even a religious one. But for Cyrano personally it is at least not a conflict of interests. Both supernatural and divine intervention must be eliminated as possible causes—not set aside or temporarily dismissed—before rational inquiry can be undertaken. In this Cyrano stands apart from the most enlightened of his contemporaries.

2

❧

MIRACLE:
ALTERNATIVES

Cyrano's answer to the miraculous is the natural. Having eliminated miracles from the realm of causation, he explains natural phenomena by his particular variety of materialism and by concepts drawn from the new astronomy. His alternatives do not constitute a philosophical system; the *Autre Monde* is a philosophical novel—one of the first philosophical novels in French[1]—and not a scientific treatise. His only treatise, the *Fragment de physique*, although an effort to systematize his thought, is incomplete and presents certain contradictions with the *Autre Monde*. Cyrano's writings reflect the attempts of an author who has pillaged works of the most advanced thinkers of his and former times to impose upon the plunder his own conclusions, without necessarily developing them into a philosophical unity.[2] His conclusions set him apart from his contemporaries and predecessors on several important issues.

❧

MIRACLE: ALTERNATIVES

MATERIALISM

In the *Estats et empires de la lune,* the *fils de l'hôte* rejects the Biblical idea of creation, replacing it with the Lucretian atomism espoused by Gassendi:

Il fault, ô mon petit Animal près avoir séparé mentalement chaque petit corps visible en une infi..ité de petits corps invisibles, s'imaginer que l'Univers infini n'est composé d'autre chose que de ces Atomes infinis très solides, très incorruptibles et très simples, dont les uns sont cubiques, d'autres ronds, d'autres pointus, d'autres piramidaux, d'autres exagones, d'autres ovales, qui tous agissent diversement chacun selon sa figure. (I, 76)[3]

It is necessary, O my little Animal! after mentally separating each little visible body into an infinity of little invisible bodies, to suppose that the infinite Universe is composed of nothing other than these very solid, very incorruptible, very simple infinite Atoms, some of which are cubic, others round, others pointed, others pyramid-shaped, others hexagonal, others oval, and which all act in diverse ways, each one according to its shape.

It is ridiculous to consider the creation of any particular thing a miracle, the *fils de l'hôte* argues, following Lucretius here,[4] for it is only the result of a certain combination of atoms.

Quand ayant jetté trois dez sur une table, il arrive ou rafle de deux, ou bien trois, quatre et cinq, ou bien deux six et un, dirés-vous: "O le grand Miracle! à chaque dé il est arrivé mesme point, tant d'autres points pouvant arriver; ô le grand Miracle! il est arrivé en trois dez trois points qui se suivent; ô le grand Miracle! il est arrivé justement deux six, et le dessous de l'autre six!" (I, 77)

When you throw three dice on a table and you get all twos; or else three, four, and five; or else two sixes and a one, do you say, "O what a great Miracle! each die turned up the same number; there could have been so many others; O what a great Miracle! the three dice

turned up three successive numbers; O what a great Miracle! exactly
two sixes and the bottom of the other six turned up!"

But his interlocutor may be disinclined to accept the non-
miraculous Lucretian concept of chance expounded by the *fils de
l'hôte*. He may ask how chance alone could provide everything
needed for the production of an oak tree. Implied in this questioning is the doubt that chance can account for what had hith-
erto been assigned to Providence. The reply offered by the *fils de
l'hôte* diminishes even the role of chance and emphasizes the disposition of matter, which itself is sufficient to produce all things:

Mais, me dirés-vous, comment le hazard peut-il avoir assemblé en un
lieu touttes les choses nécessaires à produire ce Chesne? Je responds
que ce n'est pas merveille que la Matière ainsi disposée n'eust pas
formé un Chesne, mais que la merveille eust esté bien grande si la
Matière ainsy disposée, le Chesne n'eust pas este formé; un peu
moins de certaines figures, c'eust esté un Orme, un Peuplier, un
Saule, un Sureau, de la Bruyère, de la Mousse; un peu plus de
certaines autres figures, c'eust esté la plante sensitive, une Huistre à
l'escaille, un Ver, une Mouche, une Grenoüille, un Moineau, un
Singe, un Homme. (I, 76–77)

But, you will say to me, how could chance have assembled in one
place all the things necessary for the production of this Oak? I answer
that it is no wonder that Matter so arranged should form an Oak,
but that the wonder would have been much greater if with Matter so
arranged, the Oak had not been formed; a little less of certain shapes
and it would have been an Elm, a Poplar, a Willow, an Elder-tree,
some Heather, some Moss; a little more of certain other shapes and
it would have been a sensitive plant, an Oyster in a shell, a Worm,
a Fly, a Frog, a Sparrow, a Monkey, a Man.

The same argument used for the creation of the oak tree may be
applied to the creation of man. Chance again rules in the place

of Providence. But Cyrano does not stress the fortuitous coming together of atoms as much as he does the idea that since matter is constantly in flux, capable of producing all varieties of things, it is not surprising that all that exists, including man, has been formed by different combinations of matter.

Mais vous ne sçavés pas que cent millions de fois cette Matière, s'acheminant au dessein d'un homme, s'est arrestée à former tantost une pierre, tantost du plomb, tantost du corail, tantost une fleur, tantost une Comette, pour le trop ou le trop peu de certaines figures qu'il falloit ou ne falloit pas à designer un homme; si bien que ce n'est pas merveille qu'entre une infinie quantité de Matière qui change et se remue incessamment, elle ayst rencontré à faire le peu d'animaux, de végétaux, de minéraux que nous voyons, non plus que ce n'est pas merveille qu'en cent coups de dé il arrive un rafle. (I, 77)

But you do not know that hundreds of millions of times this Matter, marching toward the formation of a man, stopped to form here a stone, here some lead, here some coral, here a flower, here a Comet, on account of the excess or lack of certain shapes that were or were not needed to form a man; so that it is no wonder that in the infinite quantity of Matter which changes and moves about incessantly, such Matter has chanced to make the few animals, vegetables, and minerals that we see, no more than it is any wonder that in one hundred throws of dice there is one pair royal.

Certain critics have seen in the two passages just quoted harbingers of evolutionary theories.[5] Although there is a certain progression toward man in the examples of the different products of combined atoms enumerated by Cyrano, there is no indication that he had formulated any notion of progressive development from one form to another.[6] But the deliberately diversified enumerations suggest Cyrano's preoccupation with the enormous variety of forms matter can assume. This is one of the central themes of the *Autre Monde*, and its insistent recurrence in both voyages supports Brun's theory that the two were meant to be one work.[7] It is one of the elements which creates at least an esthetic whole.

If Cyrano reiterates the variety of forms found in nature, it is to render more dramatic the unity of the matter of which they are composed. The starting point of Cyrano's materialism is Epicurean and Lucretian atomism, but it is the unity of matter which he most emphasizes. His presentation of this concept reveals certain interesting departures from Lucretian atomism and forms his individual contribution to materialistic thought.

Gonzalès, one of Cyrano's lunar mentors, definitely states the unity of matter, using a comparison similar to one found in La Mothe Le Vayer's *Physique du Prince*:

À pénétrer sérieusement la matière, vous trouverés qu'elle n'est qu'une, qui comme une excellente comédienne joue icy bas touttes sortes de personnages sous touttes sortes d'habits. (I, 46)[8]

If you think seriously about matter, you will find that it is a unity and, like an excellent actress, plays here on earth all kinds of parts in all kinds of costumes.

Gonzalès indignantly rejects the Aristotelian doctrine of separate elements, each of which can be transformed into another, substituting for it the dictum that "tout est en tout" and that contained potentially in each of the Peripatetics' elements is every other one (I, 49). The potential omnipresence of all forms of matter may lead to the possibility of spontaneous generation,[9] but Gonzalès does not insist on this point and mentions it only in passing. After illustrating his idea with examples of the simple elements, he turns to compound substances. The Aristotelians say that when a log is burned the wood becomes fire, but according to Gonzalès, the fire was already in the log before a match was ever applied to it, and is simply liberated by the match.

MIRACLE: ALTERNATIVES

Prenés, je vous prie, une busche, ou quelque autre matière combustible, et mettes-y le feu; ilz diront, eux [vos Péripatéticiens], quand
elle sera embrasée que ce qui estoit bois est devenu feu; mais je leur
soustiens que non, moy, et qu'il n'y a point davantage de feu, mainte-
nant qu'elle est toutte en flammes, que tantost auparavant qu'on en
eust approché l'allumette; mais celuy qui estoit caché dans la busche,
que le froid et l'humide empeschoient de s'estendre et d'agir, secouru
par l'éstranger, a rallié ses forces contre le flegme qui l'estouffoit, et
s'est emparé du champ qu'occupoit son ennemy: aussy se monstre-t-il
sans obstacle et triomphant de son geollier. (I, 50–51)

Take, I beg of you, a log or some other combustible matter, and set
fire to it. They [the Peripatetics] will say that once it is burning,
what was wood has become fire; but I myself hold the contrary, that
is, that there is no more fire, now that it is entirely in flames, than
just before the match was set to it; but the fire hidden in the log, that
the cold and humidity prevented from expanding and acting, aided
by the stranger, rallied its forces against the phlegm that was stifling
it, and took hold of the field occupied by its enemy. Therefore, it
appears without an obstacle, in triumph over its jailer.

A. Juppont found considerable difficulty in explicating this
passage; he puzzled especially over the terms "le secours de
l'étranger" (the stranger's aid), "le champ qu'occupoit son ennemy"
(the field occupied by its enemy), and "le triomphe du feu sur
son geollier" (the triumph of the fire over its jailer).[10] If, however,
it is borne in mind that Gonzalès is here simply illustrating the
principle of the unity of matter, in an imaginative, literary manner, to be sure, the meaning is clear. Gonzalès states that the fire
had been prevented from leaving the log in which it had been
contained. The match or the "secours de l'étranger" (stranger's
aid) permits it to escape and inflame the log, previously controlled
by cold and humidity, two forces contrary to fire. "Le champs
qu'occupoit son ennemy" (the field occupied by its enemy) is

therefore the log controlled by cold and humidity which is eventually overtaken by fire. The fire thus "triumphs" over its "geollier" or the hostile forces which had kept it imprisoned in the log. Juppont thinks that by "fire" Cyrano really meant "energy" (I, 50, n. 2). Whether or not this is true, the passage is obviously a picturesque example of the potential presence of varied forms within a unified matter.[11]

Cyrano expands the idea that each element contains the others by showing the interdependence of all the elements and thus of everything of which they are composed, that is, of everything in the universe. All of the elements chased from the wood by the fire will return to it in various ways and forms: the air returns as dew drunk by the leaves, the water as rain, the earth as fertilizer (I, 51–52).

De cette façon, voilà ces quatre Elémens qui recouvrent le mesme sort dont ilz estoient partys quelques jours auparavant; de cette façon, dans un homme il y a tout ce qu'il fault pour composer un arbre; de cette façon, dans un arbre il y a tout ce qu'il fault pour composer un homme. Enfin de cette façon, touttes choses se rencontrent en touttes choses, mais il nous manque un Prométhée pour faire cet extraict. (I, 52)

In this way, the four elements return to the situation from which they had departed several days ago; in this way, in a man there is all that is necessary to form a tree; in this way, in a tree there is all that is necessary to form a man. And finally, in this way, everything is found in everything else, but we lack a Prometheus to perform the extraction.

The missing Prometheus, with the ability to extract from all compound substances the "primary matter" (I, 52, variant f) or first principles of which everything is composed and thus to effect all the transformations of which such matter is capable, is supplied by the author Cyrano, significantly, in his *Estats du soleil*. It is on the sun, home of Prometheus's fire, that Cyrano demonstrates these transformations to be at least theoretically possible. It is perhaps no coincidence that a Prometheus is needed to extract the primary matter required for the transformations, and that such transformations do occur on the sun. Fire is for Cyrano, as it is for Gassendi, a main principle of creation (as well as of destruction).

Or le feu, qui est le constructeur et destructeur des parties du tout de l'Univers, a poussé et ramassé dans un Chesne la quantité des figures nécessaires à composer ce Chesne. (I, 76)[12]

Now fire, which is the builder and destroyer of the parts of the entire Universe, has cultivated and assembled in an Oak the quantity of shapes necessary to make that Oak.

The transformations to be executed on the sun by the Promethean author of the *Voyages* are prefigured in a most curious and humorous passage of the *Estats de la lune*.

As Cyrano has shown the interdependence of the elements, so he now shows the interdependence of all living things. The character Cyrano, shaken by the impious tirade of the *fils de l'hôte* against the soul's immortality, consults the *démon de Socrate* on this matter. The demon, who perhaps plays the role of deist to the *fils de l'hôte's* atheist,[13] replies to the argument that God, the Father of all creatures, would have been unjust to endow only man with an immortal soul. We cannot, he says, resorting to what had become a platitude in theological debate, measure God's justice by ours. However, he partially refutes his own reasoning by describing the interpenetration of all living things, proving that man is the result of his assimilation of all other substances.[14] This is to show that once all of life has culminated in the production of man, then the day of judgment will arrive. The demon's argument is to be understood as a satire on the doctrines of the immortality of the soul, the last judgment, and resurrection. It may be compared to the satirical fable of the Christian eating a Mohammedan. The notion that man is the end of all creation, the point of perfection in this world, is scoffed at, and a passing barb is directed at the authority of the pope and of religion. Man does not at all emerge from the demon's chain of ideas as the most privileged creature of the universe, but as one who simply partakes of the matter common to all. This passage is primarily an exercise in materialistic thinking. The "metamorphoses" mentioned here will be enacted later on the sun. The "metempsychosis" is not of the Pythagorean kind,[15] but is the reappearance of the same matter in another form.

Vous sçavez, ô mon filz, que de la terre quand il se faict un arbre, d'un arbre un pourceau, d'un pourceau un homme, ne pouvons-nous donc pas croire, puisque tous les estres en la Nature tendent au plus parfaict, qu'ilz aspirent à devenir hommes, cette essence estant l'achèvement du plus beau mixte, et le mieux imaginé qui soit au Monde, estant le seul qui fasse le lien de la vie brutale avec l'angélicque. Que ces métamorphoses arrivent, il faut estre pédant pour le nier: Ne voyons-nous pas qu'un Pommier par la chaleur de son germe comme par une bouche, succe et digère le gazon qui l'environne; qu'un pourceau dévore ce fruict et le faict devenir une partie de soy-mesme? et qu'un homme mangeant le pourceau reschauffe cette chair morte, la joint à soy, et faict enfin revivre cet animal sous une plus noble espèce? Ainsy ce Grand Pontife que vous voyez la mitre sur la teste estoit il n'y a que soixante ans, une touffe d'herbe en mon jardin. Dieu donc, estant le Pere commun de touttes ses créatures, quand il les aymeroit touttes esgalement, n'est-il pas bien croyable qu'après que, par cette métempsicose plus raisonnée que la Pitagoricque, tout ce qui sent, tout ce qui végète enfin, après que toutte la matière aura passé par l'homme, alors ce grand jour du Jugement arrivera où font aboutir les Prophètes les secrets de leur Philosophie? (I, 90–91)

MIRACLE: ALTERNATIVES

You know, O my son, that since a tree is made from earth, a hog from a tree, a man from a hog, may we not believe, since all beings in Nature strive toward perfection, that they aspire to become men, this essence being the end result of the finest and the most ingeniously conceived compound substance in the World, the only one linking brute life with the angelic. You would have to be a pedant to deny that these metamorphoses occur: Do we not see that an Apple tree sucks and digests the grass surrounding it by the heat of its seed, as if by a mouth; that a hog devours this fruit and makes it a part of itself? And that a man eating the hog warms the dead flesh, joins it to himself, and thus gives the animal a new life in a nobler species? Thus the Great Pontiff whom you see with his mitre on his head was a tuft of grass in my garden only sixty years ago. Since God is the common Father of all his creatures and should love them all equally, is it not very plausible that, by this more reasonable metempsychosis than the Pythagorean, after everything that feels, everything that vegetates, and finally after all of matter shall have passed through man, then the great day of Judgment will arrive, on which the Prophets would have all the secrets of their Philosophy come to fruition?

The "pommier" in this passage reappears on the sun as a jeweled fruit tree with a golden trunk under which Dyrcona (the anagram of Cyrano, used as the protagonist's name in the *Estats du soleil*) awakens shortly after his arrival.[16] On top of the tree a nightingale is perched. There follow two metamorphoses. Dyrcona's eye is attracted by one pomegranate. As he watches, it changes into a little man, whom Cyrano calls a "pomme raisonnable" (I, 139). The creature announces that he is king of the people who make up the tree and that he will call upon them to follow him. Thereupon the whole tree is transformed into similar little men:

Tout l'arbre tomba par pièces en petits Hommes voyans, sentans, et marchans, lesquels, comme pour célébrer le jour de leur naissance mesme, se mirent à danser à l'entour de moy. (I, 139–140)

64 ह

The whole tree fell into pieces, into little seeing, feeling, and walking Men, who, as if to celebrate the very day of their birth, began to dance about me.

The nightingale alone retains its original form. Dyrcona asks the little king why the bird did not change also, and he is told that the nightingale was not able to because he is a "real bird" who is exactly what he appears to be (I, 140). The second metamorphosis is preceded by a dance of the king and his miniature people, which Dyrcona finds contagious in its movement.

Je ne pouvois regarder cette danse que je ne fusse entraisné sensiblement de ma place, comme par un vortice qui remuoit, de son mesme bransle et de l'agitation particulière d'un chacun, toutes les parties de mon corps; et je sentois epanɔüir sur mon visage la mesme joye qu'un mouvement pareil avoit étendu sur le leur. (I, 141)

I could not look at the dancing without actually being drawn from my place, as if by a vortex moving all the parts of my body by its own motion and by the particular motion of each dancer; and I felt my face radiating the same joy that a similar movement had imparted to theirs.

The result of the dance is that all of the tiny creatures become amalgamated into one extraordinarily handsome young man.

The metamorphoses, concrete illustrations of the ideas on the unity of matter found in the *Estats de la lune*, reveal some of the aspects peculiar to Cyrano's materialism. The little men are obviously meant to be the atomistic units of which, in the Epicurean tradition, matter is composed. They first appear in the form of the jeweled tree. As Spink has remarked, Cyrano borrows from literary tradition such devices as the golden tree and the nightingale.[17] Spink places Cyrano's thinking midway between the scientific and the literary.[18] One of the important innovations of the *Autre Monde* is indeed that it presents "scientific" notions in a literary context, and, without necessarily being a work of science fiction, Cyrano's literary work serves as a frame for philosophical ideas in much the same way as will Fontenelle's or Voltaire's. In no passage perhaps as clearly as in these do the scientific and the literary intermingle so freely. The jeweled tree, however, is not a purely literary element, but has another significance as the starting point of the metamorphoses. It is an inanimate tree, and yet it is a tree. It is as if Cyrano wished to suggest that the inanimate jewels of the tree were potentially vegetative and potentially even animal, thus underlining the universality of the atoms. Dyrcona's unaccountable desire to join the little men in their dance prior to their transformation into one man indicates that the dance may be a reenactment of his own formation from similar particles. Again without hinting at a progressive development from one form to another, there is a certain progression in these metamorphoses, for the inanimate is transformed into the animated little men.

The reader may at this point begin to wonder what exactly was Cyrano's concept of the atoms. We know that for Cyrano, as for Lucretius, Gassendi, and Descartes, the first principles are not perceptible. Cyrano reiterates this point in various ways. The *démon de Socrate*, a native of the sun (I, 36), tells Cyrano on the moon that his senses are inadequate to perceive all that is perceptible to the superior demon:

Si je voulois vous expliquer ce que je perçois par les sens qui vous manquent, vous vous le représenteriés comme quelque chose qui peut estre oüy, veu, touché, fleuré, ou savouré, et ce n'est rien cependant de tout cela. (I, 38)

If I were to explain to you what I perceived by the senses which you lack, you would imagine it as something that could be heard, seen, touched, smelled, or tasted, and yet it is nothing like that.

On the sun, Dyrcona's guide, Campanella, discourses on Descartes's philosophy and mentions the Cartesian notion of infinitely divisible matter. He states that such a divisibility is not perceptible but only conceivable:

> Mais . . . quoy que cela ne puisse tomber sous les sens, nous ne laissons pas de concevoir que cela se fait par la connoissance que nous avons de la matière; et nous ne devons pas . . . hésiter à déterminer nostre jugement sur les choses que nous concevons. (I, 185)

> But . . . although it cannot fall within the province of the senses, we do not fail to conceive that it occurs, by the knowledge we have of matter; and we must not . . . hesitate to apply our judgment to the things which we conceive.

If the atoms do not possess sensible qualities for Cyrano, what of the "petits Hommes voyans, sentans, et marchans" (little seeing, feeling, and walking Men), into which the inanimate tree is metamorphosed and which in turn will be metamorphosed into the handsome young man? How does Cyrano treat the problem of the transition from the inanimate to the animate, which seems to be suggested here? The passage is strangely reminiscent of several passages in the *De Rerum Natura*[19] in which Lucretius ridicules the notion that atoms are endowed with sensation. Lucretius and the Greeks rejected the theory of sentient atoms; according to Lucretius, the sentient being is formed from non-sentient particles.[20] He rejects Anaxagoras's theory that all things are literally in all things, that is, that things are made up of smaller particles similar in nature to the whole. If this were true, Lucretius says, the particles would emerge from the whole in their own form, and those things subject to destruction would be totally destroyed. But this is not the case. Things are composed of particles alien to their nature, and nothing is totally destroyed; matter simply changes in the combination of its components.

Fire as such is not within wood, but the "seeds of heat" are.[21] If the first-beginnings are like the whole, "it will come to be that they will be shaken with quivering mirth and laugh aloud, and wet face and cheeks with salt tears."[22] Cyrano also gives the example of the fire and the wood, but in his work it does not reflect Anaxagoras's concept of little particles similar in nature to the whole. It does represent a modification of the Lucretian idea in a direction indicated by Gassendi. For Gassendi, as for Cyrano and Lucretius, the atoms of fire exist in different combinations in the wood.[23] But Gassendi, if François Bernier may be trusted here, mentions the example of fire in a passage dealing precisely with the development of the sentient from the nonsentient. Frederick Lange quotes the following from Bernier's *Abrégé* to show that Gassendi appreciated this problem, and that he wished to modify the position of Lucretius by suggesting the possibility of the sentient even at the stage of the nonsentient:

On ne peut pas absolument dire que les choses sensibles se fassent de choses insensibles, mais plutost qu'elles se font de choses qui bien qu'elles ne sentent pas effectivement, sont néanmoins, ou contiennent en effet les principes du Sentiment, demesme que les principes du feu sont contenus et cachez dans les veines des cailloux, ou dans quelque autre matière grasse.[24]

It cannot be absolutely stated that sentient things are formed from the nonsentient, but rather that they are formed from things which, although they do not effectively possess sensation, nevertheless are or in effect contain the principles of Sensation, in the same way that the principles of fire are contained or hidden in the veins of pebbles, or in some other oily substance.

It is, of course, difficult to determine what is meant by the "principes du Sentiment." Lange has understood them as simple combinations of atoms.[25]

The laughing little men with tears running down their cheeks, Lucretius's mockery of Anaxagoras's atomism, reappear in another satirical passage in the *De Rerum Natura*. Lucretius again denies the sensibility of atoms, associating it with the infinite divisibility of matter, which he also denies. If the little particles can think and feel, they will reflect on what particles they in turn are composed of; those particles will do the same thing, and so on ad infinitum.

Again, if, in order that all living things may be able to feel, we must after all assign sensation to their first-beginnings, what of those whereof the race of men has its peculiar increment? You must think that they are shaken with quivering mirth and laugh aloud and sprinkle face and cheeks with the dew of their tears. And they have the wit to say much about the mingling of things, and they go on to ask what are their first-beginnings; inasmuch as, being made like to whole mortal men, they too must needs be built of other particles in their turn, and those again of others, so that you may never dare to make a stop; nay, I will press hard on you, so that, whatsoever you say speaks and laughs and thinks, shall be composed of other particles which do these same things.[26]

The comparison of Cyrano's "petits Hommes voyans, sentans, et marchans" with Lucretius's laughing little men impresses itself on the reader. Since the men are transmuted from the inanimate but potentially vegetative tree, it may be assumed that the tree was potentially animal or human, in the same way wood is potentially fire, without necessarily bearing the implication that, as Anaxagoras would have it, like is composed of like. It is only when the particles acquire sensation, or when the fruit turns into the little men, that an actual man is formed. The man, it is true, does not really come to life until he swallows the tiny king, but this does not suggest that he was not previously sensitive. The king is evidently a principle of unity, for Cyrano contrasts the chaos of the little men grouped together with the one finished man who emerges after the king is swallowed: "Tout cet amas de petits Hommes n'avoit point encore auparavant donné aucune marque de vie; mais si-tost qu'il eut avalé son petit Roy, il ne se sentit plus estre qu'un" (I, 141–142). (This entire mass of little Men had not previously given any sign of life; but as soon as it swallowed its little King, it no longer felt itself to be anything other than a whole.) Henri Weber considers the king to be the soul,[27] and since Cyrano says the king seemed to be attracted to the body "par la respiration du corps mesme" (by the respiration of the body itself) (I, 141), the word "esprit" (spirit) comes naturally to mind. It is to be noted that this "âme" (soul) or "esprit" is simply another one of the same materialistic particles which make up the whole man. The soul is thus not to be understood in the Cartesian sense.

If the contradiction to Lucretius is logically extended, the sensitive particles will imply the infinite divisibility of matter, and they will be corpuscular rather than atomistic. If this is the case, Spink may not have included all aspects of the metamorphoses in calling them "a Gassendist parable."[28] Corpuscular matter and its infinite divisibility are, of course, Cartesian notions.[29] The dance of the little men and the use of the word "vortice" suggest still another Cartesian element: the *tourbillon* theory which explains all physical phenomena by matter and motion.[30]

Spink in his article on the metamorphoses stresses the fact that Cyrano, contrary to the Aristotelians, identifies form with structure, as does Gassendi.[31] A change in form is a change in structure, and there is no form separated from its structure. What is perhaps more to be emphasized in an analysis of the metamorphoses is one of Cyrano's departures from Gassendist thought, or what Spink calls the "pure act."[32] Spink develops the explanation of this idea elsewhere,[33] showing it to be a perfectly self-generating act, not imposed from without. If form and the arrangement of matter are one, as they are in the metamorphoses, then intelligence will be merely a certain disposition of atoms. No intelligence from without can therefore impose a form on these self-ordering atoms.[34] The little men group themselves together to form the whole man, and the final sensitive, intelligent human being is nothing more than their constitution as such.[35] Form and structure, mind and matter—all the dualisms are dispelled in Cyrano's metamorphoses,[36] justifying Spink's judgment that Cyrano "aims at a thoroughgoing monism."[37] It is Cyrano's materialistic monism which gives a special significance to the metamorphoses. His materialism goes beyond the thought of Descartes and Gassendi, for both of whom God was the First Cause, no matter how small a role he may actually have played in their philosophical systems. Cyrano's materialistic monism was better couched in the fantastical language of the metamorphoses than it would have been in a philosophical work, for its boldness belonged more to Diderot and the eighteenth century than to even the most avant-garde of the seventeenth-century thinkers.

At the completion of the metamorphoses with the formation of the handsome young man, Dyrcona is less impressed by his beauty than by the speed with which the transformation is effected: "La liaison de toutes les parties qui achevèrent ce parfait microcosme se fit en un clin d'oeil" (I, 141). (The grouping together of all the parts which completed this perfect microcosm was effected in the twinkling of an eye.) The time required for the formation of the man is a "clin d'oeil," relative to eternity.[38] The same metamorphoses on earth, Cyrano seems to imply, would require an immeasurable length of time. But on the sun, source of life's creation, the processes of formation and transformation are accelerated. Dyrcona witnesses the metamorphoses at the very center of light and heat in the universe: the "régions éclairées" (light regions) of the sun. And the little particles are natives of these "régions éclairées," the newly formed man tells Dyrcona (I, 142). The nightingale that remained unchanged, the "real bird," comes from an opaque region of the sun (I, 142) and therefore cannot participate in the continuous, rapid transformations of those particles that proceed from the source of life.[39] At this source, "le principe de la matière est d'estre en action" (the principle of matter is to be in action) (I, 145).

For Cyrano, the sun is the "grande âme du Monde" (great World-Soul) (I, 125), the "Père" (Father), and the "Autheur de toutes choses" (Author of all things) (I, 186). The world-soul, without necessarily connoting animism or pantheism, is probably more than an image; as the primary generating force it would correspond to the world-soul of Democritus, the principle of material diffusion of atoms throughout the universe.[40] Cyrano's fiery world-soul is in turn made up of the souls of all living things; pulsating with their life, it is termed "ce grand et parfait animal." Again, the individual souls are each a material principle, centers of heat necessary for procreation. After leaving their earthly dwelling places, they return to the source of all creation to form the "vital spirits" of the sun (I, 182). This is explained to Dyrcona by Campanella, the logical person to lecture on the importance of the sun.

Ainsi dès qu'une Plante, une Beste ou un Homme expirent, leurs âmes montent, sans s'éteindre, à sa sphère [du soleil]. . . . Or toutes ces âmes unies qu'elles sont à la source du jour, et purgées de la grosse matière qui les empeschoit, elles exercent des fonctions bien plus nobles que celles de croistre, de sentir et de raisonner; car elles sont employées à former le sang et les esprits vitaux du Soleil, ce grand et parfait animal: Et c'est pourquoy vous ne devez point douter que le Soleil n'opère de l'esprit bien plus parfaitement que vous, puis que c'est un élixir, qu'il connoist le secret de la vie, qu'il influë à la matière de vos Mondes la puissance d'engendrer, qu'il rend des corps capables de se sentir estre, et enfin qu'il se fait voir et fait voir toutes choses. (I, 182)[41]

Thus as soon as a Plant, a Beast, or a Man expires, the soul, without being extinguished, rises to its sphere [the sun's]. . . . Now when all these souls are united at the source of daylight, and are purged of the heavy matter which was an impediment to them, they perform much nobler functions than those of growing, feeling, and reasoning; for they serve to form the blood and the vital spirits of the Sun, that great and perfect animal. And this is why you should not doubt that the Sun's mind works much more perfectly than yours, since it is an elixir, since it knows the secret of life, infuses into the matter of your Worlds the power of procreation, renders bodies sentient, and finally renders itself and all things visible.

The peculiar type of regeneration, the non-Pythagorean metempsychosis, is due to the continuing material principle of life which makes possible the re-formation of matter. The Lucretian consolation on death, offered to Dyrcona, appropriately, by two birds of paradise[42] in the "Histoire des Oiseaux," includes the same materialistic concept: death means only the rearrangement of matter, and so Dyrcona himself will reappear one day as an entirely different creature or substance.

La matière qui, à force de se mesler, est enfin arrivée à ce nombre, cette disposition et cet ordre nécessaires à la construction de ton estre, peut-elle pas [sic] en se remeslant arriver à une disposition requise pour faire que tu te sentes estre encor une autre fois? Oüy mais me diras-tu, je ne me souviendray pas d'avoir esté. Hé! mon cher frère, que t'importe, pourveu que tu te sentes estre? . . . Mais j'ay un secret à te decouvrir . . . c'est qu'estant mangé, comme tu vas estre, de nos petits oiseaux, tu passeras en leur substance: Oüy,

tu auras l'honneur de contribuer quoy qu'aveuglement, aux opéra-
tions intellectuelles de nos Mouches, et de participer à la gloire, si
tu ne raisonnes toy-mesme, de les faire au moins raisonner. (I, 162)

Cannot this matter which, by dint of intermingling, has finally arrived at the number, arrangement, and order necessary for the construction of your being, by remingling arrive at an arrangement
required to make you sentient once again? Yes, you will say to me,
but I do not remember having existed. Ah! my dear brother, what do
you care, provided that you can feel your existence? . . . But I have
a secret to reveal to you . . . which is that once eaten, as you are going
to be by our little birds, you will pass into their substance. Yes, you
will have the honor of contributing, although blindly, to the intellectual operations of our Flies, and, if you yourself do not reason, you
will at least participate in making them reason.

That the sun is the source of the permanent material principle of life is one of the reasons Cyrano alleges for placing it at the
center of the world.[43] All the little centers of life found in each
terrestrial being correspond to the one great sun, center of life and
of the universe.

Premièrement, il est du sens commun de croire que le Soleil a pris
place au centre de l'Univers, puis que tous les corps qui sont dans la
Nature ont besoin de ce feu radical, qui habite au coeur du Royaume
pour estre en estat de satisfaire promptement à leurs nécessitez, et que
la cause des générations soit placée esgallement entre les corps où elle
agit; de mesme que la sage Nature a placé les parties génitales (au
milieu) dans l'homme, les pépins dans le centre des pommes, les
noyaux au milieu de leur fruit; et de mesme que l'ognon conserve à
l'abry de cent escorces qui l'environnent le précieux germe où dix millions d'autres ont à puiser leur essence: Car cette pomme est un petit
univers à soy-mesme dont le pépin, plus chaud que les autres parties,
est le soleil qui respand autour de soy la chaleur conservatrice de son
globe; et ce germe dans cet ognon est le petit soleil de ce petit monde
qui reschauffe et nourrit le sel végétatif de cette masse. (I, 11–12)

First of all, it is just common sense to believe the Sun is located in the center of the Universe, since all bodies in Nature need this essential fire, which dwells in the center of the Kingdom so as to be in a position to satisfy their needs promptly, and since the cause of generation must be placed equidistant from the bodies on which it acts; just as wise Nature has placed the genital parts (in the center) in man, pips in the centre of apples, pits in the center of their fruit; and just as an onion shelters within a hundred surrounding skins the precious seed from which ten million others must draw their essence. For the apple is a little universe in itself, whose pip, warmer than the other parts, is the sun, radiating about it the conserving heat of its globe; and the seed in the onion is the little sun of that little world, which warms and nourishes the vegetative salt of the mass.

It is no accident that Cyrano describes the completely formed man resulting from the metamorphoses as "ce parfait microcosme" (this perfect microcosm).[44] If an apple is a "little universe," so man who dwells within the larger universe is like a little world within a great animal. If the sun is an animal, so is the universe, which is composed of lesser animals. To creatures smaller than man, man is a universe.

Représentés-vous donc l'Univers comme un grand animal, les estoilles qui sont des Mondes comme d'autres animaux dedans luy qui servent réciproquement de Mondes à d'autres peuples, tels qu'à nous, qu'aux chevaux et qu'aux elephans, et nous, à nostre tour, sommes aussy des Mondes de certaines gens encore plus petits comme des chancres, des poux, des vers, des cirons; ceux-cy sont la terre d'autres imperceptibles, ainsy de mesme que nous paroissons un grand Monde à ce petit peuple. (I, 71)

Imagine, then, the Universe as a great animal; the stars, which are Worlds, as other animals inside it, serving in turn as Worlds to other peoples, such as to us, to horses, and to elephants; and we in our turn, are also the Worlds of certain even smaller people, such as cankers, lice, worms, mites; these creatures are the earths of other imperceptible beings, just as we appear as a great World to this little people.

Cyrano borrows from Campanella and Sorel here (I, 71, n. 1),[45] and the passage may be compared also to Pascal's "disproportion de l'homme" (disproportion of man). What is most striking is how Cyrano himself utilizes the ideas of macrocosm and microcosm. The sun as the center of life finds smaller equivalents in all life-producing centers of animate beings. Living things, all composed of one matter, correspond to each other as worlds within worlds or animals within animals.

The metamorphoses on the sun may be seen not only as transformations, but also as successive births. Corresponding to the birth of the microcosm, then, is the birth of the macrocosm. The different parts of the microcosm were formed by the coming together of similar "dancers" or particles at certain points:

Tels d'entre les plus agiles de nos petits danseurs s'elancèrent par une capriole à la hauteur, et dans la posture essentielle à former une teste; tels plus chauds et moins déliez, formèrent le coeur; et tels beaucoup plus pesans, ne fournirent que les os, la chair, et l'embonpoint. (I, 141)

The most agile of our little dancers leapt to the height and in a stance necessary to form a head; others, warmer and less supple, formed the heart; and others, much heavier, supplied only the bones, flesh, and plumpness.

The macrocosm was similarly formed. Like particles joined with each other to form certain parts of the universe.

Resvant depuis aux causes de la construction de ce grand Univers, je me suis imaginé qu'au debroüillement du Cahos, après que Dieu eut créé la matière,[46] les corps semblables se joignirent par ce principe d'amour inconnu avec lequel nous expérimentons que toute chose cherche son pareil. Des particules formées de certaines façons s'assemblèrent, et cela fit l'air; d'autres à qui la figure donna possible un mouvement circulaire, composèrent en se liant les globes qu'on appelle Astres. (I, 127)

Reflecting afterwards on the causes of the construction of this great Universe, I thought that at the disentanglement of Chaos, after God created matter, like bodies joined to like bodies by that unknown principle of love by which we have observed that everything seeks its kind. Particles formed a certain way came together and they made air; others whose shape perhaps gave them a circular movement fashioned in joining together the globes which we call Stars.

The association of like particles to form a particular thing, common to Cyrano's descriptions of the birth of the microcosm and of the macrocosm, is a distinctly Lucretian notion.[47] But Cyrano develops his ideas on the formation of the macrocosm essentially after the manner of Descartes. (Juppont, however, sees in him a forerunner of Laplace.)[48] Dyrcona muses, while traveling to the sun, that the various planets could at one time have been suns. The suns, over a considerable length of time, would have gradually lost their light and heat, turning into cold, dark bodies. The sunspots may be a crust forming on the surface of the sun, a sign that it is perhaps slowly losing its light and heat and becoming an earth (I, 127–128). Cyrano speaks a little differently in the *Estats de la lune*. There he says that earths are formed from matter which the sun casts off and that the various worlds are really "l'escume des soleils qui se purgent" (the dross of suns purging themselves) (I, 15). Spots can be observed with the telescope, he states, which are worlds in the process of being formed (I, 16).

In Descartes's hypothesis of a world created without God, the earth, without being a "purgation," was also once a sun. The sunspots forming on its surface will be part of the future earth:

MIRACLE: ALTERNATIVES

Feignons donc que cette terre où nous sommes a été autrefois un astre composé de la matière du premier élément toute pure, laquelle occupoit le centre d'un de ces quatorze tourbillons qui étoient contenus en l'espace que nous nommons le premier ciel, en sorte qu'elle ne différoit en rien du soleil, sinon qu'elle étoit plus petite: mais que les moins subtiles parties de sa matière s'attachant peu à peu les unes aux autres, se sont assemblées sur sa superficie, et y ont composé des nuages, ou autres corps plus épais et obscurs, semblables aux taches qu'on voit continuellement être produites, et peu après dissipées sur la superficie du soleil, et que ces corps obscurs étant aussi dissipés peu de temps après qu'ils avoient été produits, les parties qui en restoient, et qui, étant plus grosses que celles des deux premiers éléments,[49] avoient la forme du troisième, se sont confusément entassés autour de cette terre, et, l'environnant de toutes parts, ont composé un corps presque semblable à l'air que nous respirons: puis, enfin, que cet air étant devenu fort grand et épais, les corps obscurs qui continuoient à se former sur la superficie de la terre n'ont pu si facilement qu'auparavant y être détruits, de façon qu'ils l'ont peu à peu toute couverte et offusquée; et même que peut-être plusieurs couches de tels corps s'y sont entassées l'une sur l'autre, ce qui a tellement diminué la force du tourbillon qui la contenoit, qu'il a été entièrement détruit, et que la terre avec l'air et les corps obscurs qui l'environnoient est descendue vers le soleil jusques à l'endroit où elle est à présent.[50]

Let us therefore imagine that this earth we are on was formerly a star composed purely of matter of the first element, and that it occupied the center of one of the fourteen vortices contained in the space we call the first heaven, so that it differed in no way from the sun, except that it was smaller. But the less subtle parts of its matter fastened gradually onto each other, gathered together on its surface, and there formed clouds or other thicker, obscure bodies, similar to the spots you see continually being produced and then soon afterward dissipated on the surface of the sun. Since these obscure bodies were also dissipated shortly after being produced, the remaining particles, thicker than those of the first two elements, with the form of the third, piled confusedly about the earth; and surrounding it on all sides, they formed a body almost like the air we breathe. Finally, when this air became very large and thick, the obscure bodies which were continuing to form on the surface of the earth could not so readily as before be destroyed, so that they gradually covered and blocked it entirely, and perhaps even several layers of such bodies piled up one on top of the other, which so diminished the strength of the vortex containing the earth that this vortex was entirely destroyed and the earth with the air and obscure bodies surrounding it descended toward the sun right to the place in which it is presently located.

Before reaching the sun Dyrcona alights on a sunspot where a little man tells him about the formation of its first inhabitant. Following Lucretius and Gassendi,[51] he gives a highly fantastic account of the spontaneous generation of the man, a phenomenon which, Cyrano is careful to say, cannot occur on the earth (I, 131). It is understandable that since for Cyrano everything is the result of different combinations of matter undirected by an outside agent, he would have been tempted by the idea of spontaneous generation. He does not, however, continue to develop his thinking along this line.

In the light of the borrowings from Descartes, particularly in the passage on the formation of the macrocosm, it is not surprising that Cyrano's Campanella should have as much respect for Descartes's "Physique" (undoubtedly the *Principes de la philosophie*) as for oracles (I, 183). But Cyrano's materialism includes Gassendist, Lucretian, and Cartesian elements. If the Cartesian strain is dominant in his theory of the world's formation, Gassendist and Lucretian influences can be discerned in his atomism. Microcosm and macrocosm are welded together by Cyrano in a unity of composition and formation. The autonomous arrangement and rearrangement of matter accounts for the creation of all things. Cyrano draws heavily upon his sources, but the result is ubiquitous monism, the most daring and original feature of his materialism.

COSMOLOGY

As Cyrano's answer to Creation is his atomistic materialism, so his answer to the miracle of Joshua is heliocentrism. But the Copernican theory, however bold it may have seemed in Cyrano's day, is only one aspect of Cyrano's audacious enthusiasm for the new cosmological ideas. The extravagant settings of the sun and moon voyages prove to be suitable to Cyrano for the expression of the most startling concepts contributed by the new astronomy.

Cyrano's first attempt to reach the moon ends with his unwitting descent into Canada. Seeing that it is noon when he arrives there, instead of midnight, as it should be by his calculations, he jokingly ascribes this strange occurrence to a miracle like that of Joshua (I, 9). He is happy to make the acquaintance of the viceroy of Canada, Monsieur de Montmagnie, a man who will understand the real explanation.

Mon bonheur fut grand de rencontrer un homme capable de hautes opinions, et qui ne s'estonna point quand je luy dis qu'il falloit que la Terre eust tourné pendant mon élévation, puis qu'ayant commencé à monter à deux lieuës de Paris, j'estois tombé par une ligne casi perpendiculaire en Canada. (I, 11)

I was very happy to find a man capable of lofty ideas, and who was not amazed when I told him that the earth would have had to turn during my flight, considering that I had begun to rise two leagues from Paris, and had fallen in an almost perpendicular line into Canada.

But Cyrano is soon undeceived as to Montmagnie's degree of intellectual enlightenment, and their subsequent conversation takes on the fervor of an attempt by a Copernican zealot to convert a religious heathen. The viceroy speaks for the Jesuit fathers who are absolutely convinced that Cyrano is a "magician" (I, 11). He counters Cyrano's statement that the earth turned while he was in the air by saying it could just as well have been the sun that turned, in accordance with "Ptolémée, Ticobraé, et les Philosophes modernes" (I, 11). He adds the most powerful argument of all: do not our senses tell us that it is the sun that moves and the earth that stands still?

Et puis, quelle grande vraisemblance avés-vous pour vous figurer que le Soleil soit immobile, quand nous le voyons marcher, et que la terre tourne autour de son centre avec 'tant de rapidité, quand nous la sentons ferme dessous nous? (I, 11)

And then what likelihood leads you to believe that the Sun is immobile, when we see it move, and that the earth turns about its center with such rapidity, when we feel it motionless beneath us?

Cyrano answers Montmagnie with his own argument. If the movement of the earth is deduced from its roundness, it would be possible to deduce an analogous movement from the heavens, if they were round. But there is no way of knowing, through sensory perception or through experimentation,[52] if the heavens are in fact round; if they are not, they certainly cannot move.

Encore nous qui sommes asseurés de la rondeur de la Terre, il nous est aisé de conclure son mouvement par sa figure: Mais pourquoy supposer le Ciel rond, puisque vous ne le scauriés sçavoir, et que de touttes les figures, s'il n'a pas celle-cy, il est certain qu'il ne se peut pas mouvoir? (I, 12)

Furthermore, it is easy for us who are certain of the Earth's roundness to deduce its movement from its shape. But why assume that the Heavens are round, since you cannot know it, and since if, of all shapes, it has not this one, it is certain that it cannot move?

MIRACLE: ALTERNATIVES

This is perhaps not Cyrano's most persuasive argument, but it is significant in that it shows his preoccupation with the problems of sensory evidence and experimentation. He emphasizes the dubiousness of sensory evidence by offering Montmagnie the image of a man on a ship who thinks the shore and not the ship is moving (I, 13).[53]

The other reasons for accepting heliocentrism are ones of common sense. The smaller earth turns around the larger fiery sun to receive its light and warmth in the same way that a lark is roasted over a fire. It would be absurd to think the fire turns instead of the bird (I, 12). The greatest advantage of heliocentrism is that it is a purely natural explanation.

Parlons seulement des causes naturelles de ce mouvement. Vous êtes contraints, vous autres, de recourir aux intelligences qui remuënt et gouvernent vos globes! Mais moy, sans interrompre le repos du Souverain Estre . . . moy, dis-je, je trouve dans la Terre les vertus qui la font mouvoir. (I, 13)

Let us speak only of the natural causes of this movement. On your part, you are obliged to resort to intelligences to move and govern your globes! But I, without interrupting the peace of the Sovereign Being . . . I, so I say, find in the Earth all the properties which make it move.

Montmagnie will finally subscribe to heliocentrism, but only as explained to him by a priest. Cyrano parodies all attempts at religious interpretation of the theory by putting these ludicrous words in the mouth of the Jesuit:

Le feu d'Enfer, ainsy que nous apprend la Saincte Escriture, estant enclos au centre de la Terre, les damnez, qui veulent fuïr l'ardeur de la flamme, gravissent pour s'en éloigner, contre la voûte, et font ainsy tourner la Terre. (I, 13)

The fire of Hell, as Holy Scripture teaches us, being enclosed in the center of the Earth, the damned, who wish to flee the flame's heat to escape it, climb up against the vault, and thus make the Earth turn.

In championing heliocentrism, Cyrano underlines its value as a natural cause by opposing it to supernatural or miraculous ones. The heliocentric theory for him is a product of reason and common sense.

Cyrano's clever reply to Montmagnie's objection that heliocentrism contradicts the evidence of our senses is not his definitive one. He has a far more effective way to deal with this obstacle. In Bernier's *Abrégé* of Gassendi's philosophy, it is stated that although a man on a ship can get out of it to determine if it or the shore was moving, a man on earth cannot do the equivalent to determine if the earth moves or not.[54] Now this is exactly what Cyrano will do. His aerial travels serve as experimental verifications of his theoretical pronouncements.[55] While on his way to the sun he actually sees incontrovertible confirmation of what he had earlier only postulated rationally.

Je connus très distinctement, comme autrefois j'avois soupçonné en montant à la Lune, qu'en effet c'est la Terre qui tourne d'Orient en Occident à l'entour du Soleil, et non pas le Soleil autour d'elle; car je voyois, en suite de la France, le pied de la bote d'Italie, puis la mer Méditérranée, puis la Grèce, puis le Bosphore, le Pont-Euxin, la Perse, les Indes, la Chine, et enfin le Japon, passer successivement vis à vis du trou de ma loge; et quelques heures après mon élévation, toute la mer du Sud ayant tourné, laissa mettre à sa place le continent de l'Amérique. . . .

Je costoyay la Lune qui, pour lors, se trouvoit entre le Soleil et la Terre, et je laissay Vénus à main droite. Mais à propos de cette estoille, la vieille Astronomie a tant presché que les planètes sont des astres qui tournent à l'entour de la Terre, que la moderne n'oseroit en douter. Et je remarquay, toutefois, que durant tout le temps que

MIRACLE: ALTERNATIVES

Vénus parut au deçà du Soleil, à l'entour duquel elle tourne, je la vis toujours en croissant; mais, achevant son tour, j'observay qu'à mesure qu'elle passa derrière, les cornes se raprochèrent et son ventre noir se redora. Or cette vicissitude de lumières et de ténèbres montre bien évidemment que les planètes sont, comme la Lune et la Terre, des globes sans clarté qui ne sont capables que de réfléchir celle qu'ils empruntent. (I, 127)[56]

I very distinctly recognized, as I had previously suspected in rising to the Moon, that in effect it is the Earth which turns from East to West around the Sun, and not the Sun around it; for I saw in succession France, the foot of the boot of Italy, then the Mediterranean, then Greece, then the Bosporus, the Black Sea, Persia, the East Indies, China, and finally Japan pass in front of my cabin's hole; and several hours after my elevation, the entire South Seas turned and gave way to the continent of America. . . .

I coasted alongside of the Moon which, at that time, was located between the Sun and the Earth, and I left Venus on the right. But speaking of this star, the old Astronomy has so loudly preached the doctrine that the planets are stars which turn around the Earth that modern Astronomy would not dare to doubt it. I nevertheless noticed that during the whole time Venus appeared on this side of the Sun, around which it turns, I always saw it as a crescent; but, when it completed its circle, I noticed that as it passed behind the Sun the horns drew together and its black underbelly became golden once more. Now these vicissitudes of light and darkness show with great evidence that the planets, like the Moon and the Earth, are globes without their own light, capable only of reflecting that which they borrow.

Cyrano's open advocacy of Copernicanism assigns him a special place among his contemporaries. As Busson has amply shown, the Copernican theory met a generally unenthusiastic response in France in Cyrano's time.[57] Such luminaries of the little circle of seventeenth-century *savants* as Mersenne and Guy

Patin rejected heliocentrism.[58] Even those who were well-informed about it did not necessarily accept it. Such is the case with Montaigne, Pontus de Tyard, du Bartas, possibly Pascal,[59] and even Pierre Bayle, who in his *Pensées diverses sur la comète* (1680) professes indifference as to which cosmological system is correct.[60] Kircher, writing after Cyrano, steadfastly adheres to the Ptolemaic.[61] And LeBret, in his preface to the 1657 edition of the *Voyage dans la lune,* disengages himself from the Ptolemaic-Copernican dispute by admitting ignorance and unconcern.[62] Dorothy Stimson states that even as late as 1750 there was almost no open support of Copernicanism in France.[63]

The chief impediment to acceptance of the Copernican theory was, of course, theological opposition. Busson notes that Cyrano appropriately makes the Jesuits the opponents of heliocentrism.[64] Descartes held up the publication of his *Monde* precisely because the heliocentrism he expounded therein was considered heretical.[65] And he took pains to employ the transparent subterfuge of supposing that the world he described was only imaginary. The same cautiousness with respect to religion is shown by Gassendi, who on the occasion of Galileo's release wrote to him advising submission to the Church. Descartes and Peiresc evidently shared his sentiments on this issue.[66] In his writings, Gassendi seems to waver between the Tychonic and Copernican systems,[67] and Pintard stresses that his arguments for Copernicanism are *prudently* accumulated.[68] His ultimate attitude is ostensibly a fideistic resignation to not knowing the causes of natural things, which will have to be left to God.[69]

Cyrano, who shows no signs of wanting to reconcile heliocentrism with religious dogma, vigorously makes known his views on the new astronomy. He upholds Galileo and mocks the Inquisition in a scene in the *Estats de la lune* which is obviously an allusion to Galileo's trial.[70] Cyrano is tried for his belief that our earth, the lunarians' "moon," is a world, and is finally forced to recant (I, 60). This satirical passage implicitly defending Galileo and Copernicus reflects Cyrano's acute awareness of the widespread opposition with which the two astronomers' endeavors were met.

The more radical of Cyrano's cosmological notions, however, have little to do with Copernicanism. One of the guiding ideas of the *Estats de la lune* is the principle which Cyrano is forced to retract in the mock trial, and which he sets forth in the first paragraph of the moon voyage: "La Lune est un monde comme celuy-cy à qui le nostre sert de Lune" (I, 5). (The Moon is an earth like this one for which ours serves as a Moon.) Cyrano will prove that the moon is an earth and the earth its moon in the same empirical way he proves the motion of the earth: he will go and see for himself. It is an enterprise as Promethean as realizing the materialistic transformation supposedly possible in theory alone through the metamorphoses on the sun. And Cyrano sees himself as a second Prometheus when he reflects on his plan to go to the moon: "Et pourquoy non? . . . Promethée fut bien autrefois au Ciel dérober du feu" (I, 9). (And why not? . . . After all, Prometheus once went off to Heaven to steal fire.)

Cyrano's belief that the moon is an earth stems from a long tradition, beginning with the Greeks, such as Heraclitus, Democritus, and the Pythagoreans, and given added piquancy by Lucian's fanciful voyages to the moon in *The True History* and *Icaromenippus*. Plutarch attempts a more realistic description of the moon in his *De Facie in orbe lunare*. Francesco Patrizzi, in his *Nova de universis philosophia* (1591), states that the earth and the moon are similar and that the earth is the moon's moon as that globe is our moon.[71] In the supplement to the *Satyre Ménippée*, the *Nouvelles Régions de la lune* (1593), the moon is found to be an earth. After the appearance in 1610 of Galileo's

Sidereus Nuncius, as Marjorie Nicolson points out, the idea of a world in the moon takes on a new realism.[72] The empirical evidence offered by the telescope that the moon indeed does possess terrestrial features is evident in Kepler's *Dream*, in Wilkins's *Discovery of a New World*, and in Godwin's *Man in the Moone*. The *Selenographia* (1647) of Johannes Hevelius, mentioned by LeBret in his preface to Cyrano's moon voyage,[73] contains numerous maps of the moon bearing a noticeable resemblance to maps of the earth.

The moon-world idea acquires added significance when put forth in association with the idea of the plurality of worlds. Cyrano confides to Montmagnie his belief in the latter theory. Not only are the planets around our sun worlds like ours, he says, but the fixed stars are suns, about which revolve other planets or worlds.

Je crois que les planettes sont des mondes autour du Soleil, et que les estoilles fixes sont aussy des soleils qui ont des planettes autour d'eux, c'est-à-dire des mondes que nous ne voyons pas d'icy à cause de leur petitesse,[74] et parce que leur lumière empruntée ne sçauroit venir jusques à nous. (I,14)

I believe that the planets are worlds around the Sun, and that the fixed stars are also suns which have planets around them, that is to say, worlds which we do not see from here because of their smallness, and because their borrowed light cannot reach us.

Cyrano's lunar adventure will be empirical proof that the moon is an earth and, by implication, that if the moon is an earth, the other globes can also be worlds. He will find evidence for the plurality of worlds in the course of his ascension to the sun when he will actually pass globes similar to our own, incidentally noting the attractive power of each:

Je laissay sur ma route, tantost à gauche, tantost à droite, plusieurs terres comme la nostre où, pour peu que j'atteignisse les sphères de leur activité, je me sentois fléchir. (I, 127)

MIRACLE: ALTERNATIVES

I left along my path, sometimes on the left, sometimes on the right, several earths like ours, toward which I felt myself bend whenever I reached the spheres of their activity.

Cyrano also notices that all the planets have satellites or "little worlds" revolving about them: "Je remarquay encore d'autres petits mondes qui se meuvent à l'entour d'eux" (I, 127). (I noticed still other little worlds moving about them.)

Illustrating the plurality of worlds by the moon-world is a device found not only in Cyrano's works. Wilkins presents the two ideas in conjunction with each other, as may be seen in the list of the propositions to be proven in his discourse:

That a Plurality of Worlds does not contradict any Principle of Reason or Faith.

That there is a World in the Moon, hath been the direct Opinion of many ancients, with some modern Mathematicians; and may probably be deduced from the Tenents of others.

That as their World is our Moon, so our World is their Moon.[75]

Citing two moons of Saturn and four of Jupiter, Wilkins states that these are worlds, but shies away from a strong endorsement of the plurality of worlds, preferring to take one step at a time.

You shall find it probable enough that each of them [the moons] be a several World. Especially since every one of them is allotted to a several Orb, and not altogether in one, as the fixed stars seem to be. But this would be too much for to vent at the first: The chief thing at which I now aim at this Discourse, is to prove that there may be one in the Moon.[76]

Pierre Borel, whose *Discours nouveau prouvant la pluralité des mondes* exerted a strong influence on Cyrano, according to Spink[77] and Camille Flammarion,[78] entitles one of the chapters

PD
1793.H3

of his treatise "prouvant la pluralité des mondes par une raison tirée de la conformité de la lune avec la terre"[79] (proving the plurality of worlds by a reason taken from the conformity of the moon with the earth).

Despite the support of a long and impressive tradition, Cyrano, Wilkins, Godwin, and Borel all are painfully conscious of the relative oddity and unacceptability of their ideas. At the opening of his book Wilkins mildly warns against considering his opinions strange: The strangeness of this Opinion [that the Moon may be a World] is no Sufficient Reason why it should be rejected; because other certain Truths have been formerly esteemed ridiculous, and great Absurdities entertain'd by common Consent.[80] He gives examples of truths originally rejected: Columbus's suggestion that other parts of the world remained to be discovered was greeted with incredulity;[81] the antipodes were denied and ridiculed.[82]

To support his theory that the many worlds are purgations from the sun, Cyrano also argues that this notion is no more strange than others which are now accepted as truths. Saint Augustine, he affirms with a maliciously irreverent note lacking in Wilkins, thought the earth was flat.

Ce grand personnage, dont le génie estoit esclairé du Sainct-Esprit, asseure que de son temps la Terre estoit platte comme un four, et qu'elle nageoit sur l'eau comme la moitié d'une orange couppée. (I, 16)

This august personage, whose mind was illuminated by the Holy Ghost, asserts that in his time the Earth was as flat as an oven, and that it floated on the water like half of a sliced orange.

Borel and Godwin similarly argue, in favor of a world in the moon, that the antipodes were at first disbelieved.[83]

To dissipate fears of the new doctrine, especially on the part of the Church, Borel devotes several chapters of his treatise to an attempt at reconciling the plurality of worlds with Scripture. He aims especially at interpreting the Bible in accordance with his ideas.[84] Wilkins hopes to allay fears of heresy by separating as much as possible his scientific ideas and the Bible. Cyrano is inhibited by no such scruples. This permits him to carry the notion of the plurality of worlds to its logical conclusion and assert their infinite number, which few of his contemporaries dared to proclaim. Dassoucy, anxious to please the Church authorities during his imprisonment, evidently thought it expedient to denounce Cyrano's belief in the infinity of worlds. In his *Pensées dans le Saint-Office de Rome* (published posthumously in 1676), he derides the philosophical extravagances of his former friend:

Il n'y a rien de si ridicule ny de si extravagant dont il ne se fist une très-constante vérité. . . . Il vouloit qu'on crût que chaque estoille estoit un Monde, et qu'outre ceux-là il y en avoit encore une infinité d'autres, et qu'il y avoit plusieurs Soleils.[85]

There is nothing too ridiculous or foolish which he did not adopt as a certain truth. . . . He would have had us believe that every star was a World, and that in addition to these Worlds, there were yet an infinity of others, and that there were several Suns.

That the infinity of the world follows upon the idea of their plurality is quickly perceived by Montmagnie in his conversations with Cyrano.

Mais . . . si, comme vous asseurés, les estoilles fixes sont autant de soleils, on pourroit conclurè de là que le Monde seroit infiny, puisqu'il est vraysemblable que les peuples de ces mondes qui sont autour d'une estoille fixe que vous prenés pour un soleil, descouvrent encore au-dessus d'eux d'autres estoilles fixes que nous ne sçaurions appercevoir d'icy, et qu'il en va éternellement de cette sorte. (I, 14)

But . . . if, as you assert, the fixed stars are so many suns, you could conclude from this that the World was infinite, since it is likely that the peoples of these worlds around a fixed star, which you take for a sun, discover above themselves yet other fixed stars which we cannot perceive from here, and that such is eternally the case.

It is interesting that only when infinity is the issue does Cyrano bolster his arguments with religious reasons. His answer to Montmagnie is a variation of the traditional principle that God's power cannot be limited by restricting the scope of his creation. It is, of course, logical that Cyrano should invoke God when speaking of the infinite, particularly since his interlocutor's thought is dominated by the Jesuits. It is not unlikely that Cyrano's reply was dictated more by his desire to answer the Jesuits than by his own beliefs. If God could create an immortal soul, he says, then he could create an infinite world. But we know that Cyrano ridiculed belief in the immortality of the soul. Cyrano's reasoning is probably a bit of rhetoric designed to make the infinity of worlds palatable and logically possible to a religious man like Montmagnie. If you believe that God could create man's soul immortal, Cyrano appears to be saying, then you can believe that he could create the world infinite.

Comme Dieu a peu faire l'Ame immortelle, il a peu faire le Monde infiny, s'il est vray que l'Eternité n'est rien autre chose qu'une durèe sans bornes, et l'infiny une estenduë sans limites: Et puis, Dieu seroit finy luy-mesme, supposé que le Monde ne fut pas infiny, puisqu'il ne pourroit pas estre ou il n'y auroit rien, et qu'il ne pourroit acroistre la grandeur du Monde qu'il n'adjoutast quelque chose à sa propre étenduë, commençant d'estre où il n'estoit pas auparavant. (I, 14).[86]

As God was able to make the soul immortal, so he could make the World infinite, if it is true that Eternity is nothing other than a duration without bounds, and the infinite, an extension without limits. And then, God himself would be finite, if you supposed that the World were not infinite, because he could not exist where there was nothing and he could not increase the size of the World without adding to his own dimensions, beginning to exist where he had not previously existed.

To please Montmagnie Cyrano draws upon the Christian tradition of God's plenitude, or the concept that infinite causes produce infinite effects. The principle of plenitude was invoked as one of the major arguments in favor of the plurality of worlds in the late Middle Ages.[87] So orthodox was this argument considered that in 1277 the bishop of Paris, Etienne Tempier, with the pope's authority, officially condemned the teaching that God could not create a plurality of worlds.[88]

Cyrano brings certain modifications to the argument which can be found also in the writings of Giordano Bruno. Bruno reasons that an infinite cause produces an infinite effect,[89] but he identifies infinite space with God himself.[90]

Why should or how can we suppose the divine potency to be idle? Why should we say that the divine goodness which is capable of communicating itself to an infinity of things and of pouring itself without limit, is niggardly? . . . Why should that center of deity which is able to expand itself into an infinite sphere (if we may so speak) remain barren, as if it were envious? Why should the infinite capacity be frustrated, the possibility of infinite worlds be cheated, the perfection of the divine image be impaired—that image which ought rather to be reflected back in a mirror as immeasurable as itself?[91]

Cyrano also identifies God with infinite space, and it is as a geometer that he speaks when he says that it would be impossible for God to add to his own "étendue" (dimensions). This is undoubtedly the basis for Spink's judgment that the passage in

Cyrano quoted above can mean only "that God is to the World what the intelligence is to the body; space and intelligence are two aspects of the same infinite Being."[92] The confusion of deity and the spatially infinite is a product of the new astronomy, which had so expanded the universe as to shift the application of the adjective "infinite" from God to space.[93] Cyrano thus adds an important feature to the traditional argument. He insists less on the principle of plenitude, that is, on God as creator of an infinite universe, than he does on the identity of an infinite God with an infinite universe. His position is deceptive; although his reasoning appears in a traditional framework, it is in reality not quite acceptable to the orthodox, who would prefer to reserve the attribute of infinity to God alone.

Cyrano recapitulates in a sentence the reasoning which has led to his statement of the infinity of worlds. As we see other planets from the earth (starting with the moon-world), so from other planets will we see still others, stretching to infinity.

Il faut donc croire que, comme nous voyons d'icy Saturne et Jupiter, si nous estions dans l'un ou dans l'autre, nous descouvririons beaucoup de mondes que nous n'appercevons pas d'icy, et que l'Univers est éternellement construict de cette sorte. (I, 14)

You must believe, then, that, as we see Saturn and Jupiter from here, if we were on one or the other of them, we would discover many worlds that we do not perceive from here, and that the Universe is eternally constructed in this way.

The variant for "eternellement" in the 1657 edition, "à l'infiny,"[94] indicates an awareness of the dangerous implications of the last step of Cyrano's reasoning. The infinity, as opposed to the plurality, of worlds poses a threat to God's infinity. Eternellement" generally refers to the action of God; it is accordingly modified for the 1657 edition. Nevertheless the bold step from plurality to infinity has been taken. Even Borel, whose treatise on the plurality of worlds should logically conduct him to the infinite, hedges on this question. He feels called upon to reply to the charge that the notion of the plurality of worlds is followed logically by that of the infinity of worlds. His rather feeble rejoinder is based on the teleological concept of the stars' utility, which he himself largely rejects. Thus, afraid to make an outright statement of the infinity in which he undoubtedly believes, he wavers.

Quelqu'un oppose . . . que s'il y avoit d'astres habitez, il faudroit d'autres astres pour y influer, et d'autres cieux à l'infiny, à quoy je responds que je ne me persuade pas puissamment que les Estoiles nous soyent utiles, excepté le Soleil et la Lune, il peut estre que ces astres se communiquent et servent les uns aux autres mutuellement, et par ainsi il n'est pas besoin d'une infinité de cieux.[95]

Someone objects . . . that if there were inhabited stars, you would need other stars to influence them and other heavens ad infinitum, to which I reply that I am not so easily persuaded that the Stars are useful to us, except the Sun and the Moon. Perhaps these stars influence each other and serve each other mutually, and thus you would not need an infinity of heavens.

Descartes restrains himself from applying the epithet "infinite" to space. He prefers instead to qualify it, as Nicholas of Cusa had done before him,[96] with the term "indefinite." God alone, he says, is infinite: "Et nous appellerons ces choses indéfinies plutôt qu'infinies, afin de réserver à Dieu seul le nom d'infini."[97] (And we will call these things indefinite rather than infinite, so as to reserve for God alone the name of infinite.) Gassendi does assume the infinity of space, but he has a tendency to conceive of it negatively; space for him is infinite because it is not finite.[98]

McColley draws a distinction between the conception of a

plurality or infinity of worlds, on the one hand, and the related idea of one infinite world, on the other.[99] For Cyrano the two ideas are definitely linked; a development of the latter follows an exposition of the former. Cyrano's presentation of the infinity of the world is Lucretian and materialistic in tone. As Lucretius demonstrates the inconceivability of nothingness beyond the universe by imagining a dart hurled from its edge,[100] so Cyrano answers Montmagnie's complaint that he cannot understand the infinite by telling him it would be even harder to understand nullity surrounding finitude.[101]

—Ma foy! me réplicqua-il, vous avés beau dire, je ne sçaurois du tout comprendre cet infiny.
—He, dites-moy, luy dis-je, comprenés-vous mieux le rien qui est au-delà? Point du tout. (I, 14–15)

—My word! he replied, Say what you will, I cannot at all understand your infinity.
—Well, tell me, I said to him, Do you understand any better the nothingness beyond? Not at all.

The infinite is actually quite easy to comprehend, Cyrano says, because it is composed of exactly those elements which we already know. Cyrano abandons the domain of theology and speaks now strictly as a materialist. The world is a unity; the heavens are not incorruptible, but consist of the same substance as the earth.

Quand vous songés à ce néant, vous vous l'imaginés tout au moins comme du vent, comme de l'air, et cela est quelque chose; mais l'infiny, si vous ne le comprenés en général, vous le concevés au moins par parties, car il n'est pas difficile de se figurer de la terre, du feu, de l'eau, de l'air, des astres, des cieux. Or l'infiny n'est rien qu'une tissure sans bornes de tout cela. (I, 15)

MIRACLE: ALTERNATIVES

When you reflect on this nothingness, you imagine it at least as wind or air, and that is something; but as for infinity, if you do not understand it in its generality, you can conceive of it at least in parts, for it is not difficult to imagine earth, fire, water, air, stars, heavens. Now the infinite is nothing other than a boundless tapestry of all this.

On his trip to the sun Dyrcona will perceive something of this unlimited space. As he approaches the sun, he and his flying machine become transparent. Not realizing what is happening at first, Dyrcona mistakes his transparent machine for the sky. When he stretches out his arms he meets an obstacle, occasioning an ironic allusion to the concept of the crystalline sphere.

Encor ce qui m'effraya davantage, ce fut de sentir, comme si le vague de l'air se fut pétrifié, je ne sçay quel obstacle invisible qui repoussoit mes bras quand je les pensois étendre. Il me vint alors dans l'imagination qu'à force de monter, j'estois sans doute arrivé dans le firmament que certains Philosophes et quelques Astronomes ont dit estre solide. (I, 134)

And what frightened me even more was to feel some kind of invisible obstacle which repulsed my arms when I attempted to extend them, as if the space of air had become petrified. It then occurred to me that by rising so high I had undoubtedly reached the firmament that certain Philosophers and some Astronomers have said to be solid.

If any suspicion remains that Cyrano held to the theological principle of plenitude in his exposition of the plurality or infinity of worlds and of infinity itself, it is quelled by his satirical interpretation of the unique Biblical Creation. The viceroy asks: How could infinite worlds in an infinite universe have been created, since the Bible speaks only of the one created by God? Cyrano's impious reply invites the charge of placing a severe limit on God's power and will.

Que si vous me demandés de quelle façon ces mondes ont esté faicts,
veu que la Saincte Escriture parle seulement d'un que Dieu créa, je
responds qu'elle ne parle que du nostre à cause qu'il est le seul que
Dieu ayst voulu prendre la peine de faire de sa propre main, mais
tous les autres, qu'on voit ou qu'on ne voit pas, suspendus parmy
l'azur de l'univers, ne sont rien que l'escume des soleils qui se
purgent. (I, 15)

If you ask me how these worlds were made, in view of the fact that
Holy Scripture speaks of only one created by God, I will reply that
it speaks only of ours since it was the only one God wished to take
the trouble to create with his own hands, but all the others, which
can or cannot be seen suspended in the azure of the universe, are
nothing but the dross of suns purging themselves.

This explanation is considerably weakened in the variant for the
1657 edition, in which Cyrano falls back on a profession of fideism (I, 15, variant f).

The truly radical features, then, of the cosmology presented
by Cyrano have little relationship to Copernican heliocentrism.
That he so openly subscribed to Copernicanism was, to be sure,
sufficient grounds for the majority of his contemporaries to regard
him with a wary eye. But, as Arthur Lovejoy observes, Copernicanism in Cyrano's time did not have the revolutionary impact
of certain other ideas. Lovejoy lists five of these:

1) the assumption that other planets of our solar system are inhabited
by living, sentient, and rational creatures; 2) the shattering of the
outer walls of the medieval universe, whether these were identified
with the outermost, crystalline sphere or with a definite "region" of
the fixed stars, and the dispersal of these stars through vast, irregular
distances; 3) the conception of the fixed stars as suns similar to ours,
all or most of them surrounded by planetary systems of their own;
4) the supposition that the planets in these other worlds also have
conscious inhabitants; 5) the assertion of the actual infinity of the

physical universe in space and of the number of solar systems contained in it.[102]

As is apparent from the preceding discussion, all of these cosmological innovations are present in the *Autre Monde*. Lovejoy derives these notions from the principle of plenitude,[103] which is a starting point for Cyrano. But in the course of amplifying his ideas, Cyrano wanders far from where he set out. His assertions of infinite worlds in an infinite universe are ultimately those of a materialist who does little to conceal that in his universe a creator would be superfluous.

Apart from what the telescope revealed, the innovations so readily accepted by Cyrano did not have a "scientific" basis, in the sense that they could not be corroborated by any direct observation or experimentation.[104] Heliocentrism, too, was of necessity based primarily on experimentally unverifiable data. As Descartes insisted, a reliance on reason was demanded. Cyrano, however, was not just a theoretician, and his flights of fancy betray his desire for empirical evidence. Paradoxically enough, his imaginings serve as empirical proofs projected onto what he probably saw as a bright future. Borel had spoken seriously of the possibility of constructing an airship.[105] Cyrano's various flying machines reflect a knowledge of theories and experiments in this field by his contempories.[106] He was an innovator as well. Marjorie Nicolson thinks he may have been the first lunar traveler to use a rocket ship.[107] Fantastic as some of his aerial chariots may seem, they represent efforts to fulfill realistically what had previously been only fabulous dreams of interstellar travel.[108] For the readers of his voyages, at least, the new universe would be visible as well as theoretically conceivable, translating Cyrano's firm belief in the reality of heliocentrism and of infinite worlds in an infinite universe.

MIRACLE: ALTERNATIVES

MATERIALISM, COSMOLOGY, AND THE FRAGMENT DE PHYSIQUE

Cyrano's incomplete *Fragment de physique*, first published in the *Nouvelles Oeuvres* of 1662, presents some apparent contradictions to the ideas of the *Autre Monde*. Lachèvre feels that the differences between the *Voyage dans la lune* and the *Fragment* are so striking that the reader might well wonder if the *Fragment* was even written by Cyrano.[109] An examination of the text in its relationship to the *Autre Monde* will reveal that Lachèvre's doubts were not a little exaggerated. There are similarities as well as differences between the two works, and the differences, although important, are not unexplainable.

Both Lachèvre[110] and Brun,[111] following the biblicphile P. L. Jacob,[112] find Cyrano s *Fragment* and the *Traité de physique* by the Cartesian Jacques Rohault comparable, but Brun believes Rohault plagiarized the *Fragment* whereas it is Cyranc that Lachèvre accuses of plagiarism. Spink, who leans toward crediting Rohault with the original works, deems it more important to note that the *Fragment* follows Descartes.[113] A. W. Loewenstein considers the *Fragment* simply a restatement of Cartesian ideas;[114] Lachèvre sees the *Fragment* as Cartesian, the *Voyage dans la lune* as Gassendist.[115]

The nature of matter is explained differently in the *Estats de la lune* and in the *Fragment*. In the former, the *fils de l'hôte* expounds the Lucretian and Gassendist theory according to which the atoms of various shapes are solid, impenetrable, and indivisible.[116] In the *Fragment de physique*,[117] Cyrano equates matter with extension, as do Descartes[118] and Rohault.[119] Contrary to the Gassendist exposition in the *Estats de la lune*, Cyrano in the *Fragment* holds with Descartes that matter is infinitely divisible.[120] Although he had hinted at infinitely divisible matter in the *Estats du soleil*, Cyrano's materialism is there at once eclectic and original.

The *Estats du soleil* may well be a key in determining the relationship of the ideas in the *Autre Monde* and in the *Fragment*. In the second voyage, Cyrano seems at times to be holding a philosophical debate with himself, reflecting on ideas he had put forth in the *Estats de la lune* and on some he had possibly acquired since writing it. On the question of the vacuum, for instance, he takes opposite stands in the *Estats de la lune* and in the *Fragment*, but it is perhaps in the *Estats du soleil* that his thought on this problem presents the most interest.

In the *Estats de la lune*, Gonzalès informs Cyrano that he was almost prosecuted by the Inquisition for having asserted the existence of a vacuum in nature (I, 45).[121] The threat of the Inquisition alone would cause the *libertin* Cyrano to favor the opinions of Gonzalès. If all matter is a unity, as Gonzalès believes, then the only difference between hard and soft substances, for example, is that in the former the particles of matter are more closely packed together, whereas in the latter they are loosely joined, with little vacuums in between them (I, 45–47). The weight of all matter is the same, the impression of lightness or heaviness created by more or fewer vacuums in between the particles. This exposition of the theory of the vacuum is strictly Lucretian and Gassendist.[122] Cyrano rightly objects that Gonzalès has proceeded on the assumption that a vacuum exists without first having proved it (I, 47). Gonzalès in response points out that since according to his theory of matter the atoms are impenetrable, there is no way to explain expansion or contraction except by postulating the vacuum. Again he follows Gassendist reasoning.[123] To prove his point he cites several examples, found also in Gassendi,[124] of how nature does not abhor a vacuum. Water will burst a frosty vase or rise in a tube not to avoid a vacuum but because of the weight of air (I, 48–49). Another argument, also Gassendist and Lucretian in inspiration, is that if there were no vacuum there could be no movement (I, 48).[125]

In the *Fragment de physique* Cyrano denies the possibility of a vacuum, as does Descartes.[126] To the classic question, could God remove all the air from a room and leave the walls in the same place, Cyrano replies in the negative. If there were truly nothing, no atoms whatsoever, the walls would touch each other, since a complete vacuum is impossible.[127]

In the *Estats du soleil* Dyrcona questions his philosopher-guide Campanella, a great admirer of Descartes, on the latter's denial of the vacuum. Descartes modified Epicurean materialism, Dyrcona says, by assuming that chaos, at first solid, was later divided into innumerable little squares moving in different directions which by contact with each other were worn into various shapes.[128] But, he queries, how could the particles of matter have moved if there was no space between them (I, 184)? To this Gassendist objection Campanella gives no definitive answer, saying that Dyrcona will have to wait to hear from Descartes himself, who will most certainly be able to furnish him with the information needed since he is the most venerated thinker among the solar philosophers (I, 184). The reply is of course never proffered, because the *Estats du soleil* ends before Descartes has a real opportunity to philosophize. Whether the abrupt conclusion of the sun voyage was deliberate or not,[129] it strengthens the impression created by such passages as the one on the vacuum that much of the voyage is a philosophical dialogue representing reflection and meditation rather than definitive positions. Dyrcona's questioning of Campanella on the subject of the vacuum suggests not that he has decided for or against it, but that he would merely like to know more about it. Campanella does continue to summarize the Cartesian view that if matter is extension and space extended matter, a vacuum cannot exist. But he quickly abandons the discussion, remarking that Dyrcona has not yet developed enough independence from his senses and reliance on reason to follow his thinking (I, 185).

The same lack of decision is evident in the *Estats du soleil* on the problem of the divisibility of matter. Implicit in the Lucretian and Gassendist materialism of the *Estats de la lune* is the indivisibility of the atoms. In the *Fragment de physique* Cyrano clearly affirms the divisibility of matter.[130] The metamorphoses on the sun may suggest the infinite divisibility of matter, but nowhere in the sun voyage does Cyrano state that view as positively as in the *Fragment*. In the course of Dyrcona's conversation with Campanella, however, the philosopher brings up the question, saying that Descartes did believe in the infinite divisibility of matter, a notion which must be conceived by reason alone since it cannot be confirmed by the senses (I, 185).[131] Dyrcona does not have the chance to reply to Campanella and no solution is reached. A few days later Dyrcona and Campanella encounter an old man dying in a peculiar way. His head has swollen enormously and is pierced in several places. Campanella explains to Dyrcona that the man is a philosopher whose tripartite brain, consisting of memory, imagination, and judgment, has become filled to the bursting point with little corporeal images. In this manner—"crever d'esprit" (bursting with wit) (I, 191)—do all solar geniuses die. Dyrcona had previously visited the allegorical rivers of Memory, Imagination, and Judgment, and had learned that on the sun the atoms of dead bodies, before rearranging themselves in another form, are first soaked in the waters of these rivers (I, 189–190). It may be assumed then, that the little corporeal images in the dying philosopher's brain are these same presoaked atoms. Their multiplication to the bursting point would appear to be a satirical treatment of the infinite divisibility of atoms.[132] But again Cyrano takes no definitive stand. The Cartesian notion of the infinite divisibility of matter is both suggested and satirized. The reader is once more left with the impression that Cyrano is debating with himself in the *Estats du soleil* on issues which he will resolve as a Cartesian in the *Fragment*.

The *Fragment*, obviously designed as a systematic treatise, is consistent and coherent in a way that the fantastic voyages, by their nature, cannot be. As is to be expected, Cyrano follows Descartes on most points. His theory of movement is Cartesian.[133] Instead of proclaiming the world infinite, as he had done in the *Estats de la lune*, he now terms it indefinite with Descartes.[134]

He remains a confirmed Copernician in the *Fragment*, which is not inconsistent with the Cartesian ambiance since Descartes too had favored heliocentrism in his *Monde*. Cyrano's presentation of the Copernican theory, however, retains his own touch. It is not actually part of the fragment itself, but figures only in the "idée générale de la physique," a sort of table of contents as well as an outline of the whole treatise. The plan of the second part is entitled "De la Cosmographie" and is in fact an exposition of heliocentrism. The method of presentation proves ultimately to be a reductio ad absurdum of the opposing view which Cyrano takes alternately with the Copernican. He begins by supposing the "masse élémentaire" mobile. He next supposes it immobile, but examines the disadvantages incurred by assuming that the heavens move.[135] Cyrano then examines one by one the "appearances" of various astronomical phenomena: the sun, the fixed stars, the moon, the planets, the comets, and the new stars, satisfying them by first making the "masse élémentaire" immobile, then mobile.[136] The conclusions he reaches after his seemingly impartial study are the following:

> Que, posant la masse élémentaire immobile, le Monde total est un monstre composé de pièces rapportées sans aucune liaison.
>
> Liaison et simplicité du Monde, attribuant du mouvement à la masse élémentaire.[137]

That, supposing the elemental mass immobile, the whole World is a monster formed of pieces brought together without any interconnection.

Harmony and simplicity of the World, attributing movement to the elemental mass.

Cyrano's final argument by simplicity links him to the group of thinkers Lovejoy has called the "esprits simplistes" (simplistic minds), typically found in the period of the Enlightenment, who believed in generally simple solutions, recognizing at once the importance and the limitations of human reason.[138] As in the discussion on Copernicanism in the *Estats de la lune*, Cyrano's ultimate appeal is to reason and common sense.

The craftily sarcastic Cyrano of the *Estats de la lune* can be seen in somewhat diluted form in the sixth chapter of the *Fragment de physique*, innocuously entitled "Des Causes du mouvement et du repos." The ostensible subject of this chapter is the concept of perpetual motion. God, as the Creator of all things in time, has imparted movement to certain parts of the world and he will continue the action by which he moves things to conserve them.[139] On this idea of movement Cyrano concurs with Descartes and Rohault.[140] Although God for Descartes is a primary cause who can be easily dispensed with, whose presence is not felt in the "new world" of the *Monde*, he yet is unquestionably there, even if only for the sake of propriety. Neither Descartes nor Rohault wishes to explore the problem of creation; Descartes rather wishes to dismiss it as unobtrusively as possible and deal with the physical laws of the universe, in which he is more interested. Cyrano, who had denied Creation in the *Estats de la lune*, returns to the question here, but with a little more caution. After prudently supposing God as the primary cause, Cyrano modifies slightly the reply in the *Estats de la lune* to the objection that God could not have created a plurality of worlds since the Bible mentions only one. We will consider, he says, those things "outside" of God, and according to our mortal judgment only.[141] In trying to imagine the world before our birth, then, we can only imagine it as it is today, and if we reach farther back to the beginning of time, we can again imagine it only as the same. With reasoning based once more on the Aristotelian *ex nihilo nihil*, we arrive at the conclusion that the world is eternal.

Toutefois, quand nous considérons les êtres hors de lui, et seulement selon notre façon de raisonner, parce que nous nous apercevons comment le Monde auroit pu être créé de rien; de là provient que recherchant quel il auroit pu être avant notre naissance, nous penchons à croire qu'il étoit comme il est aujourd'hui; et lorsqu'en remontant vers nos premiers Pères, nous recherchons encore quel il auroit été, nous nous le figurons encore le même; car, ne pouvant jamais faire le saut de l'être au non-être, nous ne saurions établir le Monde si ancien, que nous ne le puissions concevoir encore plus vieux, c'est-à-dire éternel, d'une éternité pour le moins antérieure.[142]

Nevertheless, when we consider those beings outside of him, and only according to our mode of reasoning, because we can see how the World could have been created from nothing, we inquire what it might have been like before our birth, we are inclined to believe that it was like it is today; and when looking back as far as our first Ancestors, we inquire what it might have been like, we imagine it still the same; for, never being able to make the leap from being to nonbeing, we cannot declare the World so old that we could not imagine it yet older, that is to say, eternal, of an eternity at least anterior.

Much more openly than his scholarly peers, Cyrano argues against the world's having been created. One of the more impressive features of Cyrano's *Fragment* is that, unlike such *libertins érudits* as Gassendi and La Mothe Le Vayer, he does not simply report the opinions of various thinkers on a given subject, leaving it up to his initiated public to read between the lines and deduce his personal opinion; he does state his views, although, admittedly, the greater part happen to be Cartesian. Here, however, he departs at least in technique from his master and repeats the bold line of thinking of the *Estats de la lune*. His audacity is even more readily perceived by a comparison to a discussion of the same question by La Mothe Le Vayer, the influence of whose *Physique du Prince* on Cyrano's *Fragment* has been greatly exaggerated by Brun.[143] La Mothe Le Vayer practices his usual equivocation on the problem of creation. He reports the answers of several philosophies and religions to the dilemma posed by the judgment *ex nihilo nihil* and concludes, if indeed it can be considered a philosophically tenable conclusion, that "primary matter" would have to be God's handiwork. This is either a feeble attempt at reconciling a materialistic explanation of the world's beginnings with the Bible or downright evasion.

Parce qu'un des plus récens aphorismes de toute la Physique porte, que de rien l'on ne fait rien; les Philosophes ont imaginé une matière première, de laquelle toutes choses étoient faites. Les savans du Paganisme, comme Platon, ont supposé pour cela cette matière coéternelle à Dieu, dont il s'étoit servi dans la création du Monde. Et il n'y a que les Juifs, les Chrétiens, et les Mahométans, qui sur le texte de Moyse croyent que de rien il a produit tout ce grand Univers. C'est pourquoi il faut tenir pour constant que la matière première, si l'on en doit établir une est une production de la main du Tout Puissant n'y aiant que lui seul qui puisse créer et anéantir ce que bon lui semble.[144]

Because one of the most recent aphorisms of Physics states that from nothing nothing is created, Philosophers have imagined a primary matter, from which all things were made. Wherefore, Pagan thinkers such as Plato supposed this matter coeternal with God, who used the matter in the creation of the World. And only Jews, Christians, and

Mohammedans, going by the text of Moses, believe that he produced this whole huge Universe from nothing. That is why you should consider it certain that primary matter, if you must postulate it, is a product of the hand of the Almighty, since he alone is able to create and annihilate whatever he wishes.

It must be borne in mind, of course, that La Mothe Le Vayer was writing his book for the young Louis XIV and would therefore have been obliged to be somewhat more circumspect than usual. Forthright statement in any case is simply not characteristic of his works. Cyrano, perfectly aware that prudence was the order of the day, nevertheless restrains his freethinking only up to a point in the *Fragment*. There can be no doubt that the old champion of materialism and heliocentrism has left his own imprint on the *Fragment de physique*.

If uniform characteristics can be discerned, common to the *Autre Monde* and the *Fragment*, such as a certain freethinking audacity and a levelheaded belief in heliocentrism, apparent contradictions in these works do not warrant the conclusion that Cyrano may not have been the author of the *Fragment*. The contradictions are, in fact, perhaps more indicative of continuity than the resemblances. Without necessarily demarcating the moon and sun voyages as Gassendist and Cartesian works respectively, as Aram Vartanian has done,[145] a difference in philosophical outlook must be distinguished. The *Estats du soleil* is definitely less rigorous in its presentation of scientific ideas than the *Estats de la lune*, which does adhere quite faithfully to Gassendist materialism. But the *Estats du soleil* is not an exposition of any one philosophy. If more prominence is given to the ideas of Descartes, it is to meditate upon them, to question, and to debate. As the voyage has no conclusion, so Cyrano reaches no conclusion. But fresh influences are unquestionably present, and one has the feeling that Cyrano had begun to follow a new line of thinking.

Around the year 1643, after meeting Jacques Rohault, the

disciple of Descartes and probable author of the prefaces to the *Nouvelles Oeuvres* of 1662 and to the *Fragment*,[146] Cyrano obviously became more and more intrigued with Cartesian philosophy.[147] The *Fragment*, which Brun dates posterior to the *Autre Monde*,[148] but which may have been written during roughly the same period,[149] represents Cyrano's effort to consolidate into a systematic treatise the Cartesian ideas he had mulled over in his fanciful voyage to the sun. Whether this signifies a "conversion" to the philosophy of Descartes is difficult to ascertain. It is probable that the *Fragment* was to be Cyrano's excursion into another field of writing and that the exigencies of a scientific treatise stimulated him to systematize the thoughts he had allowed to wander and develop in different directions in the fantastic voyages. It is a significant endeavor, for it indicates that Cyrano was ready to move from the unordered naturalism of the Italian philosophers and the Epicurean revival staged by Gassendi to the more mechanically ordered world of Descartes.[150]

❧

It would be tempting, but slightly misleading, to say that Cyrano replaces God with Nature. Certainly "Nature" and "God" are often confused with each other in his works. Both Lachèvre and Weber point out such confusions. Lachèvre informs us that in the variants for the 1657 printed edition in the passage on the intelligent cabbage, the word "Nature" is substituted for "God" (I, 68, variant a). This may have been to attenuate the disrespect shown to both man and God in suggesting that a cabbage is a creature just as important as man, if not more so. But having Nature and not God the creative force in the universe is also a more accurate transcription of Cyrano's materialistic concept of birth and formation. Weber notes a similar confusion in Cyrano's description of the role of chance in man's birth.[151] And even in

Cyrano's "Lettre contre Scarron" a variant for the 1654 edition bears the word "Nature" in the place of the original "God" (II, 193, variant i).

At a time when the idea of spatial infinity was encroaching upon God's infinity, these confusions are not surprising. They were in fact typical of the philosophical thought of the period and were remarked upon with shock and indignation by Father Garasse, sarcastically mentioned by Cyrano in one of his letters (II, 177). The Jesuit Garasse, one of the most virulent critics of the *libertins*, charged the freethinking disciples of Montaigne with making Nature and not God their divinity and with equating Nature with God. He would correct their error by defining Nature as the order of secondary causes which are all dependent on the primary cause, the will of God.[152] His definition coincides with the first one in the 1694 edition of the *Dictionnaire de l'Académie française*: "Tout l'Univers, toutes les choses créées" (the whole Universe, all created things), which, as the examples given indicate, implies that God is the Creator.[153]

Dassoucy, zealously attacking the *libertins* with an eye on his prison door, charges Gassendi—whom he terms a "Philosophe Athée"—and his disciples with recognizing no power above that of Nature, which they confuse with God:[154] ". . . à qui ils ostent tous les Attributs, pour les donner à celle qui n'agit que par son ordre"[155] (. . . from whom they take away all Attributes, to give them to that which acts only at his command). Nature for him is completely deprived of intelligence and acts only out of necessity. Intelligence belongs to God and not to Nature.[156] Dassoucy, in depriving Nature of intelligence, would agree with Garasse and the first definition of nature in the *Dictionnaire de l'Académie*. He would refute the dictionary's second definition, considering it to be held by such "atheists" as Gassendi: "Il se prend aussi pour Cet esprit universel qui est répandu dans chaque chose créée; et par lequel toutes choses ont leur commencement, leur progrès et leur fin."[157] (It is also taken to mean That universal spirit which is diffused in every created thing; and by which all things have their beginning, development, and end.)

Cyrano's use of the word "nature" conforms roughly to the second definition. Different arrangements of atoms are responsible for the creation of all that Garasse and Dassoucy would leave to God. In the "pure acts" on the sun, matter and intelligence are one. This does not result in pantheism or animism, but in a rigorous materialistic monism. God is unnecessary in Cyrano's world because nature creates itself.

It cannot be said, however, as Garasse would doubtlessly have believed, that the *libertin* Cyrano made Nature his divinity. He does speak of "Mother Nature," but in the sense of the second definition of the *Dictionnaire de l'Académie*, that is, as the creative force in the universe. The bronze figure adorning a lunarian and covered with male genitalia is worn as a sign of respect to reproductive power and is a symbol of nobility.

Les femelles icy, non plus que les masles, ne sont pas assés ingrattes pour rougir à la veuë de celuy qui les forgées; et les Vierges n'ont pas honte d'aimer sur nous, en mémoire de leur mère Nature, la seule chose qui porte son nom. Sçachés donc que l'escharpe dont cet homme est honoré, où pend pour médaille la figure d'un membre viril, est le symbole du Gentilhomme et la marque qui distingue le Noble d'avec le Roturier. (I, 88)

Here the females, no more than males, are not so ungrateful as to blush at the sight of what begot them; and Virgins are not ashamed to love on our person, in memory of their Mother Nature, the only thing which bears her name. Know then that the sash with which this man is honored, from which hangs a medallion in the form of a male organ, is the sign of a Gentleman and the mark distinguishing a Nobleman from a Commoner.

This passage calls to mind the description of a statue of Nature found in the *Gygès Gallus* (1658) by Zacharie Lisieux and cited by Busson. Busson compares the Lisieux statue to a personification of Nature in the *Estats du soleil*, which in fact resembles the former only in that it too consists of a personification of Nature.[158] Lisieux's representation of Nature is more comparable to Cyrano's bronze figure. Lisieux, in his essay from the *Gygès Gallus*, significantly entitled "Naturae apotheosis," imagines a group of men wishing to renounce their baptism who place a statue of Nature upon a pedestal. The statue is of a woman covered with breasts, similar to an ancient goddess who was supposedly the nourisher of all living creatures.[159] There is no pedestal in Cyrano's work, although it is true that in the passage from the *Estats du soleil* to which Busson refers, a prayer is addressed to a lady resembling the artist's depiction of Nature (I, 105). Cyrano does not specify the details of the artist's image. The bronze statue of the *Estats de la lune* signifies nobility, not divinity.

As Spink has shown,[160] Cyrano worshipped neither God nor Nature. Worship and divinity are generally absent from his writings. If by replacing God with Nature is meant the substitution of one divinity for another, this notion would be false. The confusion of Nature and God in his works is at times a precaution against too open impiety, at times a reflection of the semantic and philosophical confusion resulting from an expanded universe tending to displace the traditional God. But it is mainly a conscious confusion mirroring his conviction that natural and not divine reasons suffice to explain all that we need to know. If Cyrano does not replace God with Nature, he certainly replaces him with nature, by which is meant all the natural causes and processes operating in the world, typified by Cyrano's materialism and cosmology.

3

FROM SCEPTICISM
TO RELATIVISM:
SCIENCE AND EPISTEMOLOGY

Although he was not a systematic philosophical thinker, Cyrano did reach certain significant philosophical conclusions which are readily apparent in his works. How did he arrive at these conclusions? What criteria of knowledge did he apply to the specific problems with which he was concerned? If these questions arise in the minds of Cyrano's readers, it is because Cyrano himself was preoccupied with them. As a participant in the intellectual pageantry of his time, Cyrano was not without a role in the sceptical crisis of the sixteenth and seventeenth centuries. His particular stance in the crisis marks another distinctive feature of his work and points to his precociousness and originality in the highly sensitive area of epistemology.

Richard Popkin has outlined the three facets of the sceptical crisis treated by Montaigne in the *Apologie de Raimond Sebond* that were to influence seventeenth-century scholars and thinkers. The first of these is the theological problem of the criteria of religious knowledge, as a solution to which Montaigne proposes the Catholic rule of faith. The second is the dilemma posed by the rediscovery of the ancient world as well as by the discoveries of new lands in recent times. The diversity and relative nature of all opinions produce the "humanistic crisis of knowledge" or the doubt that any permanent or absolute truths can be found. The third or "crisis of scientific knowledge," spurred on by the general attack on Aristotle, undermines the foundations of science by questioning the reliability of the criteria employed.[1]

The first of these crises was not one for Cyrano, the unwavering foe of religion. The other two, however, play a large part in his writing. He is especially concerned with the third in the *Fragment de physique*. Both the scientific and the humanistic crises pervade the *Autre Monde* and are often fused in Cyrano's treatment of the problems of knowledge and their implications for man. From his examination of these questions emerge a new scepticism and a new epistemological outlook.

⋘§⋙

If Cyrano acquired his epistemological ideas through a series of reasoned steps, the first of these would have been the rejection of authority. Authority for Cyrano encompasses primarily Aristotle, theology, and the unlikely combination of these two in scholasticism, termed a "centaur" by Cornelius Agrippa von Nettesheim.[2] The reaction against these long-standing pillars of knowledge was of course one of the motivating forces in the intellectual crisis of the period.[3] But Cyrano rejects all authority; he bows to no one philosopher or respected individual—not even to such a relatively insignificant figure of authority as the father of a family—and he certainly does not recognize as valid the opinion of the majority simply because it is the most widely accepted. It is in his "Lettre contre les sorciers" that Cyrano makes his most intransigent disavowal of all forms of authority.[4]

Je ne deffère à l'authorité de personne, si elle n'est accompagnée de raison. . . . Ny le nom d'Aristote plus sçavant que moy, ny celuy de Platon, ny celuy de Socrate ne me persuadent point, si mon jugement n'est convaincu par raison de ce qu'ils disent . . . et puis, je sçay par expérience que les esprits les plus sublimes ont chopé le plus lourdement; comme ils tombent de plus haut, ils font de plus grandes cheutes; enfin, nos pères se sont trompez jadis, leurs neveux se trompent maintenant, les nostres se tromperont quelque jour. (II, 212)

I will defer to the authority of no one, if it is not accompanied by reason. . . . Neither the name of Aristotle, a man more learned than myself, nor that of Plato, nor that of Socrates, will sway me, if my judgment is not convinced by what they say . . . and then, I know from experience that the most sublime minds have taken the heaviest tumbles; since they fall from higher up, their falls are greater; finally, our forefathers were wrong in former times, their descendants are wrong now, ours will be wrong in the future.

The conviction that reason and not authority must be followed is reiterated in the *Estats de la lune* by Gonzalès, who is pleased by the lunarians' scorn of authority and love of truth. "Truth" here would seem to be almost synonymous with reason, since Gonzalès is speaking of the method of attaining knowledge rather than of knowledge attained. If the Spaniard chooses to remain on the moon it is because:

. . . les hommes y sont amateurs de la vérité, . . . on n'y voit point de Pédans, . . . les Philosophes ne se laissent persuader qu'à la raison, et . . . l'autorité d'un sçavant, ny le plus grand nombre, ne l'emportent point sur l'opinion d'un batteur en grange, si le batteur en grange raisonne aussi fortement. (I, 36)

114

... the men there love truth, ... you do not see any Pedants there, ... Philosophers are persuaded only by reason, and ... neither the authority of a scholar nor that of the majority prevails over the opinion of a thresher, if the thresher reasons as well.

Once truth and reason have displaced the force of authority, pedants find no harbor. Cyrano's strong distaste for pedants, comically amplified in *Le Pédant joué*, is another manifestation of his aversion to any kind of dogmatism, an attitude which Jacques Denis has characterized as "une violence de haine contre le dogmatisme" (a violent hatred of dogmatism).[5] In the "Lettre contre les sorciers" Cyrano challenges pedants to profess an absolutely true philosophy instead of the usual empty "maxims" which they are accustomed to pronounce with oracular assurance.

Pour moy, je me mcque des Pédants qui n'ont point de plus forts arguments pour prouver ce qu'ils disent, sinon d'alléguer que c'est une maxime comme si leurs maximes estoient bien plus certaines que leurs autres propositions. Je les croyray pourtant s'ils me montrent une Philosophie dont les principes ne puissent être révoquez en doute, desquels toute la Nature soit d'accord, ou qui nous ayent esté révélez d'enhaut; autrement je m'en moque, car il est aisé de prouver tout ce qu'on veut quand on ajuste les principes aux opinions, et non pas les opinions aux principes. (II, 212–213)

For my part, I have no use for those Pedants who have no better argument to prove what they say than to state that it is a maxim, as if their maxims were much more certain than their other propositions. I will believe them, however, if they present me with a Philosophy the principles of which cannot be called into question, on which all of Nature agrees, or which has been revealed to us from on high; otherwise I simply dismiss them, for it is easy to prove anything you want when you adjust principles to opinions, and not opinions to principles.

FROM SCEPTICISM TO RELATIVISM

The last formula, condemning the dogmatic use of principles to confirm prejudices, is applied by Cyrano to Aristotle in the *Estats de la lune*: "Aristote . . . accommodoit des principes à sa Philosophie au lieu d'accommoder sa Philosophie aux principes" (I, 54).[6] (Aristotle . . . adjusted principles to his Philosophy instead of adjusting his Philosophy to principles.) Selectivity and discretion must be employed in considering the opinions of Aristotle and the ancients in general. Cyrano refuses to submit blindly to their judgment; to him they are only men subject to human error, as he states in the "Lettre contre les sorciers."

Quand il seroit juste de defférer à l'authorité de ces grands hommes, et quand je serois contraint d'avoüer que les premiers Philosophes ont establ|y ces principes, je les forcerois bien d'avoüer à leur tour que ces Anciens-là, non plus que nous n'ont pas toûjours escrit ce qu'ils ont cru. Souvent les Loix et la Religion de leur pays les a contraints d'accommoder leurs préceptes à l'interest et au besoin de la politique. C'est pourquoi on ne doit croire d'un homme que ce qui est humain, c'est-à-dire, possible et ordinaire. (II, 213)

Even if it were right to bow to the authority of these great men, and if I were obliged to admit that the first Philosophers did establish these principles, I would force them in turn to admit that the Ancients, no more than ourselves, did not always write what they believed. Often the Laws and Religion of their country obliged them to adapt their precepts to the interests and needs of politics. That is why you must believe of a man only that which is human, that is, possible and ordinary.

There is an element of Pyrrhonism evident in the passages just quoted from the "Lettre contre les sorciers." Underlying Cyrano's challenge to pedants to produce an incontestably true philosophy is the belief that such a philosophy does not exist. The suggestion of Machiavellianism, that is, that the laws and religion of a country may be conditioned by political needs, places further doubt on the validity or existence of permanent principles. Cyrano's philosophical goal is, accordingly, not truth but verisimilitude.

N'embrassons donc point une opinion à cause que beaucoup la tiennent, ou parce que c'est la pensée d'un grand Philosophe, mais seulement à cause que nous voyons plus d'apparence qu'il soit ainsi que d'estre autrement. (II, 212)

Let us therefore not adopt an opinion because it is held by many, or because it is the thought of a great Philosopher, but only because we see more likelihood that it would be thus than otherwise.

LeBret, in his preface to the *Estats de la lune*, notes Cyrano's preference for Pyrrho among the ancients, and suggests that scepticism appealed to him.

Démocrite et Pyrrhon lui sembloient, après Socrate, les plus raisonnables de l'antiquité; encore, n'étoit-ce qu'à cause que le premier avoit mis la vérité dans un lieu si obscur, qu'il étoit impossible de la voir; et que Pyrrhon avoit été si généreux, qu'aucun des Savans de son siècle n'avoit pu mettre ses sentimens en servitude, et si modeste, qu'il n'avoit jamais voulu rien décider.[7]

Democritus and Pyrrho seemed to him, after Socrates, the most reasonable men of classical antiquity; even if it was only because the former placed truth in such an obscure place that it was impossible to see it; and because Pyrrho was so noble that no Scholar of his time was able to enslave his ideas, and so modest that he never wanted to decide anything.

Is LeBret transcribing faithfully the sentiments of his deceased friend? His preface must be read with great discernment, for his judgments are often determined by his loyalty to Cyrano and by his desire to gloss over or dilute the more potent ideas of the freethinker. In the matter of Cyrano's attraction to scepticism, however, it is likely that his statements are accurate. Cyrano's estimation of Democritus, Pyrrho, and Socrates, for example, parallels certain ideas which he very conceivably could have gleaned from Montaigne's *Apologie*. Montaigne remarks on the merits of the dialogue form used by Plato. Like Cyrano, Montaigne approves of devices, such as the dialogue, which render truth obscure and intangible, inviting suspension of judgment rather than dogmatic decision.

Platon me semble avoir aymé cette forme de philosopher par dialogues, à escient, pour loger en diverses bouches la diversité et variation de ses propres fantaisies.

Plato seems to me to have favored this form of philosophizing in dialogues deliberately, to put more fittingly into diverse mouths the diversity and variation of his own ideas.[8]

Le conducteur de ses dialogismes, Socrates, va tousjours demandant et esmouvant la dispute, jamais l'arrestant, jamais satisfaisant, et dict n'avoir autre science que la science d'opposer. . . . De Plato nasquirent dix sectes diverses, dict on. Aussi, à mon gré, jamais instruction ne fut titubante et rien asseverante, si la sienne ne l'est.

The leader of his dialogues, Socrates, is always asking questions and stirring up discussion, never concluding, never satisfying; and says he has no other knowledge than that of opposing. . . . From Plato arose ten different sects, they say. And indeed, in my opinion, never was teaching wavering and noncommittal if his is not.[9]

The influence of Montaigne on the seventeenth-century *libertins* is indisputable, and has been amply explored by such scholars as Alan Boase, Popkin, and Busson.[10] Leo Jordan has devoted an article to the influence of Montaigne on Cyrano.[11] Although he lists numerous examples of Cyrano's acquaintance with Montaigne in several important areas of thought, he does not discuss the role played by scepticism in the tradition of Montaigne in Cyrano's works. Boase, who calls Cyrano "the sworn enemy of dogmatism,"[12] briefly notes the influence of Montaigne. According to Boase, "Cyrano is not only a sceptic, but an anti-Christian sceptic."[13] Pierre Sage sees Cyrano as "ce disciple de Pyrrhon et de Montaigne" (that disciple of Pyrrho and Montaigne).[14]

To classify Cyrano simply as a sceptic, however, would be to describe him incompletely. That he opposed all forms of dogmatism and authority is certain. But his antidogmatic stand does not necessarily lead him to the final position of a Pyrrho, a Sextus Empiricus, or even to that of Montaigne in the *Apologie*. To understand Cyrano's basic epistemological ideas it is necessary to examine his particular adaptation and transformation of the scepticism that was revived in the Renaissance and which troubled the thinkers of the seventeenth century.

The sceptical theme of human ignorance and the impossibility of attaining certitude is reflected in two passages of the *Estats de la lune*, which may be compared to an idea in Borel's *Discours nouveau*. Cyrano relates that God, having expelled Adam from paradise, punishes him by rubbing his gums with the skin of the ignorance-producing fruit from the *Arbre de Science* (I, 29). When Cyrano himself eats one of these apples his soul is plunged into a dark night ("une espaisse nuict") of ignorance (I, 31–32). In these satirical accounts of original sin, Cyrano equates knowledge with ignorance and mocks man's belief that true knowledge is possible.

Borel cites the idea of man's ignorance being the punishment for his original sin as a very curious proof of the plurality of worlds.[15] His reasoning, ultimately quite paradoxical, would appear to be that the Biblical account of Creation serves to stimulate man's admiration and wonderment rather than to furnish him with knowledge, of which he has been deprived in any case since the original sin. It is difficult to reconcile this lack of knowledge with Borel's preachment of so debatable a theory as the plurality of worlds, but he is more concerned here with removing recourse to the authority of Scripture as a barrier to learning. A recognition of human ignorance should cause the thinking man to shun authority and dogmatism in order to free his mind to contemplate new ideas.

Cette doctrine de plusieurs mondes ou globes habités ne choque point les sainctes Escritures, qui nous baillent seulement la création de celuy que nous habitons, duquel elle nous a mesme dit ce qu'elle nous en a laissé plus en discours mystique que clairement, ne faisant que toucher légèrement les autres créatures de l'univers, afin de donner plus sujet d'admirer que de cognoistre aux esprits foibles des hommes, décheus depuis longtemps de la cognoissance des sciences, c'est [sic] obscurcissement de la vérité et ces ténèbres de l'entendement humain ont esté une partie des peines que le péché d'Adam attira sur nous, à cause duquel l'homme fut exclus des délices du Paradis, de la volupté qui est en la cognoissance des sciences, de la vraye cognoissance de la nature et des choses célestes.[16]

This doctrine of several inhabited worlds or globes does not at all offend Holy Scripture, which tells us only of the creation of the one we inhabit, about which it speaks more mystically than clearly, only touching lightly on the creatures of the universe, so as to give to the feeble mind of man, who long ago fell from a state of knowledge, greater occasion to wonder than to know. The obscuring of truth and the shadows of human understanding were part of the punishment which Adam's sin visited upon us, because of which man was denied the delights of Paradise, the pleasure of the knowledge of science, the true knowledge of nature and of heavenly things.

The "obscurcissement de la vérité" (obscuring of truth) and the "ténèbres de l'entendement humain" (shadows of human understanding) remind us of the "espaisse nuict" (dark night) of Cyrano's soul. If Cyrano was thinking of Borel, as he may well have been, when writing the *paradis terrestre* episode, his version of original sin could all the more be considered a parable of human ignorance.

Perhaps the most concrete expression of Cyrano's scepticism is to be found in the *Fragment de physique*, where it is of special epistemological value. The concern with a scientific method, the most constructive product of the sceptical crisis, was confined not only to such major works as Descartes's *Discours de la méthode*, but also found its way into various lesser-known treatises. It figures in the first part of the *Traité de physique* by the Cartesian Rohault. It is reflected in Borel's *Discours nouveau*. It is a problem for the consummate sceptic, La Mothe Le Vayer. And a large part of Cyrano's *Fragment* is devoted to epistemological considerations.

In the "Idée générale" and later in the text itself is found the ne plus ultra of sceptical questions, waived by Descartes in favor of the *cogito*: Is life a dream?[17] Since, according to Cyrano, we cannot know the nature of exterior objects but only the sensations they produce in us,[18] it would appear that we have no way of determining if life is a dream or not. This doubt is dispelled, he says, by faith.[19] But Cyrano is no fideist and, as in other similar cases in his writings, his references to God must be read with a certain amount of forewarned cynicism. He does not leave the resolution of his doubts to faith alone but adds that the way to know exterior objects is to make certain suppositions and to see if they agree with our experience. If there is no agreement, the supposition is false; if there is agreement the result is not truth but, as he had indicated in the "Lettre contre les sorciers," verisimilitude. His conclusion: "La Physique ne peut être qu'une Science conjecturale."[20] (Physics can be only a conjectural science.)

From the problem of the senses, then, the method is ultimately derived. The role played by the senses in the acquisition of knowledge in turn brings up the question of that played by reason. An examination of these issues in Cyrano's works will clarify the conclusions he seems to have reached in the *Fragment de physique*.

There is no denying that for Cyrano, as well as for Gassendi, the senses are an important means of gaining knowledge. In the allegorical land of the sun, the streams of the five senses flow into the rivers representing man's cognitive faculties: Memory, Imagination, and Judgment (I, 187–188). In the *Estats de la lune* Cyrano's interest in the senses is evidenced by a lengthy description of their operations, in terms of Lucretian atomism, given by the *fils de l'hôte* (I, 78–82). But in the *Autre Monde* Cyrano does not emphasize the contribution of the senses to knowledge as much as he does their limitations.

Those scientific theories, both materialistic and cosmological, which Cyrano was most eager to propagate, were generally not subject to confirmation by the senses. Heliocentrism was indeed contradicted by sensory evidence. And so Cyrano underlines the insufficiency and unreliability of the senses as a means of attaining knowledge. This is the argument utilized by Cyrano in his attempt to convince the hesitant Montmagnie of the truth of heliocentrism.

Monsieur . . . la plus part des hommes, qui ne jugent que par les sens, se sont laissé persuader à leurs yeux; et de mesme que celuy dont le vaisseau navigue terre à terre, croit demeurer immobile, et que le rivage chemine; ainsy les hommes, tournans avec la Terre autour du Ciel, ont creu que c'estoit le Ciel luy-mesme qui tournoit autour d'eux. (I, 13)

Sir . . . most men, who judge only by their senses, let themselves be persuaded by their eyes; and just as the man whose ship is coasting along thinks he is remaining immobile and that the shore is moving, so men, turning with the Earth around the Heavens, believed that it was the Heavens themselves which were turning around them.

The *démon de Socrate*, equipped with a superior set of expanded and very refined senses, explains to Cyrano that there are many things in the universe beyond the reach of human senses.

Il y a trop peu de rapport . . . entre vos sens et l'explication de ces mistères. Vous vous imaginés, vous autres, que ce que vous ne sçauriez comprendre est spirituel, ou qu'il n'est point; la conséquence en est très faulce, mais c'est un tesmoignage qu'il y a dans l'Univers un million peut-estre de choses, qui, pour estre connuës, demanderoient en vous un million d'organes tous différens. Moy, par exemple, je conçois par mes sens la cause de la sympathie de l'aiman avec de pôle, celle du reflux de la mer, ce que l'animal devient après la mort; vous autres ne sçauriés donner jusques à ces haultes conceptions, à cause que les proportions à ces miracles vous manquent, non plus qu'un aveugle-né ne sçauroit s'imaginer ce que c'est que la beauté d'un paysage, le coloris d'un tableau, les nuances de l'iris. (I, 37–38)[21]

There is too little correspondence . . . between your senses and the explanation of these mysteries. You think that what you cannot understand is spiritual, or else it does not exist; the consequence is very false, but it is evidence that there are in the Universe perhaps a million things, which, in order to be known, would require in you a million organs of all kinds. I, for example, understand through my senses the cause of the attraction of the loadstone to the pole, that of the ebb tides, what happens to an animal after death. You people can never hope to reach such a high level of thought, because you lack the wherewithal to approach these miracles, just as a person born blind cannot imagine the beauty of a landscape, the colors of a painting, the shades of the rainbow.

If the senses are an inadequate tool for gaining knowledge, they can be supplemented by other faculties. They are, after all, only the suppliers of materials for Memory, Imagination, and Judgment in the allegory of the *Estats du soleil*. The divisibility of matter cannot be perceived by the senses, but, Campanella tells Dyrcona on the sun, this is no reason to reject that concept (I, 185). He implies that there are certain things which must be conceived by the mind alone.

Mais . . . pauvre mortel, je sens que ces spéculations te fatiguent parce que . . . tu n'as jamais pris peine à bien épurer ton esprit d'avec la masse de ton corps, et parce que tu l'as rendu si paresseux qu'il ne veut plus faire aucunes fonctions sans le secours des sens. (I, 185)

But . . . poor mortal, I feel that these speculations tire you because . . . you never took the trouble to purify your mind of your body's mass, and because you have made your mind so lazy that it will no longer perform any function without the aid of the senses.

In the *Fragment de physique*, sensation is the starting point of Cyrano's scientific method. The goal of "physics," which he defines as "une connoissance de tout ce qui est dans la nature" (a knowledge of everything in nature),[22] is to know "l'état de toutes les choses et la cause des changemens qu'on y remarque"[23] (the state of all things and the cause of the changes which you notice in them). Knowing the cause of these changes is dependent on our "première connoissance" (first knowledge) of objects and on the impressions they create in us.[24] But it is first necessary to make a kind of tabula rasa, not unlike Descartes's project to clear his mind of "opinions reçues" (accepted opinions) before adopting new ones,[25] to rid ourselves of all prejudices. With a totally unencumbered mind, then, the seeker of knowledge will consider himself not even capable of thought, but capable only of feeling.

Mettons-nous en un état de pure ignorance: c'est pourquoi ne supposons rien du tout, dépouillons-nous de toute science, et considérons-nous seulement capables de sentir, sans pourtant que nous ayons jamais rien senti.[26]

Let us place ourselves in a state of pure ignorance: to which purpose let us suppose nothing at all; let us cast off all knowledge, and let us consider ourselves capable only of feeling, without however having ever felt anything.

The first step after the initial sceptical preparation is to examine sensation. A pin pricks the subject. As a result he may be in a state of pain, but it will not be precisely correct to state that he feels the pain of the pin, for the pain is in him and not in the pin.[27] Cyrano offers other examples of different types of sensation to show that, in varying degrees, the external object causing the sensation must always be distinguished from the sensation felt by the subject.[28]

The conclusion Cyrano draws from his exploration of the nature of sensation is that all we can know directly is sensation and not the external objects, the knowledge of which will require reasoning.

Puisque, l'épingle ou le feu étant appliqués à la main, nous ne connoissons immédiatement et distinctement que ce qu'ils y excitent, et non pas l'épingle ni le feu; de même les viandes, les parfums, l'air poussé par un canon, et la flamme, étant appliqués chacun à son organe, nous ne saurions connoître, sans raisonnement, que les seules sensations, et non pas ce qui les cause: il résulte de là cette conséquence universelle, que tout ce que nous connoissons clairement, certainement, distinctement. et sans détours, sont les sensations qui sont en nous, et que nous ne connoissons rien du tout du côté des objets, si ce n'est par conjectures et par raisonnements.[29]

Since, when the pin or fire is applied to the hand, we know immediately and distinctly only what they provoke there, and not the pin or fire; just as if meats, odors, air pushed by a cannon, and a flame were each applied to their respective organs, we could know only, without reasoning, the sensations themselves, and not what causes them; the universal result ensues that all we know clearly, certainly, distinctly, and directly are the sensations which are in us, and that we know nothing at all of the objects, except by conjectures and reasoning.

Cyrano's vocabulary is here so Cartesian as to be almost a parody of Descartes's first rule. But this conclusion marks Cyrano's divergence from the Cartesian method. Whereas the initial scepticism of Descartes is merely an introductory and transient phase, to be effaced by the certitude of the *cogito*,[30] Cyrano arrives at no such reassuring formula. His equivalent of the Cartesian *cogito*, which could be termed a *sentio*, is really only a preliminary step, upon which reasoning must be built. Scepticism, which for Descartes ends with the *cogito*, is reinforced by Cyrano's idea of the subjectivity of sensation, and will continue to permeate his method.

It may be remarked that Rohault, in his *Traité de physique*, presents a method which bears a close similarity on all points, especially on those concerning the nature and role of sensation, to that outlined in Cyrano's *Fragment*. He differs most sharply from Cyrano, however, in his adhesion to Descartes in precisely the area which distinguishes the *Fragment* from Cartesian thought. Rohault prefaces his discussion of sensation by a pale imitation of the *cogito*, "Je pense; pour penser il faut estre; donc je suis" (I think; to think it is necessary to be; therefore I am),[31] followed immediately by a brief statement of the duality of body and soul.[32]

Spink observes that with the exception of what he calls Cyrano's "sketch of an empiricist psychology," the *Fragment de physique* follows Descartes.[33] This judgment cannot be disputed, but the exception is a very significant one, for it means that Cyrano's epistemology, despite the possible influence of Rohault,[34] was distinctive.

To proceed from sensations, or effects, to the causes, or objects producing the sensations, requires reasoning. This will be in the form of certain suppositions, Cyrano says, which will either confirm appearances or contradict them. As he had indicated in the "Idée générale,"[35] one single contradiction will suffice to demonstrate the falsity of the supposition, but if no contradictions at all are found it should not be concluded that the supposition represents a certain truth. In aiming at verisimilitude instead of at truth, Cyrano does not attempt to eradicate his initial scepticism but succeeds merely in modifying it. If Descartes accepts clear and distinct ideas as truths, Cyrano thinks truth is a desirable goal but not a realistic one, given the weaknesses of human reason. He will content himself with what he believes his reason is capable of attaining.

Il ne faut pas toutefois être si vain, que de croire certainement avoir trouvé le vrai, parce que nous pourrions bien soupçonner qu'un autre, possible, quelque jour, donnera une explication différente de celle-ci, laquelle satisfera et s'accordera de même à toutes les expériences dont la nôtre rend raison. C'est pourquoi tout ce que nous pouvons juger en faveur de notre hypothèse, c'est de la faire passer pour vraisemblable, et non pas pour vraie.[36] Donc, encore que par la Physique on puisse se proposer (comme nos superbes et ridicules Pédans) une connoissance certaine et évidente des choses dans leurs causes, qui est, à la vérité, ce qu'on pourroit souhaiter, nous ne le devons pas attendre de la foiblesse de nos raisonnemens, à moins que nous ne fussions aidés des révélations d'un Dieu, qui ne peut manquer, et dont la conduite est à l'aventure tout autre que ce que nous nous figurons. C'est ce qui doit encore augmenter notre incertitude, et nous empêcher de parler avec bravade. Après cela, si nous nous confessons inférieurs à ceux qui se vantent d'avoir trouvé la vérité, nous obtiendrons au moins par-dessus eux l'avantage d'être plus justes estimateurs de la valeur des choses.[37]

You should not, however, be so vain as to believe with certitude that you have found the truth, because we could very well surmise that someone else might one day give an entirely different explanation from this one, which would meet the conditions of and be consistent with all the experiments which our explanation accounts for. That is why all that we can claim in favor of our hypothesis is to have it accepted as probable, and not as true. Therefore, although with Physics you can expect a certain and evident knowledge of things in their causes, which is, in truth, all you could hope for, we should not expect this of the weakness of our reasoning, unless we were aided by the revelations of a God who cannot fail, and whose conduct is perchance quite different from what we imagine. This is what must yet increase our incertitude and prevent us from speaking with bravado. After which, if we confess ourselves inferior to those who boast of having found truth, we will at least gain the advantage over them of being fairer judges of the value of things.

Discounting the weak fideistic note dutifully struck by Cyrano, his scepticism serves as a kind of control on human reason. It may even afford a certain optimism regarding the future of collective research. Although negatively expressed, Cyrano does seem to suggest here a scientific faith in the progress of reason. To be a "juste estimateur de la valeur des choses" (fair judge of the value of things) it must be remembered that part of seeking knowledge is an awareness of the limitations of reason. This is why Cyrano counsels a suspension of judgment on questions that are difficult to resolve.

Premièrement de tenir plutôt votre jugement en balance que de le déterminer à aucune opinion dans des choses qui ne se font pas comprendre, et dire plutôt: *Je n'en sais rien, je n'y comprends rien*, que de faire de vains efforts pour expliquer une chose obscure par une plus obscure.[38]

First, of all, to suspend your judgment rather than to determine it upon any opinion in things which are not comprehensible, and to say: *I know nothing about it, I understand nothing about it*, rather than to make useless efforts to explain an obscure thing by an even more obscure one.

Cyrano's Pyrrhonism, which serves to facilitate attainment of the limited knowledge he seeks, is comparable to that of Montaigne in nature only, not in function. If Montaigne suspends his judgment to render his mind a "carte blanche" awaiting the imprint of God,[39] Cyrano does so in order to arrive as closely as possible at scientific truth. In contrast to the scepticism of Montaigne's *Apologie*, the purpose of which is to confound human reason, Cyrano's scepticism only tempers it. Cyrano, like Descartes, believed in the power of reason; unlike him, he did not believe it capable of reaching certainty.[40] Montaigne disdained verisimilitude, since for him it was but an inadequate copy of truth. If the truth is not known, he asks, how can we know its imitation?[41] But it is just this verisimilitude which is Cyrano's goal, and once he has recognized the difficulty in knowing the essences of things he will no longer be concerned with them.

Cyrano's method, contrary to that of Descartes, is empirical and inductive. He reasons from effects, or sensations, to causes. In his "Lettre contre Scarron," Cyrano takes for granted use of the inductive method, which he cites as a way of deriding the unfortunate author:

Je pense que, comme on arrive à la connoissance d'une cause par ses effets, qu'ainsi pour connoistre la force ou la foiblesse de l'esprit de ce personnage, il ne faut que jetter la veuë sur ses productions. (II, 192, variant h)

I think that, as you arrive at knowledge of a cause by its effects, so in order to know the strength or weakness of this individual, you have only to cast your eye on his works.

The superior reason of the celestial inhabitant Cyrano meets on his way to the sun seems as adept at induction as at deduction: "Il n'est pas impossible que sa raison mobile . . . ne soit capable d'atteindre la cause par les effets, veu qu'elle peut arriver aux effets par la cause" (I, 132). (It is not impossible that his mobile reason is capable of reaching the cause by the effects, seeing that it can arrive at effects by the cause.)

The method of the *Fragment* is, moreover, experimental, for each supposition must be tested to see whether or not it describes experience accurately before it can be accepted or rejected. Within such an epistemological framework there is no place for final causes, and these are ridiculed by Cyrano in the *Estats de la lune*, particularly in a passage on the supposed precepts of God concerning chastity. The *démon de Socrate*, replying to the denunciation of chastity by the *fils de l'hôte*, would like to link to God's commandments of chastity various events generally unrelated to them:

—Vous avés tort . . . de vouloir régenter la sagesse de Dieu. Il est vray qu'il nous a deffendu l'excès de ce plaisir, mais que sçaves-vous s'il ne l'a point ainsy voulu affin que les difficultez que nous trouverions à combattre cette passion nous fît mériter la gloire qu'il nous prépare? Mais que sçaves-vous si ce n'a point esté pour aiguiser l'appétit par la deffense? Mais que sçaves-vous s'il ne presvoyoit point qu'abandonnant la jeunesse aux impétuositez de la chair, le coït trop fréquent énerveroit leur semence et marqueroit la fin du Monde aux arrière-nepveux du premier homme? Mais que sçavés-vous s'il ne voulut point empescher que la fertilité de la terre ne manquast aux besoins de tant d'affamez? Enfin que sçavés-vous s'il ne l'a point voulu faire contre toutte apparence de raison affin de récompenser justement ceux qui, contre toutte apparence de raison, se seront fiez en sa parolle? (I, 66–67)

—You are wrong . . . to want to govern the wisdom of God. It is true that he has forbidden us an excess of that pleasure, but how do you know that he did not want it thus so that the difficulties which we would find in combating this passion might make us deserve the glory he is preparing for us? How do you know that it was not in order to whet the appetite by prohibition? How do you know that he did not foresee that in abandoning youth to the impetuosities of the flesh, too frequent coitus would weaken their seed and would mark the end of the world to the descendants of the first man? How do you know that he did not want to prevent the earth's fertility from failing the needs of so many starving people? Finally how do you know that he did not want to forbid it against all semblance of reason in order to reward precisely those who, against all semblance of reason, believe in his word?

Recourse to final causes or to authority is foreign to a mind which adopts an empirical, experimental method. The full significance of Cyrano's formulation of such a method in the first half of the seventeenth century can be appreciated by examining its relationship to the epistemological thinking of Gassendi.

In the preface to his *Abrégé* of Gassendi's philosophy, Bernier states that the master was charged with scepticism.[42] In the *Exercitationes paradoxicae adversus Aristoteleos* (1624), Gassendi did indeed use the Pyrrhonian criticism of sense knowledge as a blow against Aristotle.[43] But Gassendi's thought evolved, and his later ideas on the senses and on epistemology may serve as an indication of the attitudes of his supposed disciple Cyrano.

Gassendi, according to the *Abrégé*, places the source of all ideas in the senses. Innate ideas are of course rejected; the mind for Gassendi is a tabula rasa awaiting sensory impressions.[44] Ideas are acquired through experience.[45] Gassendi notes those factors which can distort sensory evidence, as Montaigne had noted them before him: the deception of the senses, the passions, customs, prejudices.[46] But whereas Montaigne concludes with a sceptical fideism that the senses are essentially unreliable and human knowledge paltry, Gassendi would make judicious use of reason based on sensory evidence to arrive at scientific truth.[47] The provost of Digne, basically fideistic in spirit, nevertheless advocated an empirical knowledge.[48] If the antipodes were once disbelieved, according to Bernier's transcription of Gassendi, it is because men used their reason alone. Today the evidence of the senses persuades us of their existence.

Cette Raison n'est plus rien auprès de l'Évidence du Sens; et l'on a reconnu à l'égard des parties du Globe de la Terre, que tomber est tendre vers le Centre, et non pas s'éloigner du Centre, et qu'ainsi ce n'est pas merveille que les Antipodes marchent droit aussi bien que nous qui leur sommes Antipodes, et ne tombent pas plutost que nous vers le Ciel, qui est sur leur teste, et vers le haut à leur égard, comme à nous.[49]

Reason is nothing in comparison to the Evidence of the Senses; and it has been acknowledged with respect to the parts of the Globe of the Earth that to fall is to tend toward the Center, and not to move away from the Center, and that it is thus no wonder that the Antipodes move straight along just as do we, who are Antipodes to them, and do not fall any more than we toward Heaven, which is over their heads and upward to them, just as to us.

Although the testimony of the senses is considered valid evidence by Gassendi, they do not lead us beyond the world of appearances.[50] To return to Cyrano's problem of the pin, we may never know the real nature of the pin. The Pyrrhonist would here conclude with Montaigne that human knowledge is at best only very feeble. But Gassendi and Cyrano profess a less rigorous scepticism. They are content to know the nature of the pin in relation to the man who has felt pain caused by it. They analyze the experience and not the object in itself. Scientific knowledge consists, then, in rational explanations and interpretations of appearances and of the conditions of our experiences.[51]

Gassendi thus evolves from a more Pyrrhonian viewpoint in his early work against Aristotle to an intermediate position between scepticism and dogmatism in his later works.[52] Popkin sees the result of this evolution as perhaps the first formulation of the "scientific outlook,"[53] termed by him "constructive or mitigated scepticism."[54] It admits of neither the dogmatists' quest for a knowledge of reality nor the sceptics' universal doubt.[55] The importance of Gassendi's epistemology cannot be underestimated, for with its insistence on the limited knowledge of appearances and experience as opposed to that of reality it was freed from the shackles of metaphysics in order to be applied to scientific inquiry.[56] The significance of Gassendi's method is summarized in the judgment of Popkin:

Building his new outlook on a complete Pyrrhonism with regard to any knowledge of reality, or the nature of things, he was able to develop a method, and a system of the sciences which, of all those of the 17th century, comes closest to the modern anti-metaphysical outlook of the positivists and the pragmatists.[57]

Of all the aspects of Gassendist philosophy which find their way into Cyrano's work in one form or another, the attitude of constructive scepticism is perhaps the most meaningful. In stressing knowledge of appearances based on sensory evidence and reason, Cyrano closely approaches Gassendi's position. If, in the *Fragment de physique*, he applied his non-Cartesian method to Cartesian ideas, this is not necessarily to be viewed as inconsistency. Although he may have been won over by certain elements of Descartes's physics, he probably considered his epistemology a practical tool which could be used in the examination of various philosophical systems. What is most striking and original about the *Fragment* is not, in any case, the repetition of the Cartesian thinking then in vogue but the adoption of a method whose modern scientific spirit is reflected in various ways in his *Autre Monde*.

The idea of a world in the moon, fundamental to the *Autre Monde*, has several implications other than the scientific. At the very beginning of the *Estats de la lune*, Cyrano's suggestion that the moon may be an earth for which the earth would be a moon is met by laughter from his companions. Cyrano replies that this same suggestion with regard to the earth might very well be the object of similar mockery at this moment on the moon: "Ainsy, peut-estre . . . se moque-t-on maintenant dans la Lune de quelqu'autre qui soustient que ce globe-cy est un monde" (I, 5–6). (In such a fashion, perhaps . . . are they now on the Moon ridiculing someone else who is contending that this globe is a world.)

Cyrano's fantasy is soon to be translated into a ficitional reality, for when he ascends to the moon he has great difficulty in persuading the lunarians that his native land, their moon, is in fact an earth. He promises the *fils de l'hôte* that he will spread his praise on the "moon" when he returns home, but the earthling perceives that his philosophical friend does not believe the "moon" is an earth. Cyrano reverses his terrestrial argument on the moon, or rather uses exactly the same argument to prove that the "moon" is an earth.

Je vois bien que vous riés de cette promesse, parce que vous ne croyés pas que la Lune soit un Monde et encore moins que j'en sois un habitant; mais je vous puis assurer aussy que les peuples de ce Monde-là, qui ne prennent cettuy-cy que pour une Lune, se mocqueront de moy quand je diray que leur Lune est un Monde, que les campagnes icy sont de terre et que vous estes des gens. (I, 75)

I see that you are laughing at this promise, because you do not believe that the Moon is an Earth and even less that I am an inhabitant of it; but I can assure you also that the peoples of that World, who take this one for only a Moon, will make fun of me when I tell them that their Moon is a World, that the countryside here is composed of earth, and that you are people.

The anecdotes are in part a wry commentary on the nature of human knowledge, limited not only by our senses, but also by the prejudices that are products both of where we happen to live and of a perhaps universal arrogance of mind. But the voyages to the moon and sun serve especially to create a perspective aimed at destroying man's natural narrow-mindedness. If the moon is an earth and the earth a moon, how may the words "earth" and "moon" be applied? The words lose their earthbound meaning since the moon we are accustomed to thinking of as such is one for us only. Permanent criteria of truth are thus humorously eradicated and the message that knowledge can be only of a relative nature put forth with considerable tactical cleverness.

The two anecdotes create a perspective in which the relativity of knowledge can be readily discerned and at the same time illustrate the identity of the earth and moon. This identity is reiterated in the course of the interlude on the earth which forms the first part of the *Estats du soleil*. Dyrcona, having returned to earth from his aerial trip, has acquired a certain measure of renown as the author of the moon voyage. His reputation grows as the reception of his book becomes more and more divided. Soon his readers are split into two factions of pro and con: "Chaque famille se divisa, et les intérêts de cette querelle allèrent si loin, que la ville fut partagée en deux factions, la *Lunaire* et l'*Anti-lunaire*" (I, 101, italics not mine). (Each family was divided, and the interests of the quarrel went so far, that the city was split into two factions, the *Lunar* and the *Antilunar*.) The quarrel over Cyrano's work is reminiscent of the quarrel in the *Estats de la lune* over his person. The lunar population is divided on the question of the visitor's nature. Does he possess reason or not? Is he human or animal? "La définition de ce que j'estois partagea la Ville en deux factions" (I, 54). (The definition of what I was split the City into two factions.) The disputes by two warring factions over Cyrano both on the moon, in the *Estats de la lune*, and on the earth, in the *Estats du soleil*, reinforce the impression that the earth and the moon are alike. These disputes are also, incidentally, another unifying link between the two voyages, prompting the reader to treat them as one book.

It has been pointed out by Randall, R. G. Collingwood, and Lovejoy, among others, that the more significant effects of the Copernican revolution did not lie in the lowering of man's dignity by removing the earth from its central position.[58] The earth was on the contrary raised by the new cosmology from the lowest, imperfect sublunar sphere to the celestial rank of the other heavenly bodies. The astronomical discoveries of the sixteenth and seventeenth centuries destroyed the notion that the universe possesses any center at all and replaced the old Aristotelian divisions of the world into separate regions by a homogeneous matter found throughout the universe, which could be governed by scientific laws formulated by men here on earth.[59]

These effects are clearly evident in Cyrano's assertion of the similarity of the earth and the moon, a notion supported by his belief in the plurality of worlds. If man loses any of his importance through the scientific ideas of Galileo's time, it is due not to the denial of his central position but to the possibility that his may not be the only inhabited globe, with a unique destiny.[60] For Cyrano, the similarity of the formerly disparate planets and the possibility of a plurality of worlds have shattering epistemological consequences. If the moon is an earth and other orbs are peopled by creatures resembling us, we must relinquish any claim to absolute truth and acknowledge the fact of relativism. In his article on the *Autre Monde*, A. Lavers pictures Cyrano in pursuit of a pure universal Truth.[61] Nothing could be further removed from the mentality of the follower of Copernicus. The relativism which Henri Weber views as an aspect of Cyrano's rationalism[62] is one of the major themes of the *Autre Monde*.

Weber is not without justification in likening the relativism of the *Autre Monde* to that in Voltaire's *Micromégas*.[63] The reader is particularly reminded of Voltaire's "tas de boue" (pile of mud) in the course of Cyrano's flights to the moon and to the sun, during which he has the opportunity to reflect on his observations. When he has traveled three quarters of the distance from the earth to the moon, Cyrano begins to fall to our satellite. Although the two globes now resemble each other in appearance he is able to tell which is which. Nevertheless, he views the earth from a distance, in a new perspective which transforms it into just another moon.

Je connus bien, à la vérité, que je ne retombais pas vers nostre Monde, car, encore que je me trouvasse entre deux Lunes et que je remarquasse fort bien que je m'éloignois de l'une à mesure que je m'approchois de l'autre, j'estois très asseuré que la plus grande estoit nostre Terre pour ce qu'au bout d'un jour ou deux de voyage, les réfractions éloignées du Soleil venant à confondre la diversité des corps et des climats, elle ne m'avoit plus paru que comme une grande placque d'or ainsy que l'autre. (I, 20)

I could tell, in truth, that I was not falling toward our World, for, although I found myself between two Moons and I saw very well that I was moving away from one as I was approaching the other, I was very sure that the larger was our Earth, because after traveling for a day or two, the distant refractions of the Sun came to merge the diversity of bodies and climates, and it now appeared to me as no more than a big slab of gold, just like the other.

The "placque d'or" (slab of gold) has not yet reached the insignificance of the "tas de boue" (pile of mud), but in the *Estats du soleil* the earth will shrink still further in stature. As he rises to the sun, Cyrano sees it become progressively smaller, fading finally into nothingness.

La sphère de nostre Monde ne me paroissoit plus qu'un astre à peu près de la grandeur que nous paroist la Lune; encore il s'étressissoit, à mesure que je montois, jusqu'à devenir une estoille, puis une bluette, et puis rien. (I, 133)

The sphere of our World seemed nothing but a heavenly body of about the size that the Moon appears to us; it shrank yet more as I rose, so as to turn into a star, then a spark, and then nothing.

Cyrano shares Voltaire's desire to minimize the dimensions of man's dwelling place and activities. It is not coincidental that in the *Estats du soleil*, after the earth has been reduced to a non-entity, the satire on man becomes more caustic than in the *Estats de la lune*, where the earth is still at least a moon. But Cyrano's cosmic relativism has yet another purpose. In Voltaire's age, men's eyes had become more accustomed to the new universe of Copernicus, Galileo, and Newton. In Cyrano's time, with the telescope still in its infancy, men had to learn to see in a new way. Cyrano wishes particularly to create a kind of telescopic vision, by showing the earth as it is in relation to other globes and to the universe. Whereas the relativism in *Micromégas* is basically a satirical device with the intention of ridiculing the human creature, the relativism of the *Autre Monde* is at once philosophical, scientific, and satirical.

As Cyrano's constructive scepticism is a weapon against authority and dogmatism, so his relativism is a weapon against all forms of anthropocentrism [64] The abandonment of geocentrism required an adjustment of one's mental lenses. No longer was it possible for man to arrogate to himself a special place in the universe, and Cyrano condemns the overweening pride of those who do so:

. . . l'orgueil insupportable des humains qui leur persuade que la Nature n'a esté faicte que pour eux, comme s'il estoit vraysemblable que le Soleil, un grand corps quatre cens trente quatre fois plus vaste que la Terre, n'eût esté allumé que pour meurir ses neffles et pommer ses choux. (I, 13–14)

. . . the insufferable pride of humans, which convinces them that Nature was made for them alone, as if it were likely that the Sun, a huge body four hundred and thirty-four times larger than the Earth, was lit only to ripen his medlars and form the heads of his cabbages.

In this passage it is clear that the rejection of the Ptolemaic system meant not so much the loss of a central position and thereby of human dignity as it did the loss of a *unique* position. With the realization that other globes are earths which may bear life comes the necessity to give up the illusion that man occupies a privileged place, alone containing life, alone worthy of God's creation and Christ's sacrifice. Cyrano follows his condemnation of geocentric anthropocentrism by a statement of his belief in the plurality of worlds. Far from agreeing with those men so bestial as to think that their globe alone is inhabited—"bien loin de consentir à l'insolence de ces brutaux" (far from admitting the insolence of these brutes)—he believes the planets and fixed stars to be earths like ours (I, 14).

Borel also compares men who reject the plurality of worlds to animals. He calls them "bestes brutes" (brute beasts), blind to the wonders of God.[65] But Cyrano will extend the relativistic perspective of the universe engendered by the new astronomy to man and his concept of deity. Thinking that our planet is the only receptacle of life is comparable to thinking that God exists for man alone. Although by "Dieu" Cyrano is ostensibly referring to the sun in this particular context, the capitalization makes the implication quite clear. It is, incidentally, noteworthy that deity is here equated with the sun.

Car comment, en bonne foy, s'imaginer que ces globes si spacieux ne soient que de grandes campagnes désertes, et que le nostre, à cause que nous y rampons pour une douzaine de glorieux coquins, ayst esté basty pour commander à tous? Quoy! parce que le Soleil com- passe nos jours, et nos années, est-ce à dire pour cela qu'il n'ayst esté construit qu'afin que nous ne cognions pas de la teste contre les murs? Non, non! Si ce Dieu visible esclaire l'homme, c'est par accident, comme le flambeau du Roy esclaire par accident au crocheteur qui passe par la rüe. (I, 14)

For how can we, in good faith, imagine that such spacious globes as these are but vast deserts, and that ours, just because we crawl around on it for a dozen or so arrogant knaves, was built to rule over all? What! Just because the Sun regulates our days, and our years, must we conclude that is was constructed only so we would not hit our heads against the wall? No, no! If this visible God gives light to man, it is by accident, as the torch of the King accidentally gives light to a porter passing in the street.

Cyrano will later sketch the portrait of an impersonal God, as removed from man as the sun from the "crocheteur" (porter): "Estant incapable de passion, il ne sçauroit ni hair, ny aymer personne" (I, 68). (Since he is incapable of feeling, he cannot hate or love anyone.)

Montaigne too had asked what gives man the right to assume the universe exists for his use and comfort alone.[66] He too had railed against an anthropocentrism so exaggerated as to make God subject to description by man.[67] But Montaigne, intending to humble man into an awareness of the limitations of his reason, preparing him for the act of faith, was without the benefit of the new cosmic perspective, for his scepticism was also applied to the Copernican theory.[68] If Cyrano attacks the arrogance of the anthropocentric attitude, it is to open man's eyes to the relativistic nature of things. Relativism is especially well adapted to his mitigated scepticism. What he rejects is a claim to unlimited, absolute knowledge; what he proposes in its stead is a limited knowledge with relativism as a guiding principle. The anthropocentrism he scorns is that which inspires Voltaire's "petit animalcule en bonnet carré" (little animalcule with a square cap) to declare that the *Summa Theologica* of Thomas Aquinas contains all truth.[69]

Dogmatic recourse to authority is amusingly contrasted to the relativistic outlook in the interrogation on the moon of that foreign being, Cyrano. The character Cyrano, comically taking the opposite stand of the author Cyrano, is shocked by the presiding officer's theories on the origins of the world, which he holds to be eternal. Cyrano cites the authority of the Bible, and when this fails to impress the lunarians he lapses into the old dogmatic, anthropocentric way of viewing the moon.

Celuy qui présidoit m'exposa fort au long ses opinions sur la structure du Monde. Elles me semblèrent ingénieuses, et sans qu'il passast jusques à son origine qu'il soutenoit éternelle, j'eusse trouvé sa Philosophie beaucoup plus raisonnable que la nostre; mais si tost que je l'entendis soustenir une resverie si contraire à ce que la foy nous apprend, je luy demandé ce qu'il pourroit responde à l'authorité de Moyse et que ce grand Patriarche avoit dit expressément que Dieu l'avoit créé en six jours. Cet ignorant ne fit que rire, au lieu de me responde. Je ne peus alors m'empescher de luy dire que, puisqu'il en venoit là, je commençois à croire que leur Monde n'estoit qu'une

FROM SCEPTICISM TO RELATIVISM

Lune. Mais, me dirent-ilz tous, vous y voyés de la terre, des forestz, des rivières, des mers; que seroit-ce donc tout cela? —N'importe, respartis-je, Aristote asseure que ce n'est que la Lune; et si vous aviés dit le contraire dans les Classes où j'ay faict mes estudes, on vous auroit sifflés.' Il se fit sur cela un grand esclat de rire; il ne faut pas demander si ce fut de leur ignorance, et l'on me reconduisit dans ma cage. (I, 58)

The presiding officer recited to me at great length his opinions on the structure of the World. They seemed ingenious to me, and if he had not gone on to its origin, which he maintained was eternal, I would have found his Philosophy much more sensible than ours; but as soon as I heard him uphold a fantasy so contrary to what faith teaches us, I asked him what he would reply to the authority of Moses and that the great Patriarch had distinctly said that God had created the world in six days. The ignoramus just laughed, instead of answering me. I then could not help telling him that, since he was going to take that attitude, I would begin to think their World was only a Moon. But, they all said to me, you can see earth, forests, rivers, seas here; what would all of that be? It does not matter, I retorted, Aristotle asserts it is only the Moon; and if you had said the contrary in my Classes, you would have been hissed. This prompted a roar of laughter—do not ask if it was out of ignorance—and I was escorted back to my cage.

With anthropocentric relish the earthling relegates the lunarians to an inferior dwelling place because they refuse to recognize the authority which for him reigns supreme. The power of reason, in this case applied to the problem of the origins of the world, is opposed to authority. But when confronted with empirical proof that the moon is a world, that is, with the evidence of his senses, the visitor from earth only reaffirms the sway of authority. In this satirical passage Cyrano deplores the power of authority to blind reason and the senses, the two essential criteria of knowledge, to the relative nature of truth.

The tables are then turned and the message that the moon is an earth as the earth is a moon is once more underscored, for the lunarians now become the dogmatists. The character Cyrano plays the part of Galileo as the lunar inquisitors prosecute him for declaring their moon to be an earth (I, 58). The suggestion that dogmatism prevails on the moon as it does on the earth reinforces the relativism of the *Autre Monde*, for the earthlings' perspective counteracts that of the lunarians as the lunarians' does that of the earthlings.

The earth-moon relativism is applied by Cyrano to his concept of man in a giant animal universe composed of other world-animals containing still other animals that reach down to the tiniest, most imperceptible creatures. As the heavenly bodies are like animals within which the human animal dwells, so man is like a world to those smaller animals which inhabit his body. This hylozoistic image of the universe, undoubtedly inherited from Bruno, Campanella, and the Italian naturalists,[70] adds another dimension to the perspective created by the earth-moon relativism. Cyrano uses microscopic vision as he had used telescopic vision; he opens men's eyes to the new universe they live in to give them a balanced picture of their position in it.

Nous, à nostre tour, sommes aussy des Mondes de certaines gens encore plus petits comme des chancres, des poux, des vers, des cirons; ceux-cy sont la terre d'autres imperceptibles, ainsi de mesme que nous paroissons un grand Monde à ce petit peuple. Peut-estre que nostre chair, nostre sang et nos esprits ne sont autre chose qu'une tissure de petits animaux qui s'entretiennent, nous prestent mouvement par le leur, et se laissant aveuglement conduire à nostre volonté qui leur sert de cocher, nous conduisent nous-mesme et produisent tout ensemble cette action que nous appelons la vie. Car dites-moy, je vous prie, est-il mal aisé à croire qu'un pou prenne vostre corps pour un Monde, et que quand quelqu'un d'eux a voyagé depuis l'une de vos

oreilles jusques à l'autre, ses compagnons disent de luy qu'il a voyagé
aux deux bouts du Monde ou qu'il a couru de l'un à l'autre Pôle?
Oüy, sans doubte, ce petit peuple prend vostre poil pour les forests
de son païs, les pores pleins de pituitte pour des fontaines, les bubes
et les cirons pour des lacs et des estangs, les apostumes pour des mers,
les fluxions pour des déluges, et quand vous vous peignés en devant
et en arrière, ilz prennent cette agitation pour le flux et le reflux
de l'Ocean. (I, 71)

We, in turn, are also the Worlds of certain even smaller peoples
such as cankers, lice, worms, mites; these are the earth of other
imperceptible beings, just as we appear as a great World to this little
people. Perhaps our flesh, our blood, and our vital spirits are nothing
more than a tissue of little animals which hold together, impart
movement to us through their own, and, letting themselves be led
blindly by our will as by a coachman, lead us ourselves and produce
together that action which we call life. For tell me, I pray you, is it
difficult to believe that a louse would take your body for a World, and
that when one of them travels from one of your ears to the other,
his companions would say of him that he had traveled to both
extremities of the World, or that he had raced from one Pole to the
other? Yes, without a doubt, this little people takes your hair for
the forests of its country, your mucus-filled pores for fountains, your
pimples and parasites for lakes and ponds, your abscesses for seas,
your inflammations for floods, and when you comb your hair in front
and in back, they take that movement for the ebb and flow of the
Ocean.

Cyrano's description of man poised between the immensity of
the celestial spheres and the minuteness of the "ciron" (mite)
recalls Pascal's famous pensée on the "disproportion de l'homme"
(disproportion of man). René Jasinski, in an article on Pascal's
"deux infinis" (two infinities), has examined the probable influ-_
ence of certain passages from Gassendi's Syntagma philosophicum
on Pascal.[71] Could the passages from the Syntagma (published in

1658 but certainly at least in some form available to Cyrano before that)[72] have proved also a source of inspiration for the author of the *Estats de la lune*? Considering the recurrent presence of Gassendist thought in the *Autre Monde*, this is not impossible. Jasinski reproduces a passage from the *Syntagma* on the correspondence of the infinitely great and infinitely small worlds,[73] after which he cites Cyrano's description of infinite worlds in an infinite universe,[74] without, however, making any conclusions as to a possible influence.

The developments on the infinitely great and the infinitely small in the *Syntagma* lead Gassendi to reflect on the nature of our knowledge of the vast new cosmos.[75] Gassendi goes beyond strict fideism here. Allying a relativistic vision of man in the universe with a mitigated scepticism he asserts that it is worthwhile to pursue the search for verisimilitude in a world of appearances. Rather than demonstrate, as does Pascal by the "disproportion de l'homme," man's need to recognize his complete dependence upon God, Gassendi points to the limitations of human reason chiefly as a caution against exaggerated expectations of discovery.

Nous nous appliquerons de bonne foi à exposer et développer ce que nous rencontrerons de plus vraisemblable touchant les choses de la nature; mais loin de faire espérer que nous puissions ouvrir dans leurs profondeurs mêmes les secrets de la nature, nous nous arrêterons plutôt et resterons pleins d'admiration pour ainsi dire dans ses vestibules mêmes. Car cette nature est comme un temple immense et sacré, dont le sanctuaire est habité par une puissance divine, qui développe et exerce son pouvoir et sa sagesse inépuisables; mais à nous, chétifs humains, il est défendu d'avancer jusque là et d'entrer. Nous pouvons regarder d'un peu plus près l'extérieur des choses, retracer pour une part quelques-uns des ouvrages de la nature; mais ce que nous pénétrons reste bien loin de ces retraites où la Vertu divine et cachée travaille à ses merveilles. Si je m'exprime ainsi, ce n'est pas pour détourner de cette sorte de recherche et contemplation, car le peu que nous pouvons distinguer est plus précieux que n'importe quelle richesse, et c'est la meilleure occasion d'écouter le conseil du poète qui finit en ces termes: "Il vaut d'aller jusque là, meme si l'on ne peut plus loin." Si je m'empresse de donner cet avis, c'est pour que, venu plein d'espoir, on ne se plaigne pas ensuite d'être joué si l'on ne pénètre pas plus au fond de tout, mais si l'on trouve toujours à s'enquérir. Je le fais aussi pour que nostre esprit se rappelle sa faiblesse, pour que reconnaissant l'insuffisance de son bagage, il s'apprenne à laisser toute présomption, et s'accoutume à admirer non lui-même mais le Créateur, dont il faut nécessairement reconnaître inconcevables la sagesse et l'industrie. Considérons encore comme du plus grand profit de pouvoir nous élever jusqu'à constater combien étroite et mince est toute notre science; car les plus sages de jadis s'estimaient heureux de réussir à reconnaître qu'ils ne savaient rien, et que la vérité reste toujours inaccessible. . . . Accéder à ce temple [la nature] n'est ni permis ni légitime, sans avoir au préalable prié Dieu qu'il nous favorise, et nous permette d'atteindre et d'emporter à défaut de la vérité, du moins la vraisemblance.[76]

We will sincerely apply ourselves to setting forth and developing the most probable things we will find concerning natural phenomena; but far from inspiring hope that we might open up nature's secrets in their very depths, we instead halt and remain filled with wonder, as it were in its vestibules. For nature is like an immense, sacred temple whose sanctuary is inhabited by a divine force, which displays and exercises its inexhaustible power and wisdom; but we, wretched humans, are forbidden to go that far and enter. We can consider from slightly closer up the external aspect of things, retrace some of the productions of nature; but what we fathom remains far from the retreats where divine and hidden Virtue works at her wonders. If I express myself thus, it is not to discourage this kind of research and contemplation, for the little that we can discern is more precious than any kind of riches, and this is the best opportunity to listen to the advice of the poet who concludes in these terms: "It is worth it to go just so far, even if you can go no farther." If I hasten to offer this opinion, it is in order that, once you arrive filled with hope, you do not then complain of having been duped if you cannot penetrate farther into the depths of everything but still find subject for inquiry. I do so also to recall to the mind its weakness, so that recognizing the inadequacy of its equipment, it learns to abandon all pride, and acquires the habit of admiring not itself but the Creator, whose unimaginable wisdom and art must absolutely be acknowledged. Let us consider with how much profit we may ennoble ourselves by stating how narrow all our knowledge is; for the wisest men of old considered themselves fortunate to succeed in recognizing that they knew nothing and that truth always remains inaccessible. . . . Reaching this temple [nature] is neither allowed nor legitimate, without having beforehand prayed God that he might favor our plans and allow us, failing truth, to attain and carry off at least verisimilitude.

Cyrano's description of man's relationship to the two infinities is much closer in spirit to Gassendi than to Pascal. With no trace of fideism but with an awareness of man's limited intellectual capacities, Cyrano, like Gassendi, will aspire to the knowledge available to man. Unlike Pascal, he will not turn aside from the new vision of infinity, but will attempt to gain some scientific understanding of it.

Jasinski has discerned another possible influence on Pascal in Borel's *Discours nouveau*.[77] Cyrano may have had in mind Borel's contemplation of the enormous starry spaces when composing his reflections on infinite worlds in an infinite universe. He may also have been influenced by Borel's treatises on the telescope and on the microscope[73] in those passages of the *Autre Monde* that suggest to the reader the impact of these two inventions on scientific and literary imagination.

Lachèvre has quoted at length a passage from Charles Sorel's romance *Francion* (1623) (I, 71, n. 1) which he believes to be the immediate source for the passage in the *Estats de la lune* on the infinitely great and small worlds.[79] Émile Roy, ignoring Gassendi, has put forth the engaging hypothesis that if Cyrano borrowed from Sorel, it was from Cyrano that Pascal borrowed.[80] Both Sorel and Pascal, he points out, were prevented by religious scruples from conceiving of the universe as a living being. Cyrano of course was not. This lends to his reasoning a certain logical authenticity, lacking in Sorel and Pascal, who are obliged to have their living mites dwell in larger inanimate spheres.[81] It would have been possible, Roy admits, that Pascal had read Sorel, but this would be a purely gratuitous assumption, whereas it is safe to say that Cyrano definitely had read Sorel and therefore that Pascal could have read Cyrano.[82] Only Cyrano, he states, seems to have expressed the idea found in the *Pensées* of life extending to infinity.[83]

The comparison with Sorel and Pascal bears further investigation, for certain points of difference may help to illuminate the significance of Cyrano's passage. Roy remarks that neither Pascal nor Sorel adopts the Galilean view of the universe, but both represent the earth as an immobile point surrounded by an infinity of worlds.[84] It is certain that Cyrano's relativism is enhanced by the idea of man inhabiting a planet with nothing to distinguish it from any other planet. For if Pascal's avowed desire is to judge man at his "juste prix" (correct worth), he does not entirely fulfill it in making this important omission. Montaigne, too, had expressed the wish of restoring to man his proper place in the ranks of the creatures of the universe,[85] but in adhering to the old cosmology he effects no profound change in perspective.[86] Sorel's pedant Hortensius outlines a fantasy of man between the two poles of great and small as it will appear in his projected literary endeavor; Pascal depicts the anguish of man without God vainly struggling to understand the two extremes of infinity in the middle of which he finds himself caught. Cyrano's purpose is certainly not that of the Christian apologist, and it is not completely that of the fantastical novelist. His goal is a philosophical and scientific relativism, sometimes couched in the language of whimsey.

Cyrano will explain by his "cironalité universelle" (universal mite-ness) the causes of skin irruptions, the differences in effect of these upon persons of different temperaments, the healing processes of skin wounds (I, 72). His explanations are not to be taken as seriously as has been done by Juppont, who sees in them an organic cellular theory,[87] or by Mongrédien, who would like to believe that Cyrano divined a theory of the microorganism.[88] But Cyrano obviously does want to paint a picture of the world of activity within a human being. The microscopic creatures evidently do have a "scientific" function; that is, their presence and operations are described rationally in order to explain certain bodily processes. Cyrano also views them fancifully as a people with their own life, government, political aspirations, and sentiments, comparable to those of human beings.

La démangeaison ne prouve-t-elle pas mon dire? Ce ciron qui la produit, est-ce autre chose qu'un de ces petits animaux qui s'est dépris de la societe civile pour s'establir tiran de son païs? Si vous me demandés d'où vient qu'ilz sont plus grands que ces autres petits imperceptibles, je vous demande pourquoy les éléphans sont plus grands que nous, et les Hibernois que les Espagnols? Quant à cette ampoulle et cette crouste dont vous ignorés la cause, il fault qu'elles arrivent, ou par la corruption des charognes de leurs ennemis que ces petits Géans ont massacrés, ou que la peste produite par la nécessité des aliments dont les séditieux se sont gorgez ayt laissé pourrir parmy la campagne des monceaux de cadavres, ou que ce tiran, après avoir tout autour de soy chassé ses compagnons qui de leurs corps bouchoient les pores du nostre, ayt donné passage à la pituitte, laquelle, estant extravasée hors la sphère de la circulation de nostre sang, s'est corrompüe. On me demandera peut-estre pourquoy un ciron en produit cent autres; ce n'est pas chose malaisée à concevoir, car de mesme qu'úne révolte en esveille une autre, ainsy ces petits peuples, poussés du mauvais exemple de leurs compagnons séditieux, aspirent chacun en particulier au commandement, allumant partout la guerre, le massacre et la faim. (I, 71–72)

Does not itching prove what I say? Is not the mite which produces it none other than one of those little animals who freed himself from civil society to establish himself as a tyrant of his country? If you ask me why they are larger than the other little imperceptible creatures, I will ask you why elephants are larger than we, and Irishmen larger than Spaniards. As for the blister and scab, of whose cause you are ignorant, they have to occur, either by the decay of the corpses of enemies massacred by these little Giants; or else because the plague, brought about by the need for the food upon which these rebels gorged themselves, has left heaps of cadavers rotting in the fields; or else because the tyrant, after chasing away from himself his companions, whose bodies were blocking the pores of our own, allowed passage to the phlegm which, after being extravasated from the circuit of our blood's circulation, became corrupted. I will perhaps be asked why a mite produces a hundred others; this is not difficult to understand, for just as one rebellion awakens another, so these little people, goaded by the bad example of their seditious companions, each aspire to command, igniting on all sides war, massacre, and hunger.

The development planned by Hortensius for his romance is much more fantastical. He insists less on a relativism induced by a contemplation of the two extremes and by the comparison of man to each one of them than he does on the extraordinary actions that will be performed by his tiny inhabitants of man. His imaginings result in an almost surrealistic vision of the autonomous acts of different parts of the body.

Il n'y a partie en l'Univers où l'on ne se puisse imaginer qu'il y a de petits mondes. Il y en a dans les plantes, dedans les petits cailloux et dedans les fourmis. Je veux faire des Romans des advantures de leurs peuples. Je chanteray leurs amours, leurs guerres et les révolutions de leurs Empires, et principalement je m'arresteray à représenter l'estat où peuvent les peuples qui habitent le corps de l'homme, et je monstreray que ce n'est pas sans sujet qu'on l'a appelé Microcosme. Je feray quelque autre discours séparé où toutes les parties corporelles auront beaucoup de choses à démesler ensemble. Les bras et les mains feront la guerre aux pieds, aux jambes et aux cuisses; et les yeux feront l'amour aux parties naturelles, les veines aux artères, et les os à la mouëlle.[89]

There is no part of the Universe in which one cannot imagine little worlds. They exist in plants, in little pebbles, and in ants. I want to make Novels of the adventures of their peoples. I will sing their loves, their wars, and the revolutions of their Empires, and I will concentrate chiefly on portraying the state in which the people inhabiting man's body may be, and I will show that it is not without reason that the body has been called a Microcosm. I will write another separate treatise in which all the parts of the body will have a lot of things to settle with each other. The arms and hands will make war upon the feet, the legs, and the thighs; the eyes will make love to the private parts, the veins to the arteries, and the bones to the marrow.

Cyrano's imagination is not as unbridled in this matter as is that of Sorel's pedant-romancer, or it is at least more purposeful in its direction. Cyrano complements his vision of a world in the moon with his equally relativistic vision of a world in the human being. The microcosm and macrocosm counterbalance each other in his attempt to place man on an equal footing with the other inhabitants of the universe.[90]

Pascal's contemplation of the two extremes of infinity in his "disproportion de l'homme" leads to a philosophical terror which in turn leads to God. The new universe for Pascal is a source of frightening incertitude which can only destroy man's presumptuous claim to any knowledge of its operations or effects.

Qui se considérera de la sorte s'effraiera de soi-même, et, se considérant soutenu dans la masse que la nature lui a donnée, entre ces deux abîmes de l'infini et du néant, il tremblera dans la vue de ces merveilles; et je crois que sa curiosité se changeant en admiration, il sera plus disposé à les contempler en silence qu'à les rechercher avec présomption.[91]

He who contemplates himself thus will become frightened of his own self, and, judging himself suspended in the mass given him by nature between the two abysses of infinity and nothingness, he will tremble at the view of these wonders; and I think that his curiosity will change into wonderment, and he will be more disposed to contemplate them in silence than to inquire about them with presumptuousness.

Georges Mounin has called Pascal "un homme malade de l'infini" (a man ill with the infinite)[92] and has contrasted his anguished reaction to the world of Copernicus and Galileo with Cyrano's robust acceptance of it. As Mounin remarks, Cyrano, especially in his conversation with the viceroy of Canada, is combating precisely that resistance to the new ideas which is manifest in Pascal's *Pensées*.[93] Pascal's return to God in the face of the unknowable is, Mounin points out, the attitude of a man of the past. Those men willing and eager to explore the uncharted regions of the sky—Borel, Godwin, Cyrano—are looking ahead.[94]

Even Bishop Wilkins, whose *Discovery of a New World* was intended to popularize the new astronomy, and who asserts that the Copernican system cannot be disproved "how horrid soever this may seem at the first,"[95] injects a note of scepticism into his description of the world in the moon. Wilkins pictures the earth, as do Pascal and Cyrano, as a mere speck in comparison to the vastness of the universe. But although he, unlike Pascal, will not be hindered from venturing forth into the new cosmos by the prospect of its infinite mysteries, the bishop is nevertheless restrained by religious scruples.

What a little is that which we know, in respect of those many Matters contained within this great Universe? This whole Globe of Earth and Water, though it seem to us to be of a large extent, yet it bears not so great a Proportion unto the whole Frame of Nature, as a small Sand doth unto it; and what can such little Creatures as we discern who are tied to this point of Earth? or what can they in the Moon know of us? If we understand anything (saith Esdras) 'tis nothing but that which is upon the earth; and he that dwelleth above in the heavens, may only understand the things that are above in the height of the heavens.[96]

The relativism apparent in this passage is similar to that of the "disproportion de l'homme" in that it serves ultimately to underline the omnipotence of God. Wilkins was certainly a more adventurous stargazer than Pascal, but he never attained Cyrano's degree of freedom from metaphysical and theological bonds.

Marjorie Nicolson would like to divide the seventeenth-century thinkers who felt the effects of the new astronomy into those who suffered from agoraphobia and those suffering from claustrophobia.[97] The former, among whom she would undoubtedly classify Pascal, retreated from the expanded heavens, often into forms of fideism and scepticism. Those scholars whom Popkin labels the "humanistic sceptics"—La Mothe Le Vayer, Patin, Samuel Sorbière—applied their Pyrrhonism to all the sciences.[98] Jean-Pierre Camus concludes his *Essay sceptique* (1610) with an attitude of fideistic scepticism toward all fields of human endeavor.[99] For these men the scientific innovations of the day are indications that there exist no abiding principle or permanent criteria of truth.[100]

FROM SCEPTICISM TO RELATIVISM

The other group of thinkers is happy to escape from the bounds of the earth to the endless spheres beyond. When Cyrano, unexpectedly successful with the airship he has confected while in prison, sees himself being lifted over Toulouse, his reaction is one of delight at the victory of human reason over the imponderability of nature.

Ce prodige m'étonna, non point à cause d'un essor si subit, mais à cause de cet épouvantable emportement de la raison humaine au succès d'un dessein qui m'avoit mesme effrayé en l'imaginant. (I, 123)

This marvel astonished me, not because of so sudden a flight, but because of the dreadful transport of human reason upon the success of a scheme which had frightened me just to imagine it.

Knowledge for Montaigne, at least for the Montaigne of the *Apologie*, was a "fiction"; it consisted of "appearances" so subject to change that they must be considered "inventions" of the human mind.[101] Cyrano puts more trust in appearances, making them the objects of his quest for knowledge. Albert Thibaudet has classified the *Autre Monde* as a "roman de l'aventure intellectuelle" (novel of intellectual adventure),[102] thus signaling one of the unifying themes of Cyrano's work. Cyrano himself tells one of the talking trees in the *Estats du soleil* that his trip was motivated solely by the desire to learn:

Je la conjuray par toutes les choses que je crûs qui la pouvoient davantage émouvoir, qu'elle daignast instruire une personne qui n'avoit risqué les périls d'un si grand voyage que pour apprendre. (I, 168)

I entreated it by everything I thought could move it any further to deign to educate a person who had risked the dangers of so great a voyage only in order to learn.

FROM SCEPTICISM TO RELATIVISM

Recognizing the limits of human reason, Cyrano will be satisfied to open men's eyes to the relativism he has found in the new universe. At the same time his mitigated scepticism permits him a certain faith in the power of reason and an insistent pursuit of knowledge, stimulated by the awareness that it must continue to be sought, within the bounds of human powers.

4

⚜

SATIRICAL RELATIVISM:
MAN AND SOCIETY

Cyrano puts his newly discovered concept of relativism to work in the *Autre Monde* as a means of ridiculing man and society. It is doubly effective as a satiric device, for it is at once a series of technical tricks of no small artistic dexterity and an expression of one of the author's most basic philosophical tenets. Relativism, founded upon astronomical discoveries which were to revolutionize seventeenth- and eighteenth-century philosophical and scientific thought, becomes a powerful weapon in the hands of the satirist eager to expose the vanity of man and his earthly pursuits.

The cosmic relativism of the earth-moon idea, that is, the idea that the moon is an earth for which our earth is a moon, is applied to the inhabitants of these globes, fictitious and real, but is of course directed at man. When Cyrano first meets the *démon de Socrate*, he is warned by this spirit not to expect more breadth of mind of the lunarians than he would of the earthlings.

Hé bien, mon fils, vous portés enfin la peine des foiblesses de vostre Monde. Il y a du vulgaire, ici comme là, qui ne peut souffrir la pensée des choses où il n'est point accoustumé, mais, sçachez qu'on ne vous traitte qu'à la pareille, et que si quelqu'un de cette terre avoit monté dans la vostre avec la hardiesse de se dire homme, vos docteurs le feroient estouffer comme un monstre ou comme un singe possédé du Diable. (I, 33)

Well, my son, you are finally bearing the punishment for the failings of your World. There are common people, here as there, who cannot stand the thought of things to which they are not accustomed, but you should know that you are only being treated in kind, and that if someone from this earth had risen to yours with the impudence to declare himself a man, your scholars would have him choked like a monster or like a monkey possessed by the Devil.

The demon's speech is illustrative of certain satirical possibilities of relativism exploited by Cyrano. Establishing an identity between earth and moon, even if a negative one in this case, is a way of correcting man's anthropocentric vision, of pointing out to him that he is not unique. The lunarians in this instance behave like men—which they do not always do—and thus the irony of Cyrano's "voyage" is heightened. Like Montesquieu's Persians,[1] he is really no stranger among the people he visits, and the perspective afforded by this deliberately punctured illusion allows both a supposedly objective criticism of man from afar, in a wider context, and a more trenchant criticism of man by a fellow-man sharing his foibles.

The most effective and most consistently used satiric device which Cyrano draws from his earth-moon relativism is akin to what David Worcester has called the "irony of inversion."[2] Described by him as a necessity "to convert apparent praise into blame,"[3] the irony of inversion appears in a modified and perhaps more complex form in the *Autre Monde*. If the moon and the earth are similar in Cyrano's fantasy—both are terrestrial life-bearing globes whose inhabitants resemble each other in certain respects—they are also the opposite of each other. When the moon becomes an earth and the earth a moon everything in the resultant upsidedown world becomes reversed. By the technique of inversion Cyrano achieves what he himself terms a "monde renversé" (world in reverse) (I, 74).[4]

Particularly in the *Estats de la lune* are found numerous examples of inversion, which proves to be a convenient vehicle for social criticism. Cyrano, in punishment for his declaration that the lunarians' "moon" is an earth, is taxed with an "amende honteuse" (shameful amends), the "amende honorable" (honorable amends) being unknown on the moon (I, 60). He is further punished by being magnificently garbed and carried through the streets in a splendid chariot drawn by four princes (I, 60). As signs of respect to a lunarian entering a room, those already there sit down and put on their hats (I, 88).

Cyrano is surprised to learn that the "parties honteuses" (shameful parts), worn by a lunarian as a bronze ornament attached to his belt, are signs of nobility on the moon. In his world, Cyrano informs the lunarians, it is the sword which is worn as a sign of nobility. His host's rejoinder, underlying the "monde renversé" motif, points up the folly of a world in which destruction is honored: "Malheureuse contrée où les marques de génération sont ignominieuses et où celles d'anéantissement sont honorables!" (I, 88).[5] (Wretched country, where the signs of reproduction are ignominious and those of annihilation are respectable!) Brun finds that Cyrano closely imitated Béroalde de Verville in this passage,[6] but the satirical sting of the *Estats de la lune* is absent from the pages of the *Moyen de parvenir* (1620), which comprise a rather lavish Rabelaisian praise of lust. There is no implied criticism here, as in Cyrano, of war and massacre.[7]

On the moon, respect is accorded not to the aged but to the young (I, 61–65). The archangel of the *paradis terrestre* is a "bel adolescent" (handsome adolescent) (I, 29). The young have the right to mete out punishment to their elders, as is evident in the retribution exacted by the *fils de l'hôte* of his father after the failure of the latter to notify him of the time (I, 73). Lachèvre interprets this deprecation of the elderly as resulting from Cyrano's dislike of his father (I, 62, n. 2). It is more likely part of Cyrano's satirical attack on the customs and institutions of his society and in particular on the force of tradition and authority. Cyrano, who did not in truth profit by his father's death,[8] will also protest against the patrimonial prejudice in favor of the eldest son which he attributes to the weakness of fathers desirous of material assurance that their name will be perpetuated (I, 89).

The shrewdest indictment of man in the *Autre Monde* is in the form of a reversal of roles between men and beasts. This inversion follows the general relativistic pattern of the "monde renversé." Certain similarities between earthlings and lunarians are established—enough to indicate that man is being subject to ridicule by a fellow human—and at the same time the perspective created by the assumption of opposite roles reinforces the satire. Thus the lunarians, who at first appear to Cyrano to be a type of animal resembling man, turn out to be real men, even if they do walk on all fours: "Je fus bien estonné lors que je reconnus, en effect, que c'estoient des hommes, de n'en rencontrer pas un qui ne marchast à quatre pattes" (I, 32). (When I saw that they were in fact men, I was very surprised to encounter no one who did not walk on all fours.) Cyrano, in turn, a lowly biped, is to be a beast in the eyes of the Selenites, a circumstance of which he has a presentiment when he notes their reaction to his approach: "De temps en temps ils eslevoient des huées si furieuses, causées sans doubte par l'admiration de me voir, que je croyois casi estre devenu Monstre" (I, 32). (From time to time they raised such wild shouts, caused undoubtedly by wonderment at the sight of me, that I almost believed I had turned into a Monster.)

SATIRICAL RELATIVISM

Cyrano, as a visitor to the moon, if not an intruder, is at a decided disadvantage. As one of two representatives of his species (the other being the Spaniard Gonzalès), he is scoffed at and disdained by the lunarians, who do not wish to confer upon him the status of humanity. To underline the baseness of man, the author Cyrano has the character Cyrano recognize the superiority of the lunar beast almost immediately. Cyrano finds that it makes more sense to walk on all fours than to use only two legs.

Et, en effet, resvant depuis sur ce subject, j'ay songé que cette situation de corps n'estoit point trop extravagante, quand je me suis souvenu que nos enfans, lors qu'ilz ne sont encore instruits que ne Nature, marchent à quatre piedz, et ne s'eslèvent sur deux que par le soin de leurs nourisses. (I, 32)

And, in fact, in since reflecting on the subject, I thought that this posture was not too foolish, when I remembered that our children, when still the pupils of Nature alone, walk on all fours, and only stand on two through the attentions of their nurses.

This exaltation of Nature at the expense of civilization could be construed as the nostalgic sigh of a primitivist, and it does indicate a certain primitivistic penchant on the part of the author. Cyrano's purpose, however, is mainly to degrade man, and not to elevate the animals. His use of "theriophily" is basically satirical, as has been pointed out by George Boas.[9] A statement by the *démon de Socrate* ably demonstrates why Cyrano has chosen his satirical caricatures of man from the realm of the beasts. After enumerating the august personages on earth whom he has known, the demon dismisses the rest of mankind as little or no better than the animals.

Voilà les personnes considérables avec qui j'aye conversé; touttes les autres, au moins de celles que j'ay connuës, sont si fort au dessous de l'homme que j'ay veu des bestes un peu plus hault. (I, 36)

These are the important people with whom I have conversed; all the others, at least those whom I knew, are so much beneath man that I have seen beasts a little nobler.

Man's anthropocentric arrogance is humorously castigated by a comparison of his posture with that of the lunar creatures. The reversal of man and beast is now complete. The four-legged lunarians walk with bowed head. As man is wont to allege final causes in support of his belief that the human stance, with head upright, is a proof of his superiority over other beings, so the lunarians employ the same reasoning to prove their superiority.

Voyez un peu . . . comme ilz ont la teste tournée devers le Ciel! C'est la disette où Dieu les a mis de touttes choses qui les a situés de la sorte, car cette posture suppliante tesmoigne qu'ilz cherchent au Ciel pour se plaindre à Celuy qui les a créez et qu'ilz luy demandent permission de s'accommoder de nos restes. Mais, nous autres, nous avons la teste penchée en bas pour contempler les biens dont nous sommes seigneurs et comme n'y ayant rien au Ciel à quoy nostre heureuse condition puisse porter envie. (I, 53)[10]

Just look . . . how their heads are upturned toward the Heavens! It is because of the state of utter want in which God has placed them that they carry themselves thus, for this suppliant posture proves that they are casting their eyes toward Heaven to complain to him who created them and that they are asking him permission to make do with our remains. But as for us, we have our heads inclined downward to contemplate the possessions of which we are lord and as if there were nothing in Heaven which we in our happy state could covet.

Cyrano must again acknowledge the superiority of the lunarians when he discovers their more refined mode of eating, inhalation of the odors of various foods. He tacitly admits to being more grossly animal in his desire for the human form of nourishment: "Ne pouvant pas me débrutaliser si promptement, je serois bien aise de sentir un morceau palpable sous mes dents" (I, 42). (Since I am not able to debestialize myself so promptly, I would be very happy to sink my teeth into a palpable piece of food.)

Leonora Rosenfield notes Cyrano's use of inversion in depicting not man's view of the beasts but what the beasts must think of man.[11] She sees in this paradoxical spirit a reflection of the Renaissance tradition of the *paradossi*,[12] a sixteenth-century genre consisting of essays the themes of which were ideas opposite to those prevailing in the society of the time.[13] According to Mrs. Rosenfield, Cyrano satirizes the Cartesian theory of animal mechanism. The device of reversing the roles of man and beast is unquestionably inspired by the famous beast-machine controversy. But it must be borne in mind that this is not the sole reason for the presence of beasts in the *Autre Monde*. It is noteworthy, for instance, that Mrs. Rosenfield makes no reference to the *Estats du soleil*. The satire on the beast-machine is ultimately linked to the general satire on man and the two should be viewed in relationship to each other.

The satire on the beast-machine theory begins with the quarrel of the lunarians over the nature of their earthly visitor. At first treated as an animal and required to perform tricks for the public, Cyrano shows such wit that his audience is willing to grant him almost as much power of reason as their own animals on the moon (I, 38). When Cyrano begins to learn the language of the lunarians it is rumored that he and Gonzalès are two savages whose growth has been stunted by poor nourishment (the lunarians are considerably larger than the earthlings) (I, 52). The opinion that Cyrano and Gonzalès are uncivilized men is about to gain ground when the priests intervene, shocked at the possibility that the lunarians might elevate the two monsters to the status of their own species.

Cette créance alloit prendre racine à force de cheminer, sans les Prestres du païs qui s'y opposèrent, disant que c'estoit une impiété espouvantable de croire que non seulement des bestes, mais des Monstres, fussent de leur espèce. Il y auroit bien plus d'apparence (adjoustoient les moins passionez) que nos animaux domestiques participassent au privilège de l'humanité et de l'immortalité, par conséquent, à cause qu'ilz sont nés dans nostre païs, qu'une beste monstrueuse qui se dit née je ne sçay où dans la Lune. (I, 52–53)

This belief would have taken root from having circulated about, if the Priests of the country had not opposed it, saying that it was dreadful impiety to believe that not only beasts, but Monsters, were of their species. It would be much more likely (added the least impassioned) that our domestic animals share the privilege of humanity and therefore of immortality, because they were born in our country, rather than a monstrous beast who says he was born who knows where on the Moon.

Rigid anthropocentrism is doubly underscored here. Not only do the lunarians refuse to recognize any similarity between themselves and the inhabitants of another globe; they will not even admit of any between themselves and one of their own native creatures.

In mentioning immortality as a privilege denied by the lunarians to their animals, Cyrano strikes at the center of the controversy over animal mechanism. Leonora Rosenfield notes the theological advantage which Descartes recognized in his hypothesis. Atheists, Descartes observed, could strengthen their beliefs by asserting the animal soul to be of the same nature as the human.[14] The dilemma thus reached by the *libertins* puts the doctrine of the immortality of the soul in a ludicrous light, for if an identity between man and animals is postulated, it must be held that either both share in immortal souls or that both are mortal.[15] This is precisely the difficulty to be posed by the *fils de l'hôte* to ridicule the immortality of the soul. On the other hand, animal automatism was to find favor with seventeenth-century theologians, who discovered in it supporting evidence for immortality.[16] And Boas suggests that the primary reason for Descartes's steadfast adherence to the beast-machine theory was to preserve the concept of the soul's immortality.[17] It is no wonder then that in Cyrano's satire it is the priests who are the strict partisans of animal mechanism.

In a note to this passage, Lachèvre remarks that Cyrano, opposing the Cartesian doctrine, is again assuming a Gassendist position (I, 52, n. 2). Although it is obviously true that Cyrano's satire is here directed against Descartes's theory, it is an oversimplification to classify his viewpoint simply as Gassendist. Gassendi did grant intelligence to the animals, and in his fifth objection to Descartes's *Méditations* he states that the difference between animal and human reason is one of degree. Elsewhere, however, he says that since human souls alone are immortal, animal and human souls do differ in essence.[18] Cyrano, at least in this passage, makes no positive statement on the beast-machine question. His aim is satirical, but in debunking the Cartesian doctrine he himself takes no easily definable position. It would thus be ill-advised to place him in the Gassendist camp, and all the more so since the provost of Digne had certain religious convictions which Cyrano did not share. Cyrano's attack on Cartesian animal automatism is primarily that of a *libertin* who has no inclination to accept the immortality of the soul.[19] At the same time it is an illustration of his general mockery of the anthropocentric and religious view which places man above all other creatures.

That Cyrano delights especially in ridiculing the religious

aspect of animal automatism is seen by the fact that final causes are again cited in support of that theory. The religious anthropocentrism of man is the butt of the satire when the lunar priests, in another instance of inversion, describe the lunarians' four-legged gait as proof of the special status which has been conferred upon them by God.

Nous autres, nous marchons à quatre piedz parce que Dieu ne se voulut pas fier d'une chose si précieuse à une moins ferme assiette, il eut peur qu'il n'arrivast fortune de l'homme; c'est pourquoy il prit luy-mesme la peine de l'asseoir sur quatre piliers, affin qu'il ne peut tomber; mais desdaignant de se mesler de la construction de ces deux brutes [Cyrano and Gonzalès], il les abandonna au caprice de la Nature, laquelle, ne craignant pas la perte de si peu de chose, ne les appuya que sur deux pattes. (I, 53)

We walk on all fours because God did not want to entrust such a precious thing to less stable support, being afraid that man's lot might befall us, which is why he himself took the trouble to place us on four posts so that we would not fall; but not deigning to take a hand in the creation of these two brutes [Cyrano and Gonzalès], he abandoned them to the whims of Nature, who, not fearing the loss of so inconsequential a thing, propped them up on two legs alone.

The theological advantage of the Cartesian doctrine was unquestionably as clear to Cyrano as to Descartes. Aware that it became in his time a rallying point for certain theologians, Cyrano does not lose the opportunity to direct another barb at the clergy. It is the priests who dominate the thinking of the lunar people. It is they who decree that he shall be deemed a plucked parrot: "Ilz bridèrent si bien la conscience des peuples sur cet article qu'il fust arresté que je ne passerois tout au plus que pour un Perroquet plumé" (I, 53). (They had so thoroughly bridled the people's conscience on this point that it was decreed that I would at the most pass only for a feathered Parrot.) But the mastery over the lunar language which Cyrano displays causes the people so to admire his cleverness that the clergy is obliged to publish another decree: "Le Clergé fut contrainct de faire publier un Arrest par lequel on deffendoit de croire que j'eusse de la raison" (I, 54).[20] (The Clergy was obliged to publish a Decree by which it was forbidden to believe I possessed reason.) After a juridical examination, the people decide that he is a kind of ostrich, and he is remanded to his cage (I, 54).

It is evident from the foregoing passages that the bulk of Cyrano's satire on the beast-machine theory is directed against religion but that other aspects of the question amused and intrigued him also. That Cyrano should at first be adjudged a parrot by the clergy is, for instance, not without significance. It is precisely the example of parrots (and magpies, which, incidentally, will appear in the *Estats du soleil* as reasonable creatures) that figures in Descartes's *Discours de la méthode* and in a response to it by Henry More. Descartes states that although magpies and parrots are able to pronounce words like ours, they are incapable of rational discourse.

Car on voit que les pies et les perroquets peuvent proférer des paroles ainsi que nous, et toutefois ne peuvent parler ainsi que nous, c'est-à-dire en témoignant qu'ils pensent ce qu'ils disent.[21]

For you see that magpies and parrots can utter words just as we can, and nevertheless cannot speak as we do, that is, they do not show that they are thinking what they are saying.

To this More replies that the sounds emitted by these creatures do indicate rationality on their part.[22] Descartes lists as the first of the two features distinguishing men from beasts the faculty of language[23] and denies the possibility that beasts do have their own languages, incomprehensible to man.[24] Thus the clergy, in classifying Cyrano as a parrot, is adopting the Cartesian idea that the sounds produced by animals, no matter how reasonable they may seem, are simply the results of the mechanical arrangement and functioning of their organs. The attribution of language to the character Cyrano naturally forms a part of the satire by inversion on animal mechanism. How seriously Cyrano actually regarded the anti-Cartesian notion that animals do possess language is another question and will be examined in relationship to the *Estats du soleil*, in which real animals do speak.

In this scene of the *Estats de la lune* the satire is clearly that of an empiricist, for in the face of all evidence to the contrary the clergy imposes upon the people the belief that no matter how reasonable Cyrano's actions may appear, they are only the products of instinct. The people are prohibited from granting reason to the earthling:

avec un commandement très exprès à toutes personnes, de quelque qualité et condition qu'elles fussent, de s'imaginer, quoy que je peusse faire de spirituel, que c'estoit l'instinct qui me le faisoit faire. (I, 54)

with the express order to all persons, of whatever rank or class, to believe that, whatever spiritual thing I might do, it was instinct that made me do it.

One of the issues with which Cyrano is obviously concerned is the merits of the empirical outlook as opposed to the theological.

The contrast between the rigidity of the theological view and the elasticity of the relativistic view takes on a propaganda value as a lunarian who comes to Cyrano's defense makes a case for intellectual freedom. There are two possibilities, he argues before the priests. Cyrano is either a man or a beast. If he is a man, he is entitled to believe what he wants. If he is a beast, he is guided by Nature, a power to be respected.

Car, supposez qu'il soit animal sans raison, quelle raison vous-mesmes avez-vous de l'accuser d'avoir péché contre elle? Il a dit que la Lune estoit un Monde. Or, les brutes n'agissent que par instinct de Nature; doncques c'est la Nature qui le dit, et non pas luy; de croire mainte-nant que cette sçavante Nature qui a faict et la Lune et ce Monde-cy ne sçache elle-mesme ce que c'est et que vous autres, qui n'avés de connoissance que ce que vous en tenés d'elle le sçachiez plus certaine-ment, cela seroit bien ridicule. (I, 59)

For, supposing he is an animal without reason, what reason do you yourselves have to accuse him of having sinned against it? He said the Moon was a World. Now beasts act only out of an instinct of Nature; therefore it is Nature that said it and not he; to start thinking that wise Nature who made both the Moon and this World does not herself know what it is and that you, whose only knowledge is what you derive from her, know it more certainly, would be quite ridic-ulous.

Taking the other side for tactical reasons, the charitable lunarian praises the virtues of instinct with an enthusiasm worthy of Montaigne. As Cyrano had previously admired the workings of Nature in four-legged creatures, so he now extols Nature's guiding hand as manifest in brute instinct. A primitivistic note is again sounded as the Cartesian position is turned against itself to the glory of the animals and Nature.[25] Cyrano's "theriophily," if indeed it may be termed such (for it must be recalled that it is here chiefly a satiric device), is thus at once intellectual and anti-intellectual. In endowing the "animal" Cyrano with reason, the author's anti-Cartesian stand is definitely intellectual; but in hav-ing Cyrano's defense consist of a eulogy of animal instinct, his theriophily takes a decidedly anti-intellectual turn. This apparent paradox supports Boas's judgment that intellectualistic and anti-intellectualistic theriophily could coexist quite peacefully, even in one work of the same writer.[26] The anti-intellectualistic aspect of theriophily is, however, for this lover of reason, only incidental.

Cyrano's satire of animal automatism abounds with echoes of Montaigne. To attack anthropocentrism the author of the *Apologie* imagines a reversal between man and beast not unlike that in the *Autre Monde*. He points out that if animals are not capable of understanding humans, man cannot understand the animals. Why then should they not consider us beasts? "Par cette mesme raison, elles nous peuvent estimer bestes, comme nous les en estimons." (By this same reasoning they may consider us beasts, as we consider them.)[27] How do we know that animals too do not regard themselves as the center of the universe?

Pourtant disoit plaisamment Xenophanes, que si les animaux se forgent des dieux, comme il est vraysemblable qu'ils facent, ils les forgent certainement de mesme eux, et se glorifient, comme nous. Car pourquoy ne dira un oison ainsi: "Toutes les pieces de l'univers me regardent; la terre me sert à marcher, le Soleil à m'esclairer, les estoilles à m'inspirer leurs influances; j'ay telle commodité des vents, telle des eaux; il n'est rien que cette voute regarde si favorablement que moy; je suis le mignon de nature; est-ce pas l'homme qui me traite, qui me loge, qui me sert?"

Wherefore Xenophanes used to say wittily that if the animals make gods for themselves, as it is likely they do, they certainly make them like themselves, and glorify themselves as we do. For why shall a gosling not say thus: "All the parts of the universe have me in view: the earth serves for me to walk on, the sun to give me light, the stars to breathe their influences into me; I gain this advantage from the winds, that from the waters; there is nothing that the heavenly vault regards so favorably as me; I am the darling of nature. Is it not man that treats me, houses me, serves me?"[28]

Relativism is contrasted to egocentric narrowness of mind by Montaigne as an illustration of the errors of anthropocentrism. He offers examples of prejudices arising from anthropocentrism.

SATIRICAL RELATIVISM

J'ay veu autresfois parmy nous des hommes amenez par mer de lointain pays, desquels par ce que nous n'entendions aucunement le langage, et que leur façon, au demeurant, et leur contenance, et leurs vestemens estoient du tout esloignez des nostres, qui de nous ne les estimoit et sauvages et brutes?

I once saw among us some men brought by sea from a far country. Because we did not understand their language at all, and because their ways, moreover, and their bearing and their clothes were totally remote from ours, which of us did not consider them savages and brutes?[29]

The resemblance to the lunarians' reception of Cyrano is obvious.

Both Cyrano and Montaigne aim at a destruction of man's anthropocentric pride, and Cyrano could easily have adopted Montaigne's dictum "Il nous faut abestir pour nous assagir" (We must become like the animals in order to become wise)[30] as his own. But he would have altered its meaning. Montaigne has used relativism as a weapon against anthropocentrism. For Cyrano the elimination of anthropocentric views is a necessary step in the acceptance of a relativistic outlook. Relativism is an end in itself. Thus for Montaigne "abestir" (to become like the animals) is essentially an act of humility. In Cyrano's work "abestir" requires a certain humility also, but it is primarily to effect a change in perspective that man should assume the viewpoint of the beasts. It is a way of widening mental horizons, of recognizing the relativistic nature of the world. The anti-intellectual fideistic humility of Montaigne, apparent in his variety of theriophily, is excluded from Cyrano's world. Although a certain relativism, the various aspects and consequences of which have been explored by Pierre Villey,[31] pervades the *Essais*, Montaigne conveys the impression of a philosophical paradise of the absolute lost, a theme that is transposed to the religious sphere by Pascal. Villey has commented that the real novelty and "idée maîtresse" (main idea) of the *Essais* was their message that "nous n'avons aucune communication à l'estre" (we have no communication with being), that knowledge of the essence of things has been forever lost by us.[32] It is the "nostalgie de l'absolu" (nostalgia for the absolute)[33] which Villey finds in Montaigne that is noticeably absent in Cyrano. Both Montaigne and Cyrano recognize the need to confine rational inquiry to the relative, but the spirit of each is distinctive. Relativism for Montaigne is a philosophical necessity which he does not greet without some feeling of resignation. Relativism for Cyrano carries with it a certain measure of optimism, for it is a means to greater knowledge.

It is with a plea for rational judgment based on an awareness of relativism that Cyrano's defender ends his tirade. His final thrust is an acrid comment both on the clergy and on the idea of a personal God who takes an interest in all human affairs. With Voltairean gusto the lunarian places the pontiffs' prosecution of Cyrano in a larger perspective.

Rougissez à tout le moins des inquiétudes que vous causent les capriolles d'une beste. En vérité, Messieurs, si vous rencontriés un homme d'âge meur qui veillast à la police d'une fourmillière pour tantost donner un soufflet à la fourmi qui auroit faict cheoir sa compagne, tantost en emprisonner une qui auroit desrobé à sa voisine un grain de bled, tantost mettre en justice une autre qui auroit abandonné ses oeufs, ne l'estimeriés-vous pas insensé de vacquer à des choses trop au-dessous de luy, et de prétendre assujettir à la raison des animaux qui n'en ont pas l'usage? Comment donc, vénérables Pontifes, appelerés-vous l'intérest que vous prenés aux capriolles de ce petit animal? (I, 59–6c)

Deign at least to blush at the anxieties caused you by the capers of an animal. Truthfully, Gentlemen, if you were to meet an adult man who was seeing to the governing of an anthill, now by giving a slap to the ant who had made his companion fall, now imprisoning another who had stolen a kernel of corn from his neighbor, now bringing to justice another who had abandoned his eggs, would you not deem him mad to attend to things too much beneath him and to claim to subject to the laws of reason animals who have not its use? What then do you say, venerable Pontiffs, of the interest which you take in the capers of this little animal?

The relativism employed here is clearly more far-reaching than that of Montaigne.[34] The aim is to free the mind for more rational exercise and greater intellectual endeavor.[35]

The beasts play a slightly different role in the *Estats du soleil*, in which the satire on man becomes much more harsh and at times even borders on invective. Eddy, indicating the influence of Cyrano's second voyage on Swift, finds the satirical treatment of man in the *Estats du soleil* and in *Gulliver's Travels* equally bitter.[36] He notes that in both the "Histoire des Oiseaux" and in Houyhnhnmland a "ruthless condemnation" of man is pronounced by a tribunal of animals.[37] As the satire grows more sombre, the seriousness with which Cyrano accords prominence to nonhumans becomes more a question. No longer are the denizens of the other world, like the lunarians, mere creatures of fancy. They are now birds and trees, such as are found on earth.

The matter of animals possessing language is taken up with more sobriety in the *Estats du soleil*. The first bird encountered by Dyrcona in the "Histoire des Oiseaux" refutes the Cartesian position that the imitation by animals of human sounds is not indicative of reason on their part.

Je voy vostre esprit tendu à comprendre comment il est possible que je m'explique à vous d'un discours suivy, veu qu'encore que les oiseaux contrefassent vostre parole, ils ne la conçoivent pas; mais aussi quand vous contrefaites l'aboy d'un chien, ou le chant d'un rossignol, vous ne concevez pas non plus ce que le chien ou le rossignol ont voulu dire. Tirez donc conséquence de là que ny les oiseaux ny les hommes ne sont pas pour cela moins raisonnables. (I, 148)

I see your mind straining to understand how it is possible that I explain myself to you in connected speech, seeing that although birds can mimic your words they cannot understand them; but you also, when you mimic a dog's barking or a nightingale's singing, you do not understand what the dog or the nightingale meant either. Conclude from this then that neither birds nor men are less rational for all that.

Did Cyrano, in rejecting Descartes's animal mechanism, actually uphold the idea that animals have their own rational language? It is quite likely that although Cyrano conceived of the beasts as much more than mere automata, he endowed the creatures of the *Autre Monde* with language for other reasons. The first of these of course was that it was necessary to his general satiric device of inversion to do so. But in addition to this, the speaking animals are not unrelated to his half-whimsical, half-serious theory of language as set forth by the man Dyrcona meets on a sunspot before he alights on the sun itself.

This man speaks to Dyrcona in a language which he has never before heard and which he does not believe exists in any form on the earth. The traveler in space is amazed to find that he understands the new language more readily than his own. The inhabitant of the sunspot enlightens him as to the meaning of this strange occurrence by discoursing on the nature of universal language.

Il m'expliqua . . . que dans les sciences il y avoit un Vray, hors lequel on estoit toûjours éloigné du facile; que plus un idiome s'éloignoit de ce Vray, plus il se rencontroit au dessous de la conception et de moins facile intelligence. (I, 129)

He explained to me . . . that in the sciences there is a True, without which you are always removed from the simple; that the more removed a language is from the True, the further it falls beneath the intended idea and the less easily understandable it is.

Lavers cites this speech to show that Cyrano posited the existence of Universal Truth.[38] Such might appear to be the case without an examination of the passages immediately following this one. It will be apparent, moreover, that Cyrano's theory of language bears a distinct relationship to other ideas of the *Autre Monde*, whereas the concept of Universal Truth does not.

Dyrcona seizes upon the notion of a universal language with enthusiasm, offering the thought that the first man on earth must undoubtedly have used this "langue matrice" (mother tongue) (I, 129). His interlocutor interrupts him with a more detailed description of the language.

Elle n'est pas simplement nécessaire pour exprimer tout ce que l'esprit conçoit, mais sans elle on ne peut pas estre entendu de tous. Comme cet idiome est l'instinct ou la voix de la Nature, il doit estre intelligible à tout ce qui vit sous le ressort de la Nature: c'est pour-quoy si vous en aviez l'intelligence, vous pourriez communiquer et discourir de toutes vos pensées aux bestes, et les bestes à vous de toutes les leurs, à cause que c'est le langage mesme de la Nature, par qui elle se fait entendre à tous les animaux. (I, 129–130)

It is not only necessary in order to express everything conceived by the mind, but without it you cannot be understood by all. Since this language is the instinct or voice of Nature, it must be understandable to everything living under Nature's jurisdiction. That is why if you understood it you could communicate and discourse upon all your thoughts to beasts, and reciprocally the beasts to you of all theirs, because it is the very language of Nature, by which she makes herself understood to all animals.

At first glance a primitivistic laud of Nature, this discourse by the inhabitant of the sunspot emerges in fact as a foreshadowing of what is to happen on the sun itself. This is a technique not unknown to the *Autre Monde*. As the transformations of matter that are theoretically described in the *Estats de la lune* occur in fictitious reality in the *Estats du soleil*, so the concept of a universal language, put forth on the sunspot, is given practical application on the sun, where Dyrcona and the birds are able to converse with each other. (On the moon, it will be remembered, he was obliged to learn the language of the lunarians.)

The universal language coincides with the idea of the unity of matter, concretely illustrated on the sun by the metamorphoses. The "langue matrice," or language of Nature, recalls the "matrice des idées de la Nature" (womb of Nature's ideas) in which, as the *démon de Socrate* told Cyrano on the moon, the latter was located before his birth (I, 64). The "langue matrice," known to all living creatures alike, corresponds logically to the "matière première" (primary matter), the stuff of which, according to Cyrano, all life is composed.[39] It is not surprising then that on the globe where one primary matter lends itself with agility to many different forms, one "langue matrice" should be available to all those living beings partaking of the elemental matter. The "langue matrice" is thus a corollary of the principle of the unity of matter.[40] If the talking animals of the *Estats du soleil* are viewed as fanciful examples of what could be theoretically possible, granting the unity of matter, it is clear that their role in the beast-machine controversy must be distinctly defined. They are of course meant as part of the satire on the Cartesian doctrine. But it is not to be supposed that they are intended as a serious counterproposal to animal automatism. Cyrano does offer what may be considered an alternative to the beast-machine theory in the *Estats du soleil*. But his talking animals are chiefly a part of his exposition of the unity of matter and are not to be taken as proof that he believed animals to speak and reason like humans.

The reversal of animal and human roles takes place on the sun, as it did on the moon, but with renewed vigor and a tinge of cruelty in the implied commentary on human behavior. The first adventure that befalls Dyrcona on the sun, for example, is that he is carried aloft to the royal capital by four eagles who want to put out his eyes. Upon arrival, he is immediately thrown into prison (I, 149). A magpie who generously befriends Dyrcona tells him that the birds are hastening to kill him because he is becoming too thin and soon will not make a substantial enough repast. Apparently a satire by the process of inversion on man's treatment of the animals, this scene is also a satirical criticism of the administration of justice by man to man, made all the more biting by the fact that it follows the interlude on earth, where such justice is sadly decried. Dyrcona escapes from his prison on earth only to find himself once more imprisoned on the sun. The irony, resulting from the seeming reversal of roles which in reality but thinly disguises an underlying identity, is obvious.

The attack on the belief in the beast-machine is thus a convenient angle of attack on all narrowness of mind, overriding prejudice, and anthropocentrism. In defending Dyrcona against his would-be assassins who consider him devoid of reason, the magpie is not only deploring the cruelty of the partisans of automatism for whom the theory meant license to treat animals as heartlessly as they desired;[41] the bird is also condemning the lack of vision which makes such beliefs possible.

La rumeur pensa s'échauffer en sédition; car ma Pie s'estant émancipée de représenter que c'estoit un procédé barbare de faire ainsi mourir, sans connoissance de cause, un animal qui approchoit en quelque sorte de leur raisonnement, ils la pensèrent mettre en pièces, alléguant que cela seroit bien ridicule de croire qu'un animal tout nu, que la Nature mesme en mettant au jour ne s'estoit pas souciée de fournir des choses nécessaires à le conserver, fut comme eux capable de raison. (I, 150)

The report [that Dyrcona was getting too thin] threatened to inflame sedition; for my Magpie having dared to point out that it was a barbaric procedure to put to death in such a way, without full knowledge of the facts, an animal who somewhat equaled their powers of reason, they threatened to chop her to bits, alleging that it would be quite absurd to believe that a completely naked animal, which Nature herself had taken no care to supply with the things necessary to his preservation when she brought him into the world, should be, like themselves, capable of reason.

Both Dyrcona's defender and his accusers are united in condemning anthropocentrism. The enumeration of the birds' grievances against humans constitutes a complete denunciation of man.

L'Homme . . . si sot et si vain qu'il se persuade que nous n'avons été faits que pour luy; . . . l'Homme qui soutient qu'on ne raisonne que par le rapport des sens, et qui cependant a les sens les plus foibles, les plus tardifs et les plus faux d'entre toutes les Créatures; l'Homme enfin que la Nature, pour faire de tout, a créé comme les Monstres, mais en qui pourtant elle a infus l'ambition de commander à tous les animaux et de les exterminer. (I, 150)

Man . . . so foolish and so vain that he is convinced we were made just for him; . . . Man who maintains that reasoning occurs only by means of information supplied by the senses and who nevertheless has the feeblest, the most backward, and the most untrustworthy senses of any Creature; finally, Man whom Nature, in order to make a little of everything, created as she did Monsters, but yet in whom she infused the ambition of governing all animals and exterminating them.

This speech, however, represents only the most enlightened avian opinion. The majority of the birds find it unthinkable that a creature as different from themselves as Dyrcona should in any way partake of their nature or share in the privilege of immortality. "Hé quoy, murmuroient-ils l'un â l'autre, il n'a ny bec, ny plumes, ny griffes, et son âme seroit spirituelle? O Dieux! quelle impertinence!" (I, 150). (What! they murmured to each other, he has neither beak, feathers, nor claws, and his soul is spiritual? Ye gods! What impertinence!) This exclamation of wounded dignity is of course a gibe at the Cartesians' defense of man's unique claim to immortality as further enhanced by the doctrine of animal mechanism. Given Cyrano's attitudes toward religion, it is undoubtedly also another scoff at immortality itself, and recalls the parable of the Christian eating a Mohammedan. The implied question is that if it is absurd to grant immortality to only one species of living being, is it not equally absurd to grant it only to certain members of the same (human) species and not to others?

Whereas Dyrcona stood trial on the moon for declaring the lunarians' moon to be an earth, on the sun he will be tried simply for being a man. The ironic process of inversion pointing up identity continues, for the solar tribunal is not exempt from human failings. Dyrcona's trial, for instance, must be postponed because of the weather, meteorological factors being thought by the solarians to have direct effects on the magistrates' judgments.

Ils craignoient que la mauvaise température de l'air n'altérât quelque chose à la bonne constitution de l'esprit des juges; que le chagrin dont l'humeur des oiseaux se charge durant la pluye ne dégorgeât sur la cause; ou qu'enfin la Cour ne se vengeât de sa tristesse sur l'accusé. (I, 152)

They feared that the disagreeable temperature might somehow alter the good health of the judges' minds; that the sorrow with which the birds' temperament beccmes burdened in the rain might unduly influence consideration of the case; or finally that the Court might take out its sadness on the defendant.

Such, then, are the velleities upon which justice and reason depend. The distortion of man's rational faculties by his emotions is signaled also in the course of the lunar trial. The "Grand Pontife," Cyrano's prosecutor on the moon, employs a trumpet in speaking, the noise of which so frightens Cyrano that he cannot remember what he said. The pontiff uses the instrument deliberately to obliterate any impulse to reason on the part of those attending the trial.

C'estoit une trompette qu'il avoit tout exprès choisie affin que la violence de ce ton martial eschauffast leurs esprits à ma mort, et affin d'empescher par cette esmoticn que le raisonnement ne pût faire son office, comme il arrive dans nos armées, où ce tintamarre de trompettes et de tambours empesche le soldat de réfléchir sur l'importance de sa vie. (I, 58–59)

It was a trumpet that he had purposely chosen so that the violence of the martial tones would inflame in their hearts the desire for my death, and so that this emotion would prevent reason from carrying out its usual functions, as it happens in our armies, where the din of trumpets and drums prevents the soldier from reflecting on the importance of his life.

These lines are not without implications as to the role of ritual and ceremony in religion,[42] a matter mentioned by Montaigne in a passage which may have inspired Cyrano's reflections on the influence of the senses and emotions on reason:

SATIRICAL RELATIVISM

Il n'est coeur si mol que le son de nos tabourins et de nos trompetes n'eschaufe; ny si dur que la douceur de la musique n'esveille et ne chatouille; ny ame si revesche qui ne se sente touchée de quelque reverence à considerer cette vastité sombre de nos Eglises, la diversité d'ornemens et ordre de nos ceremonies, et ouyr le son devotieux de nos orgues, et la harmonie si posée et religieuse de nos voix. Ceux mesme qui y entrent avec mespris, sentent quelque frisson dans le coeur, et quelque horreur qui les met en deffiance de leur opinion.

There is no heart so faint that the sound of our drums and trumpets will not warm it, or so hard that the sweetness of music will not awaken it and caress it; no soul so crabbed as not to feel touched by some reverence on contemplating the somber vastness of our churches, the diversity of ornaments, and the order of our ceremonies, and on hearing the devotional sound of our organs and the harmony, so solemn and religious, of our voices. Even those who enter with disdain feel a certain shiver in their heart, and a certain awe, which makes them distrust their opinion.[43]

The power of emotional ritual to cloud reason is again underlined by Cyrano in his description of the "mort triste," the most ignominious of solar punishments. Dyrcona's judges show him great clemency in sparing him this penalty, which consists of ceremonies curiously resembling an earthly funeral.

C'eux [sic] d'entre nous qui ont la voix la plus mélancolique et la plus funèbre sont déléguez vers le coupable qu'on porte sur un funeste cyprès. Là, ces tristes musiciens s'amassent tout autour et luy remplissent l'âme par l'oreille de chansons si lugubres et si tragiques, que l'amertume de son chagrin désordonnant l'oeconomie de ses organes, et luy pressant le coeur, il se consume à veuë d'oeil et meurt suffoqué de tristesse. (I, 156)

Those among us [the birds] whose voices are most melancholy and funereal are assigned to the culprit, who is borne to a fatal cypress tree. There these sad musicians gather about him and fill his soul with such lugubrious and tragic songs that the bitterness of his sorrow disrupts the ordering of his organs and presses on his heart, and he wastes away before your very eyes and dies suffocated by sadness.

Cyrano's satire on funerals proceeds logically from his stoical and materialistic concept of death. On the moon, a philosopher who feels death approaching and who wishes to take leave of life notifies his friends of his intentions by inviting them to a lavish banquet.[44] They accordingly return to his house on an appointed day, kill him, and feast on his flesh and blood (I, 86–87). Death is a materialistic phenomenon; eating the corpse is symbolic of the transference of the same matter to a different form. On the sun the birds of paradise offer Dyrcona a materialistic consolation of death, which makes all funereal ritual seem like flummery. Death merits no histrionics; it is, Dyrcona is told, only the redisposition of matter:

Il faut, mon cher frère, te persuader que, comme toy et les autres brutes estes matériels, et comme la mort au lieu d'anéantir la matière, elle ne fait que troubler l'oeconomie, tu dois . . . croire avec certitude que, cessant d'estre ce que tu estois, tu commenceras d'estre quelqu'autre chose. (I, 162)

You must, my dear brother, be persuaded that, since you and the other brutes are material, and since death instead of destroying matter merely upsets its arrangement, you must . . . believe with certainty that, ceasing to be what you were, you will begin to be something else.

Appended to this rejection of immortality and the ceremonies attendant upon death is a parting thrust at man: "Je veux donc que tu ne deviennes qu'une motte de terre ou un caillou, encor seras-tu quelque chose de moins meschant que l'Homme" (I,

162). (I would that you might become a clod of earth or a pebble; you would still be something less wicked than Man.)

The inversion is especially ironic in the preparation of Dyrcona for his death by the two birds of paradise.[45] The birds, after affirming the universality of death, exempt themselves from it by virtue of their immortality.

La mort, me dirent-ils . . . n'est pas, sans doute, un grand mal, puis que Nature, nostre bonne Mère, y assujettit tous ses enfants; et ce ne doit pas estre une affaire de grande conséquence, puis qu'elle arrive à tout moment et pour si peu de chose; car si la vie estoit si excellente, il ne seroit pas en nostre pouvoir de ne la point donner; ou si la mort traisnoit après soy des suites de l'importance que tu te fais accroire, il ne seroit pas en nostre pouvoir de la donner: il y a beaucoup d'apparence, au contraire, puis que l'animal commence par jeu, qu'il finit de mesme. Je parle à toy ainsi, à cause que ton âme n'estant pas immortelle comme la nostre, tu peux bien juger quand tu meurs, que tout meurt avec toy. (I, 161)

Death, they said to me . . . is undoubtedly not a great evil, since Nature, our good Mother, subjects all her children to it; it must not be a thing of great consequence, since it occurs at every moment and for such trifles; for if life were so excellent, it would not be in our power not to give it; or if from death ensued the consequences which you are given to believe, it would not be in our power to give it. There is much likelihood, on the contrary, that since animals begin in sport, they end in the same way. I am speaking to you thus, because since your soul is not immortal like ours, you can well understand that when you die, everything dies with you.

From his satire on the beast-machine Cyrano extracts the freethinker's lesson: if a radical difference between the nature of man and beast is denied, the logical consequence is that neither man nor beast can pretend to immortality. Cyrano is thus not unwittingly taking the materialist's advantage from the theory of animal mechanism, foreseen by the authors of the sixth objections to Descartes's *Méditations*. If beasts can be likened to machines, they reasoned, why cannot man?[46] Whereas the Cartesians view animals as machines, Cyrano's fictitious animals view man as little more than a machine. Again the reversal ironically implies identity. Cyrano is of course no La Mettrie. He did not even draw, at least in the *Autre Monde*, Descartes's mechanistic picture of nature. But his identification of man with the beast is definitely the materialistic gesture of a *libertin* who stresses the unity of matter at the expense of immortality.[47]

Instead of a beast-machine readied for conversion into a man-machine, Cyrano offers a unified matter with at least theoretical manifestations of "reason" at every stage of life. Not only beasts but plants as well discourse rationally in Cyrano's fantastical worlds. A talking tree from the forest of Dodona on the sun lectures, with an eloquence reminiscent of Ronsard's celebrated elegy, on the sensitivity of trees.

Si le sot peuple de vostre Monde m'avoit entendu parler comme je fais, il croiroit que ce seroit un Diable enfermé sous mon écorce; car bien loin de croire que nous puissions raisonner, il ne s'imagine pas mesme que nous ayons l'âme sensitive, encor que tous les jours il voye qu'au premier coup dont le bucheron assaut un arbre, la coignée entre dans la chair quatre fois plus avant qu'au second; et qu'il doive conjecturer qu'asseurément le premier coup l'a surpris et frapé au dépourveu, puis qu'aussitost qu'il a esté averty par la douleur, il s'est ramassé en soy-mesme, a réüny ses forces pour combattre, et s'est comme pétrifié pour résister à la dureté des armes de son ennemy. (I, 167)

If the foolish people of your World had heard me speak as I do now, they would think that a Devil were confined within my bark; for far from believing that we can reason, he does not even think we have a sensitive soul, although he sees every day that at the first blow with

SATIRICAL RELATIVISM

a device corresponding to that of elevating the lunarians or the solar birds to the privileged rank thought by man to be occupied by him alone. In this it is an extension of the beast-machine satire. Man is no more made in God's image, the demon states, than the cabbage. Even if God existed, He would be an impersonal God, showing no preference for any one of his creatures. (Strains of deism can be detected here.) The cabbage is not only man's equal; he is in fact superior to him because he is not tainted by original sin. The satire by inversion is now amplified to include comments on traditional religion, such as the flouting of the doctrine of original sin.

De dire pourtant que Dieu a plus aymé l'homme que le chou, c'est que nous nous chatoüillons pour nous faire rire; estant incapable de passion, il ne sçauroit ny haïr, ny aymer personne; et s'il estoit susceptible d'amour, il auroit plustost des tendresses pour ce chou que vous tenés qui ne sçauroit l'offenser, que pour cet homme dont il a desjà devant les yeux les injures qu'il luy doibt faire. Adjoustés à cela qu'il ne sçauroit naistre sans crime, estant une partie du premier homme qui le rendit coupable, mais nous sçavons fort bien que le premier chou n'offensa pas son Créateur au Paradis Terrestre. Dira-t-on que nous sommes faicts à l'image du Souverain Estre et non pas les choux? Quand il seroit vray, nous avons en soüillant nostre Ame par où nous luy ressemblions, effacé cette ressemblance, puisqu'il n'y a rien de plus contraire à Dieu que le péché. (I, 68)

To say however that God has loved man more than the cabbage is to tickle ourselves to make us laugh; since he is incapable of passion, he can neither hate nor love anyone and if he were capable of love, he would feel tenderness for this cabbage that you are holding, which cannot offend him, rather than for man, whose transgressions he has before his eyes. In addition, man cannot be born without crime, since he is a part of the first man who rendered him guilty, but we know very well that the first cabbage did not offend its Creator in Earthly

Paradise. Will we say that we are made in the image of the Sovereign Being and that cabbages are not? Even if that were true, in sullying the soul by which we resembled him, we effaced the resemblance, since nothing is more contrary to God than sin.

Cyrano is unquestionably thinking of the Cartesians' tolerance of callous treatment of animals when he protests against the cutting down of plants by man. He again scoffs at the probable raison d'être of Descartes's theory, man's unique claim to immortality.

Le péché de massacrer un homme n'est pas si grand, parce qu'un jour il revivra, que de coupper un chou et luy oster la vie, à luy, qui n'en a point d'autre à espérer. Vous anéantissez l'Ame d'un chou en le faisant mourir; mais, en tuant un homme, vous ne faites que changer son domicile. (I, 68–69)

Because one day he will live again, the sin of slaughtering a man is not so great as that of chopping a cabbage and taking away its life, for it has no other to hope for. You are annihilating the Soul of a cabbage by putting it to death, but when you kill a man you only change his residence.

As an antidote to anthropocentrism and anthropomorphism, Cyrano proposes a more equitable distribution of favors to all living creatures by Nature (or God, the two terms having a synonymous value here). If the cabbages are not immortal, then, they must be endowed with some compensatory advantage. Returning to one of his favorite ideas, Cyrano imagines them equipped with a superior set of senses. But since it is evident that he does not seriously consider immortality the particular prerogative of man, the attribution of better sensory faculties to the cabbage becomes another in the series of satiric devices of inversion with the intention of debunking man. Man is depicted as coltish in comparison to the cabbage.

SATIRICAL RELATIVISM

Puisque Dieu, le Père commun de touttes choses, chérit esgallement ses ouvrages, n'est-il pas raisonnable qu'il ayst partagé ses bienfaicts esgallement entre nous et les plantes? . . . Si donc les Choux n'eurent point leur part avec nous du fief de l'immortalité, ilz furent sans doubte avantagez de quelqu'autre qui par sa grandeur récompense sa brièveté; c'est peut-estre un intellect universel, une connoissance parfaicte de touttes les choses dans leurs causes, et c'est peut-estre aussy pour cela que ce sage Moteur ne leur a point taillé d'organes semblables aux nostres, qui n'ont pour tout effect qu'un simple raisonnement foible et souvent trompeur, mais d'autres plus ingénieusement travaillez, plus forts et plus nombreux, qui leur servent à l'opération de leurs spéculatifs entretiens? Vous me demanderés peut-estre ce qu'ilz nous ont jamais communiqué de ces grandes pensées? Mais, dites-moy, que vous ont jamais enseigné les Anges non plus qu'eux? Comme il n'y a point de proportion, de rapport ny d'harmonie entre les facultez imbéciles de l'homme et celles de ces divines créatures, ces choux intellectuels auroient beau s'efforcer de nous faire comprendre la cause occulte de tous les événemens merveilleux, il nous manque des sens capables de recevoir ces hautes espéces. (I, 69)

Since God, the common Father of all things, cherishes all his works equally, is it not reasonable that he distribute his gifts equally between us and plants? . . . Therefore if Cabbages did not obtain along with us their share of the fief of immortality, they were undoubtedly favored with some other benefit, the greatness of which would compensate for its brevity; it is perhaps a universal intellect, a perfect knowledge of the causes of everything, and it is perhaps also for this reason that the wise Mover did not fashion for them organs similar to ours, the entire effect of which is but a simple, weak, and often deceptive reasoning, but gave them others, more ingeniously wrought, stronger, and more numerous, which serve them in their speculative conversations. You will perhaps ask me why they have never communicated these noble thoughts to us. But, tell me, whatever more have Angels taught you? Since there is no proportion, relation, or harmony between the imbecile faculties of man and those of these divine creatures, the intellectual cabbages would try in vain to have us understand the occult cause of all marvelous events, for we lack senses capable of receiving such lofty impressions.

In concluding his defense of the cabbages the demon brings up the question of language which so worried the participants in the controversy over Cartesian animal automatism. If plants (and, by implication, animals) cannot express their thoughts to us, this does not mean that they do not think and feel (I, 69). By the refutation of one of Descartes's two criteria for classifying animals as machines Cyrano is again upholding not the idea that brutes and plants are capable of rational discourse, but the materialistic concept of universally sensitive life composed of a unified matter.

A final touch is added to the praise of the cabbages in the form of a justification by the demon of his own imaginings. It is a sceptical quip which may be applied to the general fantasy of the *Autre Monde*: "Que si vous me demandés comme je sçay que les choux ont ces belles pensées, je vous demande comme vous sçavés qu'ilz ne les ont point" (I, 69). (If you ask me how I know that cabbages have these fine thoughts, I ask you how you know that they do not have them.) This is not the brand of scepticism summarized by the reflection that nothing is impossible, but rather by the belief that everything is possible. Such a belief is one of the motifs of the *Autre Monde* and is an example of how well-suited the genre of the fantastic voyage is to the message of relativism.[51] The little men on the sun who metamorphose themselves at will into whatever they like tell Dyrcona that their method of acquiring knowledge is to travel about and observe the customs of many lands. The nature of their knowledge then is relativistic, just as is that of the author-traveler Cyrano.

Sçache donc que nous sommes des animaux natifs du Soleil dans les régions éclairées: la plus ordinaire, comme la plus utile de nos occupations, c'est de voyager par les vastes contrées de ce grand Monde. Nous remarquons curieusement les moeurs des peuples, le génie des climats, et la nature de toutes les choses qui peuvent mériter nostre attention, par le moyen de quoy nous formons une science certaine de ce qui est. (I, 142)

Know then that we are animals indigenous to the light regions of the Sun. The most ordinary and also the most useful among our pursuits is to travel through the vast lands of this great World. We note with curiosity the customs of the peoples, the characteristics of climates, the nature of everything deserving our attention, by which means we form certain knowledge of what is.

When the episodes of the *Autre Monde* do not serve as whimsical illustrations of Cyrano's theories, they at least serve as enlargements of the reader's perspective.

◄§§►

In that section of the *Estats du soleil* subtitled the "Histoire des Oiseaux," the satire by inversion is at times more perfectly executed than in other parts of the *Autre Monde*. Particularly when it is a question of government, the customs of the birds are presented as the complete opposite of humans. The king of the birds, for instance, is not, as Dyrcona had supposed, the mighty eagle, but a peaceable dove. The king is always chosen, as the magpie explains to Dyrcona, from among the weakest citizens and not from among the strongest, as is usual on earth.

Pensiez-vous donc . . . que ce grand Aigle fut nostre Souverain? C'est une imagination de vous autres Hommes, qui, à cause que vous laissez commander aux plus grands, aux plus forts et aux plus cruels de vos compagnons, avez sotement crû, jugeant de toutes choses par vous, que l'Aigle nous devoit commander.

Mais nostre politique est bien autre; car nous ne choisissons pour nos Roys que les plus foibles, les plus doux et les plus pacifiques; encor les changeons-nous tous le six mois, et nous les prenons foibles, afin que le moindre à qui ils auroient fait quelque tort se pût venger de luy. Nous le choisissons deux, affin qu'il ne haïsse ny ne se fasse haïr de personne; et nous voulons qu'il soit d'une humeur pacifique pour éviter la guerre, le canal de toutes les injustices. (I, 155–156)

Did you think then . . . that the great Eagle was our Ruler? That is a fancy of you Men who, judging everything according to yourselves, have foolishly believed, because you entrust governing to the most powerful, strongest, and cruelest of your companions, that the Eagle must rule us.

But our politics are quite different, for we choose as our Kings only the weakest, mildest, and most pacific; moreover, we change them every six months, and we take them weak so that the humblest person whom they offend may avenge himself. We choose him mild, so that he does not hate anyone, nor incurs anyone's hatred; and we want him to be of pacific temperament to avoid war, the road to all injustice.

Weber comments that this "protestation contre le droit du plus fort" (protest against "might makes right") links Cyrano to the pacifistic and humanitarian traditions of Thomas More and Erasmus, and distinguishes him from other *libertins*, such as Hobbes, who advocated a state founded on power.[52] Other critics have regarded the *Autre Monde* as a depiction of utopian societies. Howard Harvey considers the Parliament of the Birds a "clear statement of a democratic ideal"[53] and goes so far as to propose that Cyrano was suggesting the re-creation of the golden age.[54] Eddy views the lunar country as "an imaginary commonwealth of an ideal character,"[55] and says that Cyrano and Swift were the only writers to include "Beast-Utopias" among the various lands visited by their heroes.[56] According to Pietro Toldo, Cyrano found his "modèle du gouvernement idéal" (model of ideal government) of the *Estats du soleil* in Campanella's *Civitas solis*.[57] In the judgment of Leonora Rosenfield, the *Estats de la lune* contains "thumb-nail sketches of Utopias."[58]

Since the description of a utopia is in effect a recommendation of how a state should be ordered, it is not accurate to say that the *Autre Monde* is a utopian world, for Cyrano did not really advocate any particular kind of government at all. Although Cyrano's imaginary lands contain not a few utopian elements, his purpose was not to depict a political utopia. As Weber points out, Cyrano's social and political ideas are in general more critical than constructive.[59] Weber finds a revolutionary element in Cyrano's work, not in his treatment of government but in the conflict with established conventions.[60] Richard Aldington notes the lack of a political system in the *Autre Monde*, which would be necessary to the portrayal of a utopia.[61] Contrary to Toldo, Mongrédien finds no ideal commonwealth such as Campanella's in Cyrano's voyages.[62]

Not only is there an absence of any systematized political thinking in Cyrano's work; his satire remains very general, rendering it impossible to give any special stamp to his ideas on government. Mongrédien remarks that his political satire does not go very far at all, being limited to the "monde à rebours" (world in reverse).[63] Such concepts as he does advocate remain very broad and amorphous in their application.

What, for example, does Cyrano mean by "égalité," a notion which he seems especially eager to impress upon his readers? It is more a natural than a civil law. One of the main accusations brought against Dyrcona by the lawyer for the adversary in the "Histoire des Oiseaux" is that he, as a representative of mankind, has not yet learned to live in society. Cyrano is here speaking of the society of all of Nature's creatures, the laws of which have been broken by man's predatory tendencies.

Je pense, Messieurs, qu'on n'a jamais révoqué en doute que toutes les créatures sont produites par nostre commune Mère, pour vivre en société. Or si je prouve que l'Homme semble n'estre né que pour la rompre, ne prouveray-je pas qu'allant contre la fin de sa création, il mérite que la Nature se repente de son ouvrage?

La première et la plus fondamentale loy pour la manutention d'une République, c'est l'égalité; mais l'Homme ne la sçauroit endurer éternellement; il se ruë sur nous pour nous manger, il se fait accroire que nous n'avons esté faits que pour luy, il prend pour argument de sa supériorité prètenduë la barbarie avec laquelle il nous massacre et le peu de résistance qu'il trouve à forcer nostre foiblesse. (I, 158–159)

I think, Gentlemen, that no one has ever questioned that all creatures were produced by our common Mother to live together in society. Now if I prove that Man seems to have been born only to disrupt this society, will I not prove that in betraying the intent of his creation, he deserves that Nature repent of her work?

The first and most fundamental law for the administration of a Republic is equality; but Man is unable to bear it indefinitely; he hurls himself at us to devour us; he deludes himself into thinking that we were made just for him; he uses as an argument for his alleged superiority the barbarity with which he butchers us and the little resistance he encounters in forcing our weakness.

The identical status of all living beings is in agreement with Cyrano vitalistic materialism, for if all of life participates in the same matter then a basic equality of all creatures is automatically established. The natural equality resulting from Cyrano's materialistic vision of life is his answer to anthropocentrism, and so the lawyer for the birds unites his plea for equality with a bitter condemnation of the manifestations of human pride.

Il nous égorge, il nous mange, et de la puissance de tuer ceux qui sont demeurez libres, il fait un prix à la Noblesse;[64] il pense que le Soleil s'est allumé pour l'éclairer à nous faire la guerre, que Nature nous a permis d'étendre nos promenades dans le Ciel, afin seulement que de nostre vol il puisse tirer de malheureux ou favorables auspices, et quand Dieu mit des entrailles dedans nostre corps, qu'il n'eut intention que de faire un grand livre où l'Homme pût apprendre la science des choses futures. (I, 159)

He butchers us, he devours us, and he offers as a prize to the Nobility the power of killing those who have remained free; he thinks the sun shines just to give him light to make war on us, that Nature granted us the reaches of the Heavens for our rambles, just so that he could draw favorable or unfavorable auspices from our flight, and that God put entrails in our body only to make a great book wherein Man could obtain knowledge of future things.

A more political statement of equality is made by Sejanus in *La Mort d'Agrippine*. But here again it is of the most general nature. Sejanus ridicules distinctions among men by birth, substituting for hereditary nobility a nobility based on merit.

> Mon sang n'est point Royal, mais l'héritier d'un Roy
> Porte-t-il un visage autrement fait que moy?
> Encor qu'un toict de chaume eût couvert ma naissance
> Et qu'un Palais de marbre eût logé son enfance,
> Qu'il fût né d'un grand Roy, moy d'un simple Pasteur,
> Son sang auprès du mien est-il d'autre couleur?
>
> (II, 118; Act II, iv)

> My blood is not Royal, but is the face of a King's heir
> Formed differently from mine?
> Although a thatched roof was shelter for my birth
> And a marble Palace dwelling place for his childhood,
> Though he was born of a great King, myself of a humble
>   Shepherd,
> Is his blood a different color from mine?

There is nothing startling in this sentiment, which had by Cyrano's time become a literary commonplace.

The manner of waging war on the moon is based on a scrupulous equality of both armies, forming a humorous contrast to the customs of war on earth. The description of course constitutes no positive suggestion; aided by the satiric device of inversion Cyrano is criticizing war.

Quand les arbitres . . . esleus au gré des deux partis, ont désigné le temps accordé pour l'armement, celuy de la marche, le nombre des combattans, le jour et le lieu de la bataille, et tout cela avec tant d'esgallité qu'il n'y a pas dans une armée un seul homme plus que dans l'autre, les soldats estropiez d'un costé sont tous enrollez dans une compagnie, et lors qu'on en vient aux mains, les Mareschaux de Camp ont soing de les opposer aux estropiez de l'autre costé; les géans ont en teste les colosses; les escrimeurs, les adroits; les vaillans, les courageux; les débilles, les foibles; les indisposez, les malades; les robustes, les forts; et si quelqu'un entreprenoit de frapper un autre que son ennemy désigné, à moins qu'il peut justiffier que c'estoit par mesprise, il est condamné de coüard. Aprés la bataille donée, on compte les blessez, les morts, les prisonniers, car pour les fuyards il ne s'en veoit point. Si les pertes se trouvent esgalles de part et d'autre, ilz tirent à la courte paille à qui se proclamera victorieux. (I, 55)[65]

When the arbitrators . . . elected by the will of each of the two sides, have designated the time allowed for arming, for the march, the number of combatants, the date and place of the battle, and all of this with so much equality that there is not one man more in one army than in the other, the crippled soldiers of one side are all enlisted in one company, and when they begin to fight, the Field Marshals are careful to pit them against the cripples of the other side; the giants confront the colossi; the swordsmen, the adept; the valiant, the courageous; the weak, the feeble; the unwell, the sick; the robust, the strong; and if someone should undertake to strike anyone but his appointed enemy, unless he can justify himself by attributing it to error, he is condemned as a coward. After the battle, the wounded, dead, and prisoners are counted, for no deserters have been observed.

If the losses are found to be equal on either side, they draw lots to decide who will be proclaimed victor.

As Cyrano's defense of equality is essentially a protest against anthropocentrism and the use of force, so his notion of liberty is motivated chiefly by an aversion to all forms of servitude. Again, liberty and servitude are to be construed in the widest senses of the words. The lawyer-bird upbraids man for the instinct to enslave himself that he universally displays.

Encore est-ce un droict imaginaire que cet empire dont ils se flattent. Ils sont, au contraire, si enclins à la servitude, que de peur de manquer à servir, ils se vendent les uns aux autres leur liberté. C'est ainsi que les jeunes sont esclaves des vieux, les pauvres des riches, les païsans des gentilshommes, les princes des monarques, et les monarques mesmes des lois qu'ils ont établies. Mais avec tout cela ces pauvres serfs ont si peur de manquer de maistres, que comme s'ils appréhendoient que la liberté ne leur vint de quelque endroit non attendu, ils se forgent des Dieux de toutes parts, dans l'eau, dans l'air, dans le feu, sous la terre; ils en feront plutost de bois, qu'ils n'en ayent; et je croy mesme qu'ils se chatoüillent des fausses espérances de l'immortalité, moins par l'horreur dont le non-estre les effraye, que par la crainte qu'ils ont de n'avoir pas qui leur commande après la mort. (I, 159)[66]

Moreover their supposed reign is an imaginary right. They are, on the contrary, so prone to servitude, that for fear of failing to serve, they sell their liberty to each other. Thus are the young slaves to the old, the poor to the rich, peasants to gentlemen, princes to monarchs, and monarchs to the very laws they have established. But in spite of all this, the poor slaves are so afraid of lacking masters that, as if they feared that liberty might come from some unexpected place, they create Gods on all sides, in the water, in the air, in the sky, under the ground; they would make them of wood rather than do without; and I even think they flatter themselves with false hopes of immortality, less out of the horror with which nonexistence fills them, than out of fear that they will not have anyone to rule them after death.

The semifeudal nature of seventeenth-century French society, with its hierarchy of duties and allegiances, is reflected in this passage, demonstrating Cyrano's awareness of the inequities of his time. The satirical enumeration of the various forms of slavery which man, paradoxically, is portrayed as accepting and even desiring, culminates in an attack on religion. The epitome of serfdom is for Cyrano that state of mind which permits man to enchain himself to gods. The liberty he urges, then, is basically a freedom from authority which will result in freedom of thought. Gonzalès, as well as the birds, reproaches man for his lack of such freedom, which is what caused the Spaniard to leave the earth.

Ce qui l'avoit véritablement obligé de courir toutte la terre et enfin de l'abandonner pour la Lune, estoit qu'il n'avoit peu trouver un seul païs où l'imagination mesme fust en liberté. (I, 45)

What had really forced him to wander all over the earth and finally to abandon it for the Moon, was that he had been unable to find one single country where so much as the imagination was at liberty.

And lunarians take leave of each other by employing the formula "Songés à librement vivre" (Remember to live in freedom) (I, 83), a pithy reminder that the free exercise of reason must prevail.

Denis observes that the notion of liberty common to the *libertins* of Cyrano's time was fundamentally a personal one. They sought the freedom to pursue their work as they chose, Denis claims, and did not extend their concept of liberty to political or philosophical realms. He considers Cyrano, however, an exception to this tendency.[67] Denis's estimation of Cyrano must be qualified. It is true that freedom was more than a strictly personal ideal for him. But he never elaborated upon the meaning or extent of liberty in a political context. To champion intellectual freedom at a time when a decree prohibiting teachings contradicting those of Aristotle had been published was indeed courageous. To ascribe more importance to the role of liberty in the *Autre Monde* would, however, be an exaggeration.

One might expect to find a more accurate transcription of Cyrano's political ideas in his *mazarinades*. Their subject matter is topical, inviting the supposition that they might provide an outline of Cyrano's political position. They are deserving of study as documents of the times and of certain of Cyrano's attitudes toward contemporary events. The reader seeking to extract from them Cyrano's basic opinions on government will, however, be disappointed. Mercurial essays in wit and in opportunism, they cannot be treated as a unity. They may nevertheless profitably be compared to each other and to the *Autre Monde* or others of Cyrano's works in an attempt to gain a more precise picture of his social and political ideas.

Lachèvre, after an examination of the manuscripts, has established that these eight pieces are all by Cyrano. Paul Lacroix had attributed only one to him, "Le Ministre d'état flambé" (1649), and Brun recognized only the "Lettre contre les frondeurs" (1651) as a product of Cyrano's pen (II, 233). Lachèvre has published the six important *mazarinades*, five of which are hostile to the prime minister and one, the "Lettre contre les frondeurs," sympathetic to him. Brun, to whom Cyrano greatly endeared himself by this monarchistic letter, rejected after its perusal the possibility that the "Ministre d'état flambé," an anti-Mazarin poem of the burlesque school, could have been by the same author.[68] The discrepancy between the two is indeed great. In addition to the fact that the "Lettre contre les frondeurs" ardently defends the very man vilified in the "Ministre d'état flambé," the two letters differ in tone and in style. The former is sober, lofty, and, as Brun would have it,[69] arrogant. The latter is a lusty Rabelaisian exercise in burlesque humor, with no real pretense to seriousness. Brun, adapting the disparity to his preferences, chose to believe in a pro-Mazarin, conservative, and totally *sage* Cyrano. Lachèvre, also not devoid of such prejudices, was led in this instance to a more accurate interpretation of the facts by his desire to impugn Cyrano's morality. The change of heart, according to him, would be explained by the purely materialistic impulse to obtain one's money from sources where it happens to be available at the time (II, 233–234; 278–279). The spiritual indifference with which Cyrano wrote these letters would be further attested to, in Lachèvre's opinion, by the contradictions between the sentiments expressed therein and those to be found in his other works, such as his profession of religious feeling only when it is required as an argument in support of monarchy (II, 278–279). Other inconsistencies within the letters themselves are not unusual. If Lachèvre's interpretation is granted, then Cyrano's *mazarinades*, no more than commissioned pieces written in complete disregard of his personal beliefs, would not serve as reliable indications of his political ideas.

Lachèvre's judgment may be accepted with some modifications. The contradictions in the *mazarinades* are flagrant. In "Le Conseiller fidèle" (1649), Mazarin's foreign birth is cited as one of his drawbacks; he secretly wishes to exploit France, Cyrano charges, and then return to his own country (II, 269). In the "Lettre contre les frondeurs," however, Cyrano defends Mazarin rather eloquently, in a tone that recalls Montaigne, against this same accusation: "Un honneste homme n'est ny François, ny Aleman, ny Espagnol, il est Citoyen du Monde, et sa patrie est par tout" (II, 280). (A gentleman is neither French, nor Spanish; he is a Citizen of the World, and his fatherland is everywhere.)

The evocation of this wider perspective seems more typical of the author of the *Autre Monde*, and yet it cannot be said that the rest of the letter bears much resemblance to Cyrano's other works. Again in the "Lettre contre les frondeurs" Cyrano asserts that, contrary to the imputations of some, arts, letters, and religion are flourishing under the ministry of Mazarin (II, 285). Now Cyrano himself had leveled such charges in his "Conseiller fidèle" (II, 269–270), and in his "Ministre d'état flambé" (II, 243). In the latter piece Cyrano protests against the devastating effects of the very harsh taxes (II, 245) with obvious justification, for they were indeed an impossible burden on the peasant, in particular.[70] In the "Lettre contre les frondeurs," on the other hand, Cyrano makes an attempt, of necessity feeble, to condone or at least to understate the severity of these measures. Taxes are not greater or more rigorously imposed than under Richelieu, he claims, and they are necessary to maintain the state and the army (II, 282–283).

Not only does the religious sentiment professed by Cyrano in support of monarchy form a ludicrous contrast to the spirit of the *Autre Monde*; Cyrano goes so far, in the "Lettre contre les frondeurs," as to sanctify the authority of the head of the family, an object of derision in the *Estats de la lune*.

L'Eglise Militante, qui est l'image de la Triomphante, est conduite monarchiquement par les Papes; et nous voyons que jusqu'aux maisons particulières, il faut qu'elles soient gouvernées par une espèce de Roy, qui est le Père de famille. (II, 286)

The Militant Church, which is the figure of the Triumphant, is ruled monarchically by the Popes; and we see that even private homes have to be governed by a kind of King, who is the Paterfamilias.

These inconsistencies should lead the reader to disregard the *mazarinades* (as well as most of Cyrano's other letters, in general

little more than exercises in outrageous style)[71] as serious represen-
tations of Cyrano's views. There are, however, some deductions
concerning these which may be made from an examination of the
mazarinades. The majority of these pieces are of course anti-
Mazarin. In the confusion of the Fronde, during which loyalties
were exchanged as readily and frequently as handshakes, this may
not mean very much. But Cyrano's sympathy would seem to be
with the insurgents. What then is his attitude toward the monarchy and the nobility?

In the "Gazettier des-interressé" (1649) is found the same
definition of nobility as in *La Mort d'Agrippine*; it is based not
on birth but on merit: "Notre condition est une; il n'y a que la
vertu qui nous distingue, et la noblesse ne peut pas avoir toujours
esté vieille" (II, 248). (Our rank is one; virtue alone distinguishes
us, and nobility cannot always have been ancient.) And of the
"Remonstrances des trois estats, à la reine régente, pour la paix"
(1649), the one written on behalf of the people is the most convincing in tone. Cyrano champions the rights of the people as
essential contributors to the life and functioning of the monarchy.

Les Roys ne sont appelez de ce nom qu'au regard de leurs sujets,
dont nous faisons la plus gr[a]nde et la meilleure partie, quoy que
nous n'en fassions pas la plus noble. Nous avons tousjours oüy dire
qu'il estoit du corps de l'Estat, de mesme que du corps humain, où
l'on trouve diversement des puissances qui commandent, qui con-
seillent ou qui délibèrent, des membres qui travaillent et qui exécu-
tent, et des parties qui ne se nourrissent que pour engraisser les
autres. Nous sommes de ces dernières, puisque nous fournissons
mesme aux Souverains de quoy subsister, que nous les entretenons de
nos sueurs, et que tout ce qui passe dans leur mains est sorty des
nostres. (II, 276)[72]

Kings are called such only with respect to their subjects, of which we
comprise the greatest and best part, although not the noblest. We

have always heard that the body of the State was like the human body, where there are various powers which rule, which advise or which deliberate, members who work and carry out plans, and parts which subsist only to fatten the others. We are among the last, since we supply even Sovereigns with sustenance, since we maintain them by our sweat, and since everything passing into their hands has come from ours.

But the people are treated with scorn and disdain in the "Lettre contre les frondeurs," which is a militant endorsement of the monarchy. It is the stupidity of the people, Cyrano implies in this letter, which causes their dissatisfactions.

Monsieur le Drapier se figure qu'il en va du Gouvernement d'une Monarchie comme des gages de sa chambrière, ou de la pension de son fils Pierrot. . . .

. . . Un misérable petit Mercier, en roulant ses rubans, ne trouve pas à propos que Monsieur le Cardinal fasse bastir à ses despens une Maison! (II, 283)

Mr. Clothier imagines that the Governing of a Monarchy is like the wages of his chambermaid or Junior's allowance. . . .

. . . A wretched little Haberdasher rolling his ribbons does not think it proper that the Cardinal build a House at his expense!

The people are blamed for misjudging Mazarin, who is cleared by Cyrano of the charges brought against him.

La canaille murmure encore et crie qu'il n'a aucun lieu de retraite si la France l'abandonnoit. Hé! quoy donc, Messieurs les Aveugles, à cause que pour vous protéger et conserver, il s'est fait des ennemis par toute la terre, c'est un homme détestable et abominable, et vous le jugez indigne de pardon! Sa faute, en effet, n'est pas pardonnable d'avoir si fidellement servy des ingrats. (II, 283)

The rabble still grumbles and cries that he would have no place to retire to if France abandoned him. Well then, my Blind Sirs, because to protect and take care of you he made enemies all over the earth, he is a detestable and unpardonable man, and you deem him unworthy of forgiveness! His fault, in fact, is unforgivable in that he served ingrates so faithfully.

Cyrano's attack on the people is extended with much vigor to an attack on the popular state, a concept opposed, according to his polemic, to the divinely ordered monarchy.

Il est très vray . . . que comme Dieu n'est qu'un à dominer tout l'Univers, et que comme le Gouvernement du Royaume Céleste est monarchique, celuy de la Terre le doit estre aussi. La saincte Escriture fait foy que Dieu n'a jamais ordonné un seul Estat populaire, et quelques Rabins asseurent que le péché des Anges fut d'avoir fait dessein de se mettre en République. (II, 286)

Je soustiens que le gouvernement populaire est le pire fléau dont Dieu afflige un Estat, quand il le veut chastier! N'est-il pas contre l'ordre de la Nature qu'un Bastelier ou un Crocheteur soient en puissance de condamner à mort un Général d'Armée, et que la vie du plus grand personnage soit à la discrétion des poulmons du plus sot qui, à perte d'haleine, demandera qu'il meure? (II, 287)

It is very true . . . that since God, as one, rules over the entire Universe, and since the Government of the Heavenly Kingdom is monarchical, the Earth's must be also. Holy Scripture attests the fact that God never ordered one single popular State, and some Rabbis affirm that the sin of the Angels was that they planned to constitute themselves into a Republic.

I maintain that popular government is the worst scourge with which God afflicts a State, when he wants to punish it! Is it not contrary to the order of Nature that a Ferryman or a Porter should have the power to condemn to death an Army General, and that the life of the most important personage should be left to the mercy of the lungs of the biggest fool, who will breathlessly demand that he die?

SATIRICAL RELATIVISM

How much of this kind of argument proceeds from Cyrano's ironic wit? His insincerity seems manifest in a passage upholding the authority of the king's favorites (meaning Mazarin) in so satirical a manner as to approach the ridiculous.[73]

Mais cependant celuy de Paris a bien eu la témérité de lever ses mains sur l'Oint du Seigneur, alléguant, pour prétexte, que ce n'est pas au Roy qu'il s'attaque, mais à son Favory; comme si de mesme qu'un Prince est l'image de Dieu, un Favory n'estoit pas l'image du Prince. Mais c'est encore trop peu de dire l'image, il est son fils! Quand il engendre selon la chair, il engendre un Prince! Quand il engendre selon sa dignité, il engendre un Favory. En tant qu'homme, il fait un Successeur, en tant que Roy, il fait une Créature. Et s'il est vray que la création soit quelque chose de plus noble que la génération, parce que la création est miraculeuse, nous devons adorer un Favory comme estant le miracle d'un Roy. (II, 286)

Yet nevertheless they [the people of Paris] had the temerity to raise their hands against the Lord's Anointed, alleging, as a pretext, that they were not attacking the King, but his Favorite; as if just as a Prince is the image of God, a Favorite were not the image of the Prince. But it is not enough to say the image; he is his son! When he begets according to the flesh, he begets a Prince! When he begets according to his dignity, he begets a Favorite. As a man, he makes a Successor; as a King, he makes a Protégé. And if it is true that creation is something nobler than procreation, because creation is miraculous, then we must adore a Favorite as being the miracle of a King.

That the "Lettre contre les frondeurs," so atypical of Cyrano's thought, was perhaps partially disavowed by him is suggested by a note, reproduced by Lachèvre, which Cyrano himself placed at the head of his letter as it appeared in the *Oeuvres diverses* of 1654.

Le Lecteur doit estre adverty que cette Lettre fut envoyée pendant le siège de Paris et durant la plus violente animosité des Peuples contre Monseigneur le Cardinal. On ne s'étonnera donc pas d'y voir des choses un peu moins adjustées à l'estat présent des Affaires, qui ont beaucoup changé depuis ce temps-là. (II, 279)

The Reader must be notified that this Letter was sent during the siege of Paris and during the most violent animosity of the Peoples against His Eminence the Cardinal. It will not be surprising, therefore, to see things slightly less in keeping with the present state of Affairs, which has greatly changed since that time.

Lachèvre has convincingly shown that Cyrano's claim to have written this during the siege of Paris (1649) is a lie. The letter is a response to Scarron's *mazarinade* of March 1651, Lachèvre informs us, and would thus have had to be written after this date (II, 279). It is not completely accurate to describe Cyrano's letter as an answer to Scarron's poem. The latter piece is not mentioned specifically. But the allusion to it seems clear.

Il n'appartient qu'à des Poëtes du Pont-Neuf, comme Scarron, de vomir de l'escume sur la Pourpre des Roys et des Cardinaux, et d'employer les libéralitez qu'ils reçoivent continuellement de la Cour en papier qu'ils barboüillent contre elle. (II, 288)[74]

It is only the Poets of the Pont-Neuf, like Scarron, who pour forth their foam on the Purple of Kings and Cardinals, and use up the generous gifts which they continuously receive from the Court in paper on which they scrawl things against that very Court.

Admitting, then, the discrepancy between the actual date of composition of the "Lettre contre les frondeurs" and the date given by Cyrano, the writer's motives in moving back the year would presumably spring from a desire to dissociate himself from its authorship, and not from a desire to, in Lachèvre's words, "donner le change à la postérité" (dupe posterity) (II, 279). Cyrano was right in saying things had changed since the siege of Paris. Between that time and March 1651 a new and violent front of the Fronde had been opened up at Bordeaux, only to be abruptly closed by the arrival of the king, queen, Mazarin, and an army. Hatred of Mazarin had reached a peak.[75] Had one's inclinations been at all to the side of the rebels (if the Fronde can be referred to in terms of "sides"), they were likely to be greatly intensified by then.[76] It would thus be understandable that Cyrano might attempt to disclaim some responsibility for writing his antipopular treatise at such a time by the subterfuge of changing the date.

Although Cyrano was undoubtedly not such a sworn enemy of the people as he would appear from a superficial reading of the "Lettre contre les frondeurs," it would be equally false to see him as a champion of republicanism or, as Mongrédien views him, a "révolutionnaire en politique" (revolutionary in politics).[77] If there is one general attitude toward governmental systems to be extracted from Cyrano's works, it is indifference. He simply had no carefully considered political system in mind. There is no reason to believe that, despite his rejection of authority—which for him is primarily intellectual authority—he seriously favored the replacement of the monarchy by a republic. The birds in the *Estats du soleil* live democratically but are governed by a king, albeit a mild dove. This type of government is again suggested in the "Lettre contre les frondeurs," in which Cyrano warns the people to be content with the rule of a "dove" for fear of falling into the clutches of an "eagle" (II, 285). It is not the monarchy to which Cyrano seems to object but to any form of tyranny. Ideally, it is implied in the "Gazettier des-interressé," monarchy can be benevolent and beneficent.

Il est de l'authorité du Roy comme de la lumière du Soleil, qui se respand doucement par tout et qui ne fait de mal qu'à ceux qui n'en peuvent souffrir l'éclat, et de l'authorité des Favoris comme de la Lune qui n'esclaire qu'autant qu'elle est esclairée. (II, 257)

The authority of the King is like the light of the Sun, which is gently shed everywhere and which harms only those who cannot bear its brilliance, and the authority of Favorites is like the Moon which illuminates only as much as it is illuminated.

It is the unlawful usurpation of power by kings and their favorites which must be guarded against.

Quelqu'indifférentes ou quelqu'obscures que puissent estre le loix dans les Estats, il y en a tousjours quelqu'une qui s'oppose diversement à la violence des Souverains, pour ce que la Religion qui s'y exerce explique ce qu'un Prince doit éviter et ce qu'il doit suivre. Quelle différence y auroit-il entre l'usurpation et la souveraineté légitime, entre les Tyrans et les Roys, entre les sujets et les esclaves? Depuis quand les Souverains qui sont appellez les Pasteurs du peuple en doivent-ils estre les bouchers, et quelle est la loy qui nous dispense de toutes les autres? (II, 257)

However indifferent or obscure the laws in States may be, there is always one which opposes in various ways the force of Sovereigns, for the Religion which is practiced there explains what a Prince must avoid or adhere to. What difference would there be between usurpation and legitimate sovereignty, between Tyrants and Kings, between subjects and slaves? Since when must Rulers, who are called Shepherds of the people, be their butchers, and which law is it that excuses us from all the others?

Even Sejanus in *La Mort d'Agrippine*, although plotting to kill Tiberius, envisages a republic only as a last resort, in the event that new injustices should result from the coup d'état.

> Si César massacré, quelques nouveaux Titans
> Eslevez par mon crime au Thrône où je prétens,
> Songent à s'emparer du pouvoir Monarchique,
> J'appelleray pour lors le peuple en République,
> Et je luy feray voir que par des coups si grans

SATIRICAL RELATIVISM

> Rome n'a point perdu, mais changé ses Tyrans.[78]
> (II, 119; Act II, iv)

> If, with Caesar killed, some new Titans
> Raised by my crime to the Throne to which I pretend,
> Plan to seize the Monarchical power,
> I will summon the people to form a Republic,
> And I will make them see that by such great coups
> Rome did not lose, but changed, its Tyrants.

It is really tyranny and not monarchy which the conspirators of Cyrano's tragedy wish to overthrow. Agrippina expresses an intense hatred of tyrants in announcing her intention to kill Tiberius.

> Oüy, moy, de César je veux percer le flanc,
> Et jusques sur son Thrône hérissé d'halebardes,
> Je veux, le massacrant au milieu de ses Gardes,
> Voir couler par ruisseaux de son coeur expirant
> Tout le sang corrompu dont se forme un Tyran!
> (II, 124; Act III, i)

> Yes, I myself wish to pierce Caesar's side,
> And right upon his Throne bristling with halberds,
> I wish to kill him in the middle of his Guards,
> And see flowing in streams from his dying heart
> All of the corrupt blood of which a Tyrant is formed!

Cyrano, then, is not an advocate of republicanism; he does not wish to eliminate monarchy, but he does protest against its degeneration into tyranny. It is to be assumed, from a comparison of the greater number of the *mazarinades* with the *Autre Monde*, that Cyrano did sincerely champion the rights of the people and especially their right of intellectual and personal freedom, but within a monarchistic framework. In his lack of political ideas, Cyrano was a product of his times. The Fronde, instigated by the aristocracy, was not a democratic revolution, and its net result was to be a strengthening of absolutism under Louis XIV.[79] The authors of the numerous *mazarinades* which circulated at the time expounded no political theory, recommended no change in the form of government. The Fronde, directed chiefly against Mazarin and not the monarchy, inspired no original ideas on political reforms on the part of its pamphleteers, who confined themselves mainly to denunciations of the prime minister. They were unanimous, however, in their condemnation of despotism. The Cardinal de Retz in his *Mémoires* even dates the beginning of despotism in France from the time of Richelieu. Some of the authors of the *mazarinades* did, it is true, arrive at the principle of the sovereignty of the people, but incorporated it into no political system. In demanding the ousting of Mazarin they were in reality asking for the personal rule of the king, and, far from fostering republican tendencies, their claims were to be realized in the absolutist reign of Louis XIV.[80] No one was concerned with actual steps toward the establishment of political freedom.[81]

No revolutionary voices were heard in the 1640s and 1650s. The arrest of the liberal Broussel in 1648 produced a tumultuous reaction but no revolution because, as Ernest Lavisse has remarked, no one—neither the *parlement* nor the bourgeoisie—wanted a revolution.[82] During the Fronde, Lavisse notes, there was much talk of a republic, but he asks, how was one to be established? Upon what tradition or authority would it rest?[83]

Against this background it is not astonishing to find in Cyrano no harbinger of the Revolution, no budding Jean-Jacques Rousseau. But if his ideas on political freedom were at best only rudimentary, his espousal of the cause of intellectual freedom puts him in the vanguard of the thinkers of his time. In an age of impending absolutist rule, relativism was a message of no small consequence. All but stifled during the reign of Louis XIV, it would not be heard again until the period of the Enlightenment.

❧

CONCLUSION

Cyrano de Bergerac wrote a generation too early to be a participant in the heated polemics between Ancients and Moderns which mark the seventeenth century as a decisive moment in their conflict. But the breadth of his scientific and philosophical interests justifies expanding his exclusive classification as a *libertin* to include his unsuspecting identification with the causes of the Moderns. These causes had of course been prevalent in the minds of certain thinkers long before the formal debates, but in espousing them in the thoroughgoing manner that is characteristic of his works Cyrano surpasses the modernity of his predecessors and associates himself in spirit with the band of intellectual rebels that were to follow him.

The seventeenth-century *libertins* were primarily distinguished by their desire to cast off the shackles of tradition and authority;[1] the Moderns were acutely conscious of the necessity to construct something new, imposed upon them by their very rejection of the old standards and values. Cyrano's anti-Christian destructive spirit, which has prompted Lachèvre's judgment of him as "l'initiateur de l'esprit philosophique rationaliste, ayant pour objet la destruction du christianisme" (the initiator of the rationalistic philosophical spirit, having as its object the destruction of Christianity),[2] is accompanied by a positive acceptance and propagation of the same scientific and philosophical ideas which, although not directly transmitted by Cyrano, were to have a profound impact on the minds of the eighteenth-century *philosophes*. The author of the *Autre Monde* substitutes for miracles a doctrine of materialism which retains an honorable status even today, the modern cosmology which was to require so many years to become firmly established, and an epistemological program conceived along Cartesian lines and in the experimental, empirical tradition of Francis Bacon.

In his desire to replace authority with bold new ideas Cyrano may be likened to other thinkers of contemporary or previous periods who had upheld various "modern" causes. Du Bellay, Malherbe, Corneille, and Charles Sorel, among others, had initiated diverse programs of attack on tradition. The work of Descartes is of course imbued with the very spirit of reform. What differentiates Cyrano from his fellow defenders of modernity is the completeness of his innovating goals. With the possible exception of the political domain, Cyrano unites in his battle against a centuries-old heritage tendencies scattered in the works of others. The result is a vigor and audacity rarely achieved in his day and which warrant considering him as one of the earliest Moderns. As Fellows has noted, "he was the first to link closely together a criticism of the religion of Moses and the philosophy of Aristotle."[3] Thus Cyrano, while representative of intellectual trends which had been current for at least a century, is unique in his daring amalgamation of these into a philosophical outlook that was not to find general expression until the eighteenth century.

CONCLUSION

What implications does Cyrano's modernity have for the history of ideas? What consequences arise from the premature exposition of the tenets of a Modern in an age when witch-burnings could not yet be termed a thing of the past?

Cyrano's voyages, published posthumously and then with the disfiguration of LeBret's editing, enjoyed only a limited popularity during the seventeenth century, and were largely ignored in the eighteenth-century "age of enlightenment."[4] Although he did have his imitators, and was even the addressee of a rather unflattering dedication to the *Telliamed* (published posthumously in 1748) by Bénoît de Maillet,[5] he did not have a real following.[6] There was, to be sure, a profusion of works posterior to the *Autre Monde* in the spirit of Cyrano's philosophical voyages, and it is in this sense that Lachèvre applies the word "successors" to Gabriel de Foigny, Denis Veiras, and Claude Gilbert, seventeenth-century authors of fantastic novels bearing some resemblance to Cyrano's.[7] Brun also lists numerous works in a tradition that could be dubbed "cyranesque," without, however, suggesting that there was any direct influence.[8]

It cannot be said, then, that Cyrano served as an inspiration to the Moderns, nor that he set a precedent for the *philosophes* to follow. The *Autre Monde* is one of the very few survivors of the literature of constructive protest in the period of circumspection which forms the first half of the French seventeenth century. As such, it is an unquestionably valuable indicator of the current intellectual mood, confined in general to underground expression. Cyrano's philosophical colleagues did not allow themselves the freedom so typical of the author of the *Autre Monde*. Cyrano's work, almost unparalleled in its open advocacy of a new philosophy at that time, serves as a proof that those causes to be championed by the Moderns toward the end of the seventeenth century had already become rallying points not long after its beginning.

CONCLUSION

The matters Cyrano treats constitute precisely the larger issues of the Quarrel between the Ancients and the Moderns. Their presence in his writings demonstrates that it is not possible to confine the fundamental bases of the Quarrel within definite time limits. If insistent rumblings of the historic struggle can be heard as early as the 1640s and the 1650s in the work of Cyrano de Bergerac, the questions raised therein make it clear that the repercussions of the Quarrel will reach far beyond his death in 1655 even to the "modern" world of the present.

◆§§◆

NOTES

INTRODUCTION

1. Gabriel Guéret, *La Guerre des autheurs anciens et modernes*, pp. 151–52.

2. Hippolyte Rigault, *Histoire de la Querelle des anciens et des modernes*, in *Oeuvres complètes*, vol. I. Hubert Gillot, *La Querelle des anciens et des modernes en France.*

3. Cf. Gillot, *La Querelle des anciens et des modernes en France*, pp. 33–34.

4. Ibid., pp. 279–80.

5. See J. B. Bury, *The Idea of Progress*, pp. 109–10.

6. Ibid., p. 73.

7. Ibid.

8. William James, letter to Henry James, as quoted in Alfred North Whitehead, *Science and the Modern World*, p. 10. Cf. R. F. Jones, *Ancients and Moderns· A Study of the Background of the Battle of the Books*, Washington University Studies, N.S., No. 6, St. Louis (1936), p. 51.

9. See Gillot, *La Querelle des anciens et des modernes en France*, p. 83.

10. See Bury, *The Idea of Progress*, p. 113.

11. Although Cyrano entitled only the first of his two voyages *L'Autre Monde* . . . , this title will be used in the present study, following the example of Lachèvre, to refer to both voyages. See

NOTES: Introduction

Cyrano de Bergerac, *Oeuvres libertines*, ed. Frédéric Lachèvre, vol. I, p. 1. References to the Lachèvre edition will hereafter be made in the text with the volume and page number in parentheses. In the footnotes the edition will be referred to as "Lachèvre," with the volume and page number given.

12. Otis Fellows, "Cyrano de Bergerac," *Encyclopedia of Philosophy*, II, 286.

13. Fellows states that Cyrano's chief significance is that he "epitomized the general mental attitudes among the freethinkers of his period." Ibid.

14. Jones, *Ancients and Moderns*, p. 154.

15. See Fellows, "Cyrano de Bergerac," p. 286.

16. Jones, *Ancients and Moderns*, pp. 124–25.

17. Lachèvre, I, xxiii–xcvi.

18. Among those studies, many of which appeared after Lachèvre's, to be used only with great discretion are: Cyrano de Bergerac, *Oeuvres*, ed. P. L. Jacob, pp. xiii–lxxiv; N. M. Bernardin, "Cyrano de Bergerac," in *Hommes et moeurs au dix-septième siècle*, pp. 127–52; Henriette Magy, *Le Véritable Cyrano de Bergerac*; Louis-Raymond Lefèvre, *La Vie de Cyrano de Bergerac*; Cameron Rogers, *Cyrano: Swordsman, Libertin, and Man of Letters*; Charles Pujos, *Le Double visage de Cyrano de Bergerac*.

19. Pierre Brun, *Savinien de Cyrano Bergerac, sa vie et ses oeuvres*. Henceforth referred to as *Cyrano* (1893).

20. Georges Mongrédien, *Cyrano de Bergerac*.

21. The other was the property of Bergerac, whence Cyrano took his name. Despite the particle "de" employed by his father and grandfather, the family was not noble. Indeed, a brother and cousin of Cyrano were formally charged with usurping titles of nobility. See Lachèvre, I, xx.

22. The dating of the play is aided by an allusion to the voyage of the duchess Marie-Louise de Gonzague to Poland, which took place in 1645.

23. For a detailed discussion of the dating of the *Autre Monde*, see Cyrano de Bergerac, *L'Autre Monde*, ed. Leo Jordan in *Gesell-*

schaft für Romanische Literatur, 23 (Dresden, 1910), pp. 39–40. Jordan dates the composition of this work considerably earlier than Lachèvre.

24. For Cyrano's posthumous history, see Lachèvre, I, xcvii–cxii; 1–2.

25. For the distinguishing features of the two manuscripts as well as the differences between them and LeBret's edition, see Cyrano de Bergerac, *L'Autre Monde*, ed. Jordan, pp. 21–36.

CHAPTER I. MIRACLE: THE ATTACK

1. William Eddy, *Gulliver's Travels, A Critical Study*, pp. 8–10.

2. Pietro Toldo, "Les Voyages merveilleux de Cyrano de Bergerac et de Swift et leurs rapports avec l'oeuvre de Rabelais," *Revue des études rabelaisiennes*, IV (1906), 297–99. Cyrano's voyages fall into that one of Toldo's three categories which he calls satirical, in the tradition of Lucian, a product of the Renaissance.

3. Alvin Kernan, *The Cankered Muse*, pp. 14 ff.

4. This is a common satiric device in Cyrano's work. Cf. J.-J. Bridenne, "Cyrano de Bergerac et la science aéronautique," *Revue des sciences humaines*, N.S. Fasc. 75 (July–Sept. 1954), 242.

5. See the variant c, I, 29: "mortal" for "natural" in the Munich manuscript.

6. Cf. John Wilkins, *Discovery of a New World*, in *The Mathematical and Philosophical Works*, p. 111.

7. Luciano Erba, "L'Incidenza della magia nell'opera di Cyrano de Bergerac," *Pubblicazioni*, Università Cattolica del sacro cuore (Milan), *Contributi del Seminario de Filologia Moderna*, I (1959), 53 ff.

8. Edward W. Lanius, *Cyrano de Bergerac and the Universe of the Imagination*, p. 29. In the *paradis terrestre* scene, according to Lanius, "Cyrano is not theorizing on original sin." For Lanius, despite the allowance in his conclusion (p. 103) that there is also an

"intellectual" aspect to Cyrano, the *Autre Monde* is little more than an exercise in the imagination, a series of cinematic tableaux. The effect of this interpretation is to remove all ideas from Cyrano's works. Thus on page 38 of his study Lanius tells us that there is no satirical purpose to the voyages of the *Autre Monde*, and on page 96 he informs us that the "Lettre contre les sorciers" makes no attack on the Church, but represents only rovings of the imagination and "free association." Such an interpretation, in my opinion, makes serious omissions, because it is based on false premises. There is no reason why the description of an "imagined" universe should preclude exposition of serious ideas. The present examination of Cyrano's works reveals, on the contrary, an imaginative presentation of philosophical concepts.

9. Cyrano de Bergerac, *Voyages to the Moon and the Sun*, ed. and trans. Richard Aldington, p. 40.

10. J. S. Spink, *French Free-Thought from Gassendi to Voltaire*, p. 64.

11. For discussions of Gassendi's fideism, see Richard H. Popkin, *The History of Scepticism from Erasmus to Descartes*, pp. 103–9; Henri Busson, *La Pensée religieuse française de Charron à Pascal*, pp. 299–301; René Pintard, *Le Libertinage érudit dans la première moitié du XVIIe siècle*, I, 483–98. Pintard does not see him as a "pur fidéiste."

12. Pietro Pomponazzi, *Les Causes des merveilles de la nature, ou Les Enchantements*, ed. and trans. Henri Busson, p. 76.

13. Ibid. Leo Jordan also mentions the influence of Montaigne's essay on Cyrano. See Leo Jordan, "Cyrano Bergerac und Montaigne," *Archiv für der neuren Sprachen und Literaturen*, 8° Bd. 135, N.S. Bd. 35 (1916), 391–92.

14. Montaigne, "Des boyteux," in his *Essais*, II, 480. Cf. Alan Boase, *The Fortunes of Montaigne*, pp. 258–59. Boase calls attention to the influence of this essay particularly on Cyrano's "Lettre contre les sorciers." Montaigne, "Of Cripples," in *The Complete Essays of Montaigne*, trans. by Donald M. Frame (Stanford: Stanford University Press, 1965), III: 11, p. 789. All translations of Montaigne are taken from this edition.

15. Pomponazzi, *Les Enchantements*, ed. and trans. Busson, p. 103.

16. Pomponazzi, *Les Enchantements*, p. 129.

17. Ibid., p. 118.

18. Cf. Lynn Thorndike, *A History of Magic and Experimental Science*, V, 110, and Pomponazzi, *Les Enchantements*, pp. 21–25, 33.

19. Cyrano de Bergerac, *L'Autre Monde*, ed. Henri Weber, p. 133, n. 1.

20. See Busson, *Pensée religieuse*, pp. 166–77, for Averroist ideas and other explanations of Creation.

21. Ibid., p. 174.

22. Luciano Erba makes a useful distinction between the magical and the marvelous, which can perhaps be modified to apply to the miraculous and the marvelous: "Non si presentano sotto il segno deciso della magia le situazioni originate dal meraviglioso, quasi nate a ridosso di questo et divenute in seguito autonome: inverisimili a lume di ragione, ma del tutto plausibili per il lettore che abbia accettato, sorprendendosi una volta per tutte, la prima frattura con la verisimiglianza." (Situations derived from the marvelous are not presented under the definite sign of magic, as if they had arisen close by it and had subsequently become independent: [they are] unlikely in the light of reason, but completely plausible to the reader who has accepted, experiencing surprise once and for all, the first rupture with verisimilitude.) Erba, "L'Incidenza della magia," pp. 34–35.

23. Busson, *Pensée religieuse*, p. 349.

24. Ibid., p. 349: "Cyrano, qui est décidément le plus incrédule de nos libertins, a mis en roman ce blasphème." (Cyrano, who is decidedly the most incredulous of our *libertins*, fictionalized this blasphemy.)

25. Ibid., p. 500.

26. Ibid.

27. Lucretius, *On the Nature of Things*, ed. and trans. Cyril Bailey, Bk. III, pp. 133–42.

28. Edward Lanius maintains that these lines reveal Sejanus's desire to believe in the gods, an interpretation which hardly seems

justified in the context of the philosophical tone of the entire play and of Cyrano's other works. See Lanius, *Cyrano de Bergerac and the Universe of the Imagination*, p. 72.

29. Lachèvre, II, 167. Cf. Busson, *Pensée religieuse*, pp. 105–6, and Antoine Adam, *Histoire de la littérature française au XVIIᵉ siècle*, II, 147. Adam also sees the Machiavellian strain in Cyrano.

30. Spink, *French Free-Thought*, p. 52. Cf. in "Contre le pédant": "Mais sçachez que je connois une chose que vous ne connoissez point, que cette chose est Dieu, et que l'un des plus forts arguments . . . qui m'ont convaincu de sa véritable existence, c'est d'avoir considéré que sans une première et souveraine bonté qui règne dans l'univers, foible et meschant comme vous estes, vous n'auriez pas vecu si longtemps impuny" (II, 169–70). (But know that I know a thing that you do not know, that this thing is God, and that one of the strongest arguments . . . which has convinced me of his real existence is to have considered that without a primary and sovereign goodness reigning in the universe, you, weakling and rascal that you are, would not have lived so long with impunity.)

31. Spink, *French Free-Thought*, p. 52.

32. Henry Carrington Lancaster, *A History of French Dramatic Literature in the Seventeenth Century*, II, Part III, 169. Cf. Lachèvre, I, xc.

33. Gabriel Guéret, *La Guerre des autheurs anciens et modernes*, p. 155.

34. *Menagiana* (II, 1715), quoted in Lancaster, *French Dramatic Literature*, II, Pt. III, 169. Cf. Lachèvre, I, xc.

35. Lancaster, *French Dramatic Literature*, II, Pt. III, 169.

36. Spink, *French Free-Thought*, p. 52. Cf. p. 64.

37. Lancaster, *French Dramatic Literature*, II, Pt. III, 169. In this he concurs with Gautier. See Theophile Gautier, *Les Grotesques*, pp. 188–89.

38. "Quelques très rares audacieux, Cyrano, Hénault, ont pu risquer sous le couvert d'un païen notoire une tirade matérialiste. Mais ce sont là des exceptions. Si l'on peut soupçonner que dans la vie beaucoup partagèrent leur incrédulité, ils ne l'avouaient pas."

(Some very rare bold spirits—Cyrano, Hénault—were able to risk a materialistic speech under the cover of a notorious pagan. But they are exceptions. If it may be suspected that in real life many shared their incredulity, these people did not admit it.) Busson, *Pensée religieuse*, p. 162.

39. See, for example, II, 152 (Act V, scene vii).

40. Vítor Ramos notes the admiration for Sejanus expressed by Agrippina in these lines. See Vítor Ramos, *Cyrano, Auteur tragique*, p. 26.

41. Cf. Charles Nodier, "Cyrano de Bergerac," *Bulletin du bibliophile*, No. 8, 3ᵉ série (Oct. 1838), 350. Vítor Ramos characterizes *Agrippine* as an amoral and nihilistic play, with pride and will the main motivating forces. Ramos, *Cyrano, Auteur tragique*, pp. 136–37.

42. Ramos sees him as a "héros malchanceux" (unlucky hero), and, in agreement with Pintard and Adam, a "Surhomme" (Superman). See Ramos, *Cyrano, Auteur tragique*, pp. 39, 97, 136.

43. Lancaster, *French Dramatic Literature*, II, Pt. III, 170.

44. See especially I, ii, in which Sejanus tells his wife how much he loves her and her children although he is about to divorce her; also his scene of "repentance," IV, ii. Jean Magnon, *Séjanus*.

45. Ibid., p. 59.

46. Ibid., p. 85.

47. Tacitus, *Annals*, 4. 1.

48. Tristan l'Hermite, *La Mort de Sénèque*, Act II, iv, p. 55, and notes to ll. 703–10. Among Tristan's sources are religious as well as pagan works.

49. Spink, *French Free-Thought*, p. 64.

50. For discussions of fideism and the *libertins*, see Busson, *Pensée religieuse*, chap. V, "La Raison et la Foi," pp. 225–82, and Pintard, *Le Libertinage érudit*, passim.

51. See Busson, *Pensée religieuse*, p. 557. It is interesting that the *fils de l'hôte*, in his refutation of the "pari" (wager) (I, 96), objects that if God existed he would make his presence known and not play "cligne-musette" (hide-and-seek) with man. This very ob-

jection constitutes the essence of Pascal's "Dieu caché" (hidden God) (see No. 242 in the Brunschvicg ed.), a coincidence not mentioned by Georges Mounin in his article on Cyrano and Pascal in *Le Préclassicisme français* (pp. 69–78). The resemblance to Pascal is, however, noted by Weber. See Cyrano de Bergerac, *L'Autre Monde*, ed. Weber, p. 158, n. 1.

52. Pintard, *Le Libertinage érudit*, p. 447.

53. Busson, *Pensée religieuse*, p. 340.

54. Erba, "L'Incidenza della magia," p. 14.

55. It could be adduced here that Cyrano made the opposite about-face in following his "Pour les sorciers" by a "Contre les sorciers." A careful reading of the former letter will reveal, however, that it is not a plea in favor of witchcraft but merely an exposition of all those goings-on which Cyrano will denounce as tomfoolery in the next letter. A similar satirical exposition of superstitious beliefs is to be found in the *Pédant joué*, IV, i (Lachèvre, II, 58). See Brun, *Cyrano* (1893), pp. 147–48, and Erba, "L'Incidenza della magia," p. 47.

56. Mongrédien recognizes the implications of this passage in commenting: "Argument traditionnel, d'une simplicité et d'une force irrésistibles, qui va plus loin qu'on ne pense, car, si Bergerac l'applique ici aux prétendus miracles diaboliques, ne voit-on qu'il est également valable pour les miracles divins?" (The traditional argument, of an irresistible simplicity and strength, which goes farther than you would think, for if Bergerac here applies it to alleged diabolical miracles, is it not evident that it is equally applicable to divine miracles?) Mongrédien, *Cyrano de Bergerac*, p. 119.

57. Brun remarks: "Certes, il faut que l'esprit de Cyrano ait été trempé de façon spéciale pour se dégager des superstitions de son époque et pour écrire cette lettre *Contre les sorciers* au temps où Bodin publiait *La Démonomanie*, Boguet le *Discours des sorciers*, Delancre le *Tableau de l'inconstance des mauvais anges et démons*, le P. Leloyer les *Discours et histoires de spectres*." (Most certainly, Cyrano's mind must have been specially tempered in order to have freed itself from the superstitions of his times and to have written the

letter "Contre les sorciers" at the time when Bodin was publishing "Demonomania," Boguet the "Discourse on sorcerers," Delancre the "Portrait of the inconstancy of wicked angels and demons," Father Leloyer the "Stories of specters and discourse thereupon.") Brun, *Cyrano* (1893), pp. 148–49. Cf. Mongrédien, *Cyrano de Bergerac*, p. 115.

58. Cf. Cyrano de Bergerac, *l'Autre Monde*, ed. Weber, p. 164, n. 3.

59. Cf. the famous line in *Le Pédant joué*, "Que Diable aller faire dans la Galère d'un Turc?" (What the devil would you do in a Turk's galley?) Lachèvre, II, 38. (Act II, scene iv.)

60. Kepler, *Dream*, ed. John Lear, trans. Patricia F. Kirkwood, p. 39. See also Marjorie Nicolson, *Voyages to the Moon*. She notes the enormous influence of Kepler's *Dream* on later cosmic voyages (p. 41), and indicates that he was one of the sources for Cyrano: "Here [in Cyrano's *Lune*] are elements drawn from earlier literature from Lucian to Rabelais, Kepler, Godwin" (p. 163). Charles Sorel also mentions Kepler's *Dream* in connection with Cyrano's moon voyage. See Charles Sorel, *Bibliothèque françoise*, p. 191. Cf. Lachèvre, I, c–ci.

61. Kepler, *Dream*, ed. Lear, pp. 29–30.

62. Ibid., pp. 39–40.

63. According to Leo Jordan, Cyrano may have found the idea of placing the *démon de Socrate* on the moon in Montaigne (II, 12). Jordan, "Cyrano Bergerac und Montaigne," pp. 394–95.

64. See, for example, Lachèvre, I, 33.

65. For Kepler's explanation of the Daemon's meaning, see Lear's introduction to Kepler's *Dream*, p. 5.

66. See Tristan l'Hermite, *Le Page disgracié*, chaps. XVII, XVIII, XIX, pp. 93–105.

67. Cf. Pintard, *Le Libertinage érudit*, p. 488.

68. Busson, *Pensée religieuse*, p. 495. Cf. his statement, pp. 346–47, that Cyrano seems to him to have shown the keenest critical attitude toward miracles.

69. Brun, *Cyrano* (1893), p. 283.

70. Harold W. Lawton, "Notes sur Jean Baudoin et sur ses traductions de l'anglais," *Revue de littérature comparée*, VI (1926), 673–81.

71. Cyrano de Bergerac, *Voyages*, ed. Aldington, pp. 293–94.

72. Cyrano de Bergerac, *Oeuvres*, ed. P. L. Jacob, p. 11.

73. Lachèvre, I, 45, and see n. 1. It is interesting to speculate on Cyrano's adoption of Godwin's character, Gonzales. Dorothy Singer is of the opinion that Gonzales represents Giordano Bruno in the English work. Could Cyrano have held the same opinion? See Dorothy W. Singer, *Giordano Bruno: His Life and Thought*, p. 183.

74. Leo Jordan concludes, after an examination of Godwin's work, that although Cyrano borrowed from it, he did not imitate it. See Cyrano de Bergerac, *L'Autre Monde*, ed. Jordan, p. 56. Jordan holds that Cyrano knew Godwin in the original English. See p. 49.

75. Bishop Francis Godwin, *The Man in the Moone*, ed. Grant McColley, in *Smith College Studies in Modern Languages*, XIX (Oct. 1937–July 1938), 28, and see p. 74, n. to "Iesus."

76. Ibid., introduction by McColley, p. xiii.

77. Ibid., p. 8.

78. Ibid., p. 38, and see McColley's note on magic stones, p. 75.

79. Ibid., p. 19, and see note, p. 71.

80. Brun, *Cyrano* (1893), p. 283.

81. Wilkins, *Discovery*, p. 17.

82. Ibid., p. 18.

83. Ibid., pp. 98–99.

84. See, for example, Wilkins, *Discovery*, pp. 54–55, 76.

85. The subtitle of his work is: "A Discourse, tending to prove that ('tis probable) there may be another Habitable World in the Moon." Leo Jordan also notes the differences between the two works, reflected in the different genres of each. See Cyrano de Bergerac, *L'Autre Monde*, ed. Jordan, pp. 48–49.

86. See the catalogue of his writings in the *Discovery*, pp. vii–viii. The title of another of his "scientific" works, *Mathematical Magick*, is significant. Marjorie Nicolson remarks: "John Wilkins and his contemporaries lived without contradiction in a world of 'Mathematical Magic.'" (*Voyages to the Moon*, p. 98.)

87. See Lachèvre, I, 35, 181 ff.

88. Léon Blanchet, *Campanella*, pp. 213–14.

89. Tommaso Campanella, *The City of the Sun*, in *Ideal Empires and Republics*, ed. Charles M. Andrews, p. 277.

90. Tommaso Campanella, *La Cité du soleil*, ed. Louise Colet, *Oeuvres choisies de Campanella*, p. 183.

91. Campanella, *City of the Sun*, ed. Andrews, pp. 303–4.

92. Ibid., p. 307.

93. Blanchet, *Campanella*, pp. 215–16.

94. See ibid., pp. 208–13. Blanchet traces the tradition of natural magic and explanation of miracles by occult causes from Pomponazzi through Agrippa, Wier, and Porta, and describes Bodin's reaction against it.

95. Campanella, *The Defense of Galileo*, trans. and ed. Grant McColley, in *Smith College Studies in History*, XXII, nos. 3–4, (April–July 1937), 32.

96. Luciano Erba, "L'Incidenza della magia," pp. 1–74.

97. See, for example, Erba's discussion of the anagram "Mada" (p. 23), which could have been simply a subterfuge for the 1657 editions, or his discussion of phallic symbols in the *Lune* (p. 39), or his interpretation of the metamorphoses in the *Soleil* (p. 41), passages which will be discussed later in the context of Cyrano's thought. Erba gratuitously attaches an allegorical meaning to the *Autre Monde* (see p. 51), which was the product of a distinctly nonallegorical mentality.

98. Lachèvre, in a note in his edition of Cyrano's *Oeuvres diverses*, indicates the ambiguous nature of Cornelius Agrippa von Nettesheim with respect to magic. Cyrano de Bergerac, *Oeuvres diverses*, ed. Frédéric Lachèvre, p. 370, n. 30. Agrippa attacked miracles while yet believing in occult powers. He could thus have been for Cyrano a real "sorcerer" or a rationalistic thinker.

99. See Spink's discussion of magic in Cyrano's works. Spink, *French Free-Thought*, p. 65. By "natural magic" Spink does not mean the occult but what he calls "the magic of science."

100. See Blanchet, *Campanella*, pp. 222–23.

101. See Busson, *Pensée religieuse*, p. 496, and A. Lavers, "La

Croyance à l'unité de la science dans 'L'Autre Monde' de Cyrano de Bergerac," *Cahiers du sud*, vol. 45, no. 349 (March 1959), 410.

102. Spink, *French Free-Thought*, pp. 7–8. See also p. 57 for the influence of the Italian philosophers on Cyrano.

103. Ibid., pp. 63–64. Further reference will be made to the use of panpsychism by Cyrano in a discussion of his atomism. See infra, pp. 93–94, 221–22.

104. Campanella, *City of the Sun*, ed. Andrews, p. 281.

105. Ibid., p. 296.

106. Ibid., p. 315. For an explanation of Campanella's concept of creation as presented in his *Metaphysics*, see Blanchet, *Campanella*, pp. 299–305.

107. Campanella, *City of the Sun*, ed. Andrews, p. 309.

108. Campanella, *Defense of Galileo*, ed. McColley, pp. 53–54.

109. Lachèvre informs us in a note (2) that Cyrano is here alluding to the miracle of Joshua.

110. Campanella, *Defense of Galileo*, ed. McColley, pp. 53–54.

111. Ibid., preface by McColley, p. xxxiv.

112. Cf. ibid. "Scripture remained to Campanella the basic source for theological truth. As much may be said of Galileo, of Wilkins in 1640, of Locke in 1690, of Bayle, and of other advocates of an empirical theory of knowledge."

113. See ibid., pp. xii–xiii: "Although Campanella was a true son of the Renaissance and of the scientific movement which developed with it, he was equally a faithful son of the Church. In the late sixteenth and early seventeenth centuries this meant nothing less than divided allegiance."

114. See Brun, *Cyrano* (1893), p. 282.

115. Francis Bacon, *New Atlantis*, in *Ideal Empires and Republics*, ed. Charles M. Andrews, p. 243.

116. Sir Thomas More, *Utopia*, in *Ideal Empires and Republics*, ed. Charles M. Andrews, p. 185.

117. Ibid., p. 220.

118. Ibid., pp. 216–17.

119. See John H. Randall, Jr., *The Career of Philosophy*, I,

468. Randall calls this deism an "undogmatic humanistic religion which is the purest and most complete worship of the Divine Being, a universal theism founded on reason."

120. More, *Utopia*, p. 186.

121. Lachèvre, I, 93. Cyrano of course brings up the question in order to prove that man's soul is as corporeal as the beasts'.

122. More, *Utopia*, p. 219. Brun says that Cyrano's thought on this point approaches that of More, because they both believe animals have a soul. While this may be true (a discussion of the role of plants and animals in Cyrano will follow in Chapter IV), it is to be noted that for Cyrano the soul is not immortal, whereas for More it is. See Brun, *Cyrano* (1893), p. 315.

123. Randall, *Career of Philosophy*, p. 468. He does remark that the freedom was qualified.

124. More, *Utopia*, pp. 218–19.

125. See Cyrano de Bergerac, *Histoire comique*, in *Oeuvres*, ed. P. L. Jacob, LeBret's preface to the *Voyage dans la lune*, pp. 24–25.

126. Brun, *Cyrano* (1893), pp. 34–35.

127. Ibid., p. 69.

128. Ibid., p. 321. Leo Jordan seems to share this opinion. See his edition of Cyrano's *Autre Monde*, p. 85.

129. Busson, *Pensée religieuse*, p. 496.

130. See Pintard, *Le Libertinage érudit*, p. 566.

131. Busson, *Pensée religieuse*, p. 496. For the *Quatrains du déiste*, see Busson, p. 103.

132. Jean-Jacques Bridenne, "A la Recherche du vrai Cyrano de Bergerac," *Information littéraire*, Ve année (1953), 172.

133. Adam, *Littérature française au XVIIe siècle*, II, 115.

134. Spink, *French Free-Thought*, pp. 64–65. He has also said of him: "He was the freest-thinking of the free-thinkers or libertines of the seventeenth century." J. S. Spink, "Form and Structure: Cyrano de Bergerac's Atomistic Conception of Metamorphosis," in *Literature and Science*, p. 150.

135. Pintard, *Le Libertinage érudit*, p. 626.

136. Charles Dassoucy, *Les Pensées dans le Saint-Office de Rome*, in his *Aventures burlesques*, pp. 333–36. Busson refers to his judgments (*Pensée religieuse*, p. 267).

137. Marin Mersenne, *Quaestiones celeberrimae in Genesim* (1623), cited by Boase, *The Fortunes of Montaigne*, p. 171.

138. Dassoucy, *Pensées*, pp. 337–38.

139. Ibid., p. 339.

140. Pintard, *Le Libertinage érudit*, p. 565.

141. See Pintard, *Le Libertinage érudit*, p. 625. Brun (*Cyrano* [1893], p. 70) lists Chapelle among Cyrano's friends. Lachèvre also speaks of their friendship (I, xxxv–xxxvi). Among Cyrano's letters are one against Chapelle and one to him. See Lachèvre, II, 187–89 and 189–92.

142. See Lucien Febvre, *Le Problème de l'incroyance au XVI*ᵉ *siècle: la religion de Rabelais*.

143. "A leurs disciples émancipés—si l'on peut réunir sous ce titre Christine de Suède et Cyrano de Bergerac—les érudits libertins laissent les théories scabreuses sur l'éternité de l'univers, sur la pluralité des mondes, sur la fatalité qui gouverne toutes choses." (To their emancipated disciples—if we can group together under this heading Christina of Sweden and Cyrano de Bergerac—the erudite *libertins* left the scabrous theories of the eternity of the universe, the plurality of worlds, the fatality governing everything.) Pintard, *Le Libertinage érudit*, p. 440. See pp. 437–41 for his discussion of the attitudes of the various *libertins* toward miracles, the supernatural, and the notion of divinity.

144. Ibid., p. 488.

CHAPTER 2. MIRACLE: ALTERNATIVES

1. See Lavers, "La Croyance à l'unité de la science dans 'L'Autre Monde' de Cyrano de Bergerac," p. 409. See also Spink, *French Free-Thought*, p. 53.

2. The title of Lavers's article obviously indicates such a unity,

but Lavers in fact points to a possible synthesis of several philosophical systems which Cyrano might have made, without showing that this synthesis was made by him.

3. See also Lachèvre, I, 76, n. 1.

4. Cf. Lucretius, *On the Nature of Things*, Bk. V, p. 200. As Weber points out, the same argument for chance creation is found in Diderot's *Pensées philosophiques*. See Cyrano de Bergerac, *L'Autre Monde*, ed. Weber, p. 135, n. 2.

5. See Lachèvre, I, 77, n. 4. In his recent study of Cyrano, Mongrédien also states that Cyrano anticipated Lamarckian and Darwinian theories. See Mongrédien, *Cyrano de Bergerac*, p. 165

6. Cyrano makes a similar enumeration but in a humorous vein in his letter "Pour une Dame rousse." The idea of a striving toward perfection in nature is found here ("La Nature qui tend au plus parfait . . ." [Nature who tends toward the most perfect . . .]), but not that of progressive development. See Cyrano de Bergerac, *Oeuvres diverses*, ed. Lachèvre, p. 33. Cf. Lachèvre, I, 90, where the idea of nature tending toward the perfect reappears in a satirical passage. Jacques Denis does not see evolution foreshadowed in the latter passage because progressive development is not suggested. Jacques Denis, "Sceptiques ou libertins de la première moitié du XVIIᵉ siècle," as quoted in Lachèvre, I, 91, n. 1.

7. Brun, *Cyrano* (1893), p. 253. Edward Lanius agrees with this theory. See Lanius, *Cyrano de Bergerac and the Universe of the Imagination*, p. 27.

8. Cf. François de La Mothe Le Vayer, *La Physique du Prince*, in his *Oeuvres*, II, 10: "L'amitié d'entre la forme et la matière est telle qu'on ne les voit jamais l'une sans l'autre. Mais la forme peut être comparée à un mari fidèle et constant dans son affection; au lieu que la matière . . . ressemble à ces femmes sans honneur qui s'abandonnent incessamment à toute sorte de partis." (The friendship between form and matter is such that one is never seen without the other. But the form may be compared to a faithful husband, constant in his affection; whereas matter . . . resembles those women without honor who incessantly abandon themselves to each and every suitor.)

9. "Je leur [aux Scolares] demande, premièrement, si l'eau n'engendre point du poisson. Quand ils me le nieront, je leur ordonneray de creuser un fossé, le remplir du sirop de l'esguière qu'ilz passeront encore, s'ilz veulent, à travers un bluteau pour eschapper aux objections des aveugles, et je veux, en cas qu'ilz n'y trouvent du poisson dans quelque temps, avaller toute l'eau qu'ilz y auront versée. (I ask them [the *Scolares*], first, if water does not engender fish. If they deny it, I will order them to dig a ditch, fill it with water from a pitcher which they can yet strain through a sieve, if they wish, so as to avoid the objections of the blind, and, if they do not shortly find fish there, I will swallow all the water they will have poured out.)

10. A. Juppont, "L'Oeuvre scientifique de Cyrano de Bergerac," as quoted in Lachèvre, I, 51, n. 1.

11. The conflict between the two opposing forces, heat and cold, is developed into a mortal combat between the "Salamander" and the "Remora," or fire and ice, in the *Estats et empires du soleil*. It is noteworthy that the battle is caused by the talking trees of the forest of Dodona who, after unsuccessfully attempting to ward off the fire-beast, have had to call upon the ice-beast to help them. Heat and cold are again vying for the possession of wood, but in this passage it is the force of cold that is victorious. See Lachèvre, I, 178–80. The anecdote is undoubtedly meant to be a literary exposition of the ancient principle of antiperistasis or the confrontation of two opposing forces one of which gives power to the other. Cf. Lachèvre, I, 46, and Cyrano de Bergerac, *Histoire comique des estats et empires de la lune et du soleil*, ed. Claude Mettra and Jean Suyeux, pp. 59 n., 293.

12. See Lachèvre, I, 76, n. 2. See also Frederick A. Lange, *The History of Materialism*, trans. Ernest Thomas, Bk. I, p. 264.

13. See Rachmiel Brandwajn, *Cyrano de Bergerac*, p. 216 (résumé in French).

14. The notion of assimilation is similar to the one expressed by Diderot in the *Rêve de D'Alembert*. See Cyrano de Bergerac, *L'Autre Monde*, ed. Weber, p. 151, n. 1.

15. Toldo believes it is. See his "Voyages merveilleux," p. 316.

Weber considers that Cyrano has substituted the universal circulation of matter for reincarnation, but he does see evolutionary ideas in this passage, which he views as a satire on the last judgment. See Cyrano de Bergerac, *L'Autre Monde*, ed. Weber, p. 150, n. 2; p. 151, nn. 2, 3.

16. This is an interesting parallel with the *Estats de la lune*. Cyrano, it will be recalled, upon landing on the moon, crashes into an apple from the Tree of Life, under which he falls. See Lachèvre, I, 20.

17. Spink, "Form and Structure," p. 150.

18. He notes the vogue of the metamorphoses theme, derived, of course, from Ovid. See ibid., pp. 145, 147–48.

19. Cyrano undoubtedly knew Lucretius in the original, but he possibly benefited from the 1650 translation by the abbot Michel de Marolles, whom he knew, according to LeBret. See Cyrano de Bergerac, *Oeuvres*, ed. P. L. Jacob, p. 22.

20. See Lange, *History of Materialism*, Bk. I, p. 13, n. 9; p. 143.

21. Lucretius, *On the Nature of Things*, Bk. I, pp. 56–57.

22. Ibid., p. 57.

23. See Lange, *History of Materialism*, Bk. I, p. 267.

24. François Bernier, *Abrégé de la philosophie de Gassendi*, VI, 48. See Lange, *History of Materialism*, Bk. I, p. 266, n. 11.

25. Lange, *History of Materialism*, Bk. I, pp. 266–67, n. 11. Brett, however, holds that Gassendi rejected the idea of potential presence. See G. S. Brett, *The Philosophy of Gassendi*, pp. 117–18. Mabilleau states that although Gassendi does not accept the concept of the sentient atom, which he describes in terms very similar to Lucretius's, he does suggest the possibility of development of sensibility from potentially sentient atoms, as in the passage from the *Abrégé* quoted above. See Léopold Mabilleau, *Histoire de la philosophie atomistique*, pp. 418–19.

26. Lucretius, *On the Nature of Things*, Bk. II, pp. 98–99.

27. Cyrano de Bergerac, *L'Autre Monde*, ed. Weber, p. 221, n. 2.

28. Spink, "Form and Structure," p. 149.

29. Rochot, however, points out the corpuscular nature of Gassendi's atomism, which admits neither of the mathematical point as an atom nor of the infinite divisibility of space. Gassendi's atoms do have parts, but these can never be separated. See Bernard Rochot, *Les Travaux de Gassendi sur Épicure et sur l'atomisme*, pp. 96–97.

30. See Aram Vartanian, *Diderot and Descartes*, p. 49. The movement of the atoms, however, may also be derived from the Gassendist theory of the atoms' perpetual motion, which accounts for the constant change in the forms of matter. See Bernier, *Abrégé*, II, 158–71.

31. Spink, "Form and Structure," p. 149.

32. Ibid.

33. Spink, *French Free-Thought*, pp. 60–61.

34. Ibid., p. 61.

35. That the psychical and physical are indissolubly linked in Cyrano's materialism is dramatically indicated by his explanation of the identical behavior of twins: "Mais ne voyez-vous pas qu'il estoit impossible que la composition des organes de leurs corps estant pareille dans toutes ses circonstances, il n'opérassent d'une façon pareille, puis que deux instrumens égaux, touchez également, doivent rendre une harmonie égale? et qu'ainsi conformant tout à fait mon corps au vostre, et devenant, pour ainsi dire, vostre gémeau, il est impossible qu'un mesme branle de la matière ne nous cause à tous deux un mesme branle d'esprit." (But do you not see that since the construction of the organs of their bodies was similar in all conditions, they would act in similar fashion; since two like instruments, touched alike, will render like harmony? And thus in making my body conform exactly to yours, and in becoming, so to speak, your twin, it is impossible that the same impulse of matter would not cause in us the same impulse of mind.) Lachèvre, I, 178. The two "instrumens égaux" form a striking parallel to the "clavecin sensible" (sensitive harpsichord) in Diderot's *Entretien entre D'Alembert et Diderot*.

36. Spink, *French Free-Thought*, p. 61.

37. Ibid.

38. Cyrano uses "clin d'oeil" in a similar context in the stoical passage on death in the "Histoire des Oiseaux": "Or tu vas estre comme celuy qui n'est pas né; un clin d'oeil après la vie, tu seras ce que tu estois un clin d'oeil devant; et ce clin d'oeil passé, tu seras mort d'aussi longtemps que celui qui mourut il y a mille siècles." (Now you are going to be like someone who is not born; in the twinkling of an eye after your life, you will be what you were in the twinkling of an eye before it; and once this twinkling of an eye is past, you will be dead as anyone who died a thousand centuries ago.) Lachèvre, I, 161–62.

39. Cf. Spink, "Form and Structure," p. 149: "And the sun, in Cyrano's universe, is the seat of pure act, the source of heat, light, feeling, animation, activity in the world."

40. See Lange, *History of Materialism*, Bk. I, p. 29. Cyrano's world-soul is similar to that of Gassendi, who describes it as "une espèce de feu, ou de petite flamme très subtile, très mobile, et très active, qui se trouvant tempérée, meslée, agitée, et disposée d'une certaine manière dans les diverses fibres de la Terre, devenoit en quelque façon . . . Ame" (a sort of fire, or a very thin, very mobile, and very active little flame which, tempered, mingled, stirred, and arranged in a certain way in various fibres of the Earth, became in a way . . . a Soul). Bernier, *Abrégé*, II, 95.

41. Campanella goes on to tell Dyrcona that there are three orders of spirits in the planets, of which the purest, those of philosophers, rise to the sun's sphere and are not incorporated into its mass, as are the others. The passage is similar to the conjecture of Nicholas of Cusa, that if the planets were inhabited, the most spiritual and intellectual beings would inhabit the sun, the most material the earth, those on the moon being possibly "lunatics." See Nicholas Cusanus, *Of Learned Ignorance*, trans. Fr. Germain Heron, p. 116. Gassendi also though that the sun's inhabitants would be of a nobler nature than man. See Cyrano de Bergerac, *L'Autre Monde*, ed. Weber, p. 207, n. 1.

42. Pierre Borel describes in some detail the birds of paradise which are found not on earth but on other stars. See Pierre Borel,

Discours nouveau prouvant la pluralité des mondes, pp. 35–36.

43. Among the nonastronomical arguments for the sun's central position put forth by Copernicus was the following: "In the midst of all dwells the Sun. For who could set this luminary in another or better place in this most glorious temple, than whence he can at one and the same time lighten the whole. . . . And so, as if seated upon a royal throne, the Sun rules the family of the planets as they circle round him." Quoted by Angus Armitage from the *De revolutionibus*, in *The World of Copernicus*, pp. 106–7.

44. Lavers is of the opinion that the use of the word "microcosme" indicates that the metamorphoses represent the formation of the macrocosm as well as of the microcosm. See Lavers, "La Croyance à l'unité de la science dans 'L'Autre Monde,'" p. 412. This is true insofar as for Cyrano the processes of formation of both are comparable.

45. See also Cyrano de Bergerac, *L'Autre Monde*, ed. Weber, p. 127, n. 2.

46. The reference to God seems to be only for the sake of form, since on the following page Cyrano gives a satirical account of the fall of the angels. See Lachèvre, I, 128. God is superfluous to Cyrano's materialistic theory of the world's formation.

47. See Lucretius, *On the Nature of Things*, Bk. V, pp. 200–203.

48. See Lachèvre, I, 128, n. 1.

49. Descartes defines the three elements as: (1) the sun and fixed stars, (2) the heavens, (3) the earth, planets, and comets. Descartes, *Les Principes de la philosophie*, in *Oeuvres*, ed. Victor Cousin, III, 218.

50. Ibid., pp. 331–32. See Vartanian, *Diderot and Descartes*, pp. 56–57. Vartanian remarks that Cyrano borrowed his ideas on the formation of the universe and on sunspots from Descartes. Brun also notes Descartes's influence on Cyrano's sunspot theory. See Brun, *Cyrano* (1893), p. 302.

51. See Cyrano de Bergerac, *L'Autre Monde*, ed. Weber, p. 205, nn. 2, 3.

52. See Lachèvre, I, 12, n. 3.

53. The same image used for the same purpose can be found in Bernier's *Abrégé*, IV, 223. It is also used in Borel's *Discours nouveau*, p. 18, as well as in Fontenelle's *Pluralité des mondes*.

54. Bernier, *Abrégé*, IV, 224.

55. Weber calls Cyrano's moon voyage a "vérification expérimentale, quoique imaginaire" (an experimental, although imaginary, verification). See, Cyrano de Bergerac, *L'Autre Monde*, ed. Weber, p. 28.

56. The theme of the "borrow'd light" of the moon in seventeenth-century literature is explored by Marjorie Nicolson, who sees it as in part a heritage from the Greeks, in part due to a revival of interest in the question of the source of the moon's light, prompted by the scientific discoveries of the seventeenth century. See Marjorie Nicolson, *A World in the Moon*, in *Smith College Studies in Modern Languages*, XVII, no. 2 (Jan. 1936), 11–12.

57. For a discussion of the reception of heliocentrism in seventeenth-century France, see Busson, *Pensée religieuse*, pp. 286–99.

58. Ibid., p. 287.

59. See Jean Plattard, "Le Système de Copernic dans la littérature française au XVIᵉ siècle," *Revue du seizième siècle*, I (1913), 229–36.

60. Ibid., p. 236.

61. See Camille Flammarion, *Les Mondes imaginaires et les mondes réels*, p. 396.

62. Cyrano de Bergerac, *Oeuvres*, ed. P. L. Jacob, p. 26.

63. Dorothy Stimson, *The Gradual Acceptance of the Copernican Theory of the Universe*, p. 96.

64. Busson, *Pensée religieuse*, p. 291.

65. See Vartanian, *Diderot and Descartes*, p. 104.

66. See Busson, *Pensée religieuse*, p. 299.

67. See Bernier, *Abrégé*, IV, 290–91.

68. Pintard, *Le Libertinage érudit*, pp. 488–89.

69. Busson, *Pensée religieuse*, p. 301.

70. This is also Brun's interpretation of the passage. See Brun, *Cyrano* (1893), pp. 305–6.

71. See Camille Flammarion, *Les Mondes imaginaires*, p. 329.

72. Nicolson, *Voyages to the Moon*, pp. 23–24.

73. See Cyrano de Bergerac, *Oeuvres*, ed. P. L. Jacob, p. 12. LeBret also mentions Patrizzi on this page.

74. Galileo's telescope was thought to function in one of two ways: either it made stars too small to be seen larger, or it brought stars too far away to be seen nearer. Cyrano evidently chooses the first way, in contradiction to modern thinking as well as to that of the majority of his contemporaries. See Alexandre Koyré, *From the Closed World to the Infinite Universe*, p. 94.

75. Wilkins, *Discovery*, propositions II, VI, XI.

76. Ibid., p. 101.

77. Spink, *French Free-Thought*, p. 53.

78. Flammarion, *Les Mondes imaginaires*, p. 370.

79. Borel, *Discours nouveau*, chap. IV, pp. 9-10. Even though the book was first published in 1657, Borel states that it was ready for publication by 1648. It could thus have been available to Cyrano. See Borel's preface.

80. Wilkins, *Discovery*, p. 1.

81. Ibid., p. 2.

82. Ibid., p. 3: "I shall specify that [another truth formerly held to be ridiculous] of the Antipodes, which have been denied, and laught at by many wise Men and great Scholars; such as were Herodotus, Chrysostom, Austin, Lactantius, the venerable Bede, Lucretius the Poet, Procopius and the voluminous Abulensis, together with all those Fathers or other Authors who denied the Roundness of the Heavens."

83. See Borel, *Discours nouveau*, p. 5, and Godwin, *The Man in the Moone*, p. 2.

84. See Borel, *Discours nouveau*, chaps. XLI–XLIII, pp. 60–65.

85. Dassoucy, *Pensées*, p. 339. Busson notes this passage in his *Pensée religieuse*, p. 294.

86. Leo Jordan calls this passage "echt gassendisch" (pure Gassendi). See his edition of Cyrano's *Autre Monde*, p. 86.

87. See Grant McColley, "The Seventeenth-Century Doctrine of a Plurality of Worlds," *Annals of Science*, I (1936), 391.

88. Ibid., p. 399.

89. See ibid., p. 414, and Randall, *The Career of Philosophy*, I, 331.

90. Cf. R. G. Collingwood, *The Idea of Nature*, pp. 99–100. Koyré observes that Bruno does draw a distinction between the infinity of God and that of the world, but this hardly modifies the basic identification of the two with each other. See Koyré, *From the Closed World to the Infinite Universe*, p. 52.

91. Giordano Bruno, *De imaginum compositione, Opera latine conscripta*, as quoted in Randall, *The Career of Philosophy*, p. 330. Bruno elsewhere uses the image of the infinite worlds as animals, found in the *Estats de la lune*. "These magnificent stars and luminous bodies, which are so many inhabited worlds, and great animals, and most excellent spirits, which seem and are innumerable worlds, . . . must necessarily know a principle and cause." Bruno, *De l'infinito, universo et mondi*, as quoted in Randall, *The Career of Philosophy*, p. 331.

92. Spink, *French Free-Thought*, p. 56.

93. See Marjorie Nicolson, *The Breaking of the Circle*, p. 175. Edward Lanius, in accordance with his interpretation of the *Autre Monde* as an imaginative work, chooses to give a figurative meaning to the word "infinite." "Rather than proposing a philosophical and mathematical infinity, Cyrano presents a universe as he envisions it in his imagination, unfolding in cinematic fashion as one image follows another in constant succession." Lanius, *Cyrano de Bergerac and the Universe of the Imagination*, p. 24.

94. See Lachèvre, I, 14, variant h. See also variant f for "éternellement" in the passage quoted above, p. 75.

95. Borel, *Discours nouveau*, pp. 48–49. Borel, in accumulating all possible arguments in favor of the plurality of worlds, is often led to contradictions and inconsistencies. In another passage of the *Discours*, he professes a very anthropocentric doctrine of utility, concluding that since everything in the world is made for man's use, the probable presence of plants on other planets would logically imply that they are inhabited by man. See p. 68.

96. See Koyré, *From the Closed World to the Infinite Universe,* pp. 7–8.

97. Descartes, *Principes de la philosophie,* p. 80.

98. See Brett, *The Philosophy of Gassendi,* p. 36. Rochot, however, states that for Gassendi infinity is "possible" but not "real." See Rochot, *Les Travaux de Gassendi,* pp. 146–47.

99. McColley, "The Plurality of Worlds," p. 386.

100. Lucretius, *On the Nature of Things,* Bk. I, p. 59.

101. This is the reverse of Aristotle's argument that it is as difficult to assert infinity as to deny it. See A. W. Loewenstein, "Die naturphilosophischen Ideen bei Cyrano de Bergerac," *Archiv für Geschichte der Philosophie,* Bd. XVI, N.F. (1903), 55.

102. Arthur O. Lovejoy, *The Great Chain of Being,* p. 108.

103. Ibid., p. 111.

104. Cf. ibid., pp. 110–11.

105. Borel, *Discours nouveau,* pp. 66–67.

106. For a discussion of Cyrano's flying machines, see Bridenne, "Cyrano de Bergerac et la science aéronautique," pp. 241–58. See also Marjorie Nicolson, *Voyages to the Moon,* pp. 158–180.

107. Nicolson, *Voyages to the Moon,* p. 161.

108. Cf. Bridenne, "Cyrano de Bergerac et la science aéronautique," p. 257.

109. Lachèvre, I, xcix, n. 2. Leo Jordan also feels that the discrepancies cast doubt upon Cyrano's authorship of the *Fragment.* See Cyrano de Bergerac, *L'Autre Monde,* ed. Jordan, pp. 70, 81, 90.

110. Lachèvre, I, xcix, n. 2.

111. Brun, *Cyrano* (1893), pp. 323–24.

112. Cyrano de Bergerac, *Oeuvres,* ed. P. L. Jacob, p. 283.

113. Spink, *French Free-Thought,* p. 62.

114. Loewenstein, "Die naturphilosophischen Ideen," p. 58.

115. Lachèvre, I, xcix, n. 2.

116. Ibid., p. 76. Cf. Bernier, *Abrégé,* II, Bk. I, 104–56. See also Lachèvre, I, 76, n. 1, and Cyrano de Bergerac, *L'Autre Monde,* ed. Weber, p. 133, n. 2.

117. Cyrano de Bergerac, *Fragment de physique,* in *Oeuvres,* ed. P. L. Jacob, p. 302.

118. Descartes, *Les Principes de la philosophie*, pp. 120–24. Cf. Brun, *Cyrano* (1893), pp. 333–34.

119. Jacques Rohault, *Traité de physique*, pp. 37–38.

120. Cyrano, *Fragment de physique*, in *Oeuvres*, ed. P. L. Jacob, pp. 304–5. Cf. Descartes, *Principes de la philosophie*, p. 137.

121. Brun, for reasons difficult to determine, feels that Gonzalès's stand is meant as a "raillerie" (satire) of the concept of the vacuum. See Brun, *Cyrano* (1893), p. 300.

122. See Lucretius, *On the Nature of Things*, Bk. I, pp. 38–39. See also Bernier, *Abrégé*, II, 171–90.

123. See Bernier, *Abrégé*, II, 184–85.

124. Ibid., pp. 198–2c2.

125. Cf. ibid., II, 172–73, and Lucretius, *On the Nature of Things*, Bk. I, pp. 38–40.

126. Cyrano, *Fragment de physique*, in *Oeuvres*, ed. P. L. Jacob, pp. 302–3. Cf. Descartes, *Les Principes de la philosophie*, pp. 130–33.

127. Cyrano, *Fragment de physique*, in *Oeuvres*, ed. P. L. Jacob, pp. 302–3. The same example is given in Rohault, *Traité de physique*, p. 42.

128. Descartes, *Le Monde*, in *Oeuvres*, ed. Victor Cousin, IV, 248–49.

129. Lachèvre thinks it was. See Lachèvre, I, 199, n. 1.

130. Cyrano, *Fragment de physique*, in *Oeuvres*, ed. P. L. Jacob, p. 305.

131. Cyrano repeats the idea that not everything in the world is perceptible by the senses in the *Fragment*, this time in a clearly Cartesian context. See ibid., p. 303.

132. Juppont sees reflected in this passage discussions on the divisibility of matter. See Lachèvre, I, 191, n. 1.

133. See Cyrano, *Fragment de physique*, in *Oeuvres*, ed. P. L. Jacob, pp. 305–7. Cf. Descartes, *Les Principes de la philosophie*, pp. 139–49. Cf. also Brun, *Cyrano* (1893), pp. 337–38.

134. Cyrano, *Fragment de physique*, in *Oeuvres*, ed. P. L. Jacob, pp. 303–4. Cf. Descartes, *Principes de la philosophie*, pp. 79–80.

135. Cyrano, *Fragment de physique*, in *Oeuvres*, ed. P. L. Jacob, p. 290.

136. Ibid., pp. 291–92. Rohault, in his *Traité de physique*, uses a similar method, but it does not contain the forceful gibe of Cyrano's reductio ad absurdum. See Rohault, *Traité de physique*, Table des Chapitres, Seconde Partie.

137. Cyrano, *Fragment de physique*, in *Oeuvres*, ed P. L. Jacob, p. 292.

138. Lovejoy, *The Great Chain of Being*, pp. 7–8.

139. Cyrano, *Fragment de physique*, in *Oeuvres*, ed. P. L. Jacob, p. 307.

140. Cf. Descartes, *Principes de la philosophie*, p. 153; Descartes, *Le Monde*, p. 259; Rohault, *Traité de physique*, pp. 62–63.

141. Cyrano, *Fragment de physique*, in *Oeuvres*, ed P. L. Jacob, p. 308.

142. Ibid.

143. Brun, *Cyrano* (1893), p. 324.

144. François de La Mothe Le Vayer, *La Physique du Prince*, in his *Oeuvres*, II, 6–7.

145. See Vartanian, *Diderot and Descartes*, pp. 55–57. He says that the *Estats du soleil* found its inspiration "wholly in Descartes."

146. See Lachèvre, I, xcix, n. 2, and Brun, *Cyrano* (1893), pp. 323–24. See also Cyrano de Bergerac, *Oeuvres*, ed. P. L. Jacob, p. 131, n. 1; p. 283, n. 1. LeBret, in his preface to the *Estats de la lune*, lists Rohault as one of Cyrano's friends. *Oeuvres*, ed. P. L. Jacob, p. 23.

147. Cf. Vartanian, *Diderot and Descartes*, p. 56: "[Cyrano] came under the progressive sway of Descartes's physics, largely through his friendship with Rohault." Cf. also Cyrano de Bergerac, *L'Autre Monde*, ed. Weber, p. 16: Il est assez caractéristique de voir Cyrano passer progressivement au rang des cartésiens." (It is rather typical to see Cyrano pass progressively into the ranks of the Cartesians.) Spink feels that Cyrano was influenced only by Rohault and that the *Fragment* is unrelated to any of Cyrano's other works which, according to him, contain "no trace of Cartesianism." Spink, *French Free-Thought*, pp. 62–63.

148. Brun, *Cyrano* (1893), p. 323.

149. Brun bases his date on the evidence of Rohault's preface, from which he quotes: "Lecteur, comme on était encore après les *États du soleil.* . . ." (Reader, since it was just after the *États du soleil.* . . .) Brun, *Cyrano* (1893), p. 323, n. 1. He does not, however, quote the entire opening sentence of the preface, which continues thus: ". . . un Génie obligeant, qui peut-être est celui-là même avec lequel notre Auteur a eu tant de conversations dans ses voyages, a incité une personne de qualité à nous donner ce commencement de *Physique,* que nous te présentons encore." (. . . an obliging Spirit, who is perhaps the very one with whom our Author had so many conversations in his voyages, urged a person of quality to give us this beginning of a Physics, which we now offer to you.) Cyrano de Bergerac, *Oeuvres,* ed. P. L. Jacob, p. 283. This statement indicates, in vague, figurative language, only that the *Fragment* was "given" after the *Estats du soleil* was written. Cyrano could have written the *Fragment* some time before. Vartanian believes the two were written about the same time. Vartanian, *Diderot and Descartes,* p. 56. The passages of the *Estats du soleil* in which Cyrano questions Campanella on Descartes's philosophy would suggest that he was being introduced to it at that time. It would seem logical that a coherent presentation of Descartes's philosophy would follow the speculative dialogues of the sun voyage, although there is no direct evidence to corroborate this view.

150. Randall underlines the importance of this transition in his treatment of Bruno and of Descartes. See his *Career of Philosophy,* pp. 336, 371–72. Spink does not consider Cyrano's world mechanically ordered, but this statement applies to the *Estats de la lune.* See Spink, *French Free-Thought,* p. 57. Would complete conversion to the mechanist point of view have meant that Cyrano would have had to abandon his monism? Probably, for as Collingwood states, mechanism is "fatal to monism." See Collingwood, *The Idea of Nature,* p. 100.

151. See Cyrano de Bergerac, *L'Autre Monde,* ed. Weber, p. 118, n. 1. Weber also says that for Cyrano the terms "Nature" and "God" are identical. See Henri Weber, "L'Imagination au service du

rationalisme: 'Le Voyage de Cyrano dans la lune,'" *Les Cahiers rationalistes*, no. 167 (Dec. 1957), 278.

152. See George Boas, *Dominant Themes of Modern Philosophy*, pp. 90–91.

153. *Dictionnaire de l'Académie française*, p. 109. The first example is: "Dieu est l'auteur et le maistre de la nature." (God is the author and master of nature.)

154. Dassoucy, *Pensées*, pp. 339–40.

155. Ibid., p. 340.

156. Ibid., pp. 340–41.

157. *Dictionnaire de l'Académie*, p. 109. Among the examples given: "La nature est une bonne mère." (Nature is a good mother.)

158. See Busson, *Pensée religieuse*, p. 395. Cf. Lachèvre, I, 105–6.

159. Busson, *Pensée religieuse*, p. 395.

160. Spink, *French Free-Thought*, p. 64.

CHAPTER 3. FROM SCEPTICISM TO
RELATIVISM: SCIENCE AND EPISTEMOLOGY

1. Popkin, *History of Scepticism*, pp. 53–54. Although the *Apologie* by no means represents Montaigne's definitive philosophical outlook, Popkin has focused on it as a fountainhead of scepticism. See Popkin, *History of Scepticism*, p. 45. It will be thus treated in the present study.

2. Cited by Busson in his *Pensée religieuse*, p. 226.

3. For a discussion of this reaction, see ibid., pp. 225–77.

4. Weber calls this letter "un rejet catégorique de l'argument d'autorité" (a categorical rejection of the argument of authority). Cyrano de Bergerac, *L'Autre Monde*, ed. Weber, p. 25.

5. Denis, "Sceptiques ou libertins," p. 215.

6. Gassendi, in a letter to Schickard, "De Mercurio in sole viso et venere invisa Parisiis anno" (1631), had said: "Il n'y a qu'une

seule manière légitime de philosopher, et c'est à condition de soumet-tre son esprit à la nature, et non la nature à son esprit." (There is only one legitimate way to philosophize, and it is by submitting the mind to nature, and not nature to the mind.) As quoted in Henri Berr, *Du scepticisme de Gassendi*, trans. Bernard Rochot, p. 74.

7. Henri LeBret, Preface to the *Estats de la lune*, in Cyrano de Bergerac, *Oeuvres*, ed. P. L. Jacob, p. 16.

8. Montaigne, *Essais*, I, 566. *Apology for Raymond Sebond*, in *The Complete Essays of Montaigne*, trans. Frame, p. 377.

9. *Essais*, I, 565. *Apology*, p. 377.

10. Boase, *The Fortunes of Montaigne*; Popkin, *History of Scepticism*; Busson, *Pensée religieuse* (see especially chap. IV, pp. 177–225).

11. Jordan, "Cyrano Bergerac und Montaigne," pp. 386–96.

12. Boase, *The Fortunes of Montaigne*, p. 258.

13. Ibid. For a discussion of Montaigne's influence on Cyrano, see pp. 258–59.

14. Pierre Sage, *Le Préclassicisme*, in *Histoire de la littérature française*, ed. J. Calvet, III, 227.

15. See Borel, *Discours nouveau*, p. 14. The title of chapter IX is "Confirmant la pluralité des mondes par la privation de la science des hommes après le péché d'Adam." (Confirming the plurality of worlds by man's deprivation of knowledge since the sin of Adam.)

16. Ibid.

17. Cyrano, *Fragment de physique*, in *Oeuvres*, ed. P. L. Jacob, pp. 286, 299.

18. See ibid., pp. 285–86, 292–99. Descartes discusses the same problem of the immediate objects of knowledge in his *Monde*, pp. 215–17; and in the *Principes de la philosophie*, pp. 107 ff.

19. Cyrano, *Fragment de physique*, in *Oeuvres*, ed. P. L. Jacob, p. 286.

20. Ibid.

21. Montaigne had imagined that certain "occult" properties, such as that of the magnet to attract iron, could be perceived by senses more refined than man's. See the *Apologie*, in *Essais*, I, 664.

22. Cyrano, *Fragment de physique*, in *Oeuvres*, ed. P. L. Jacob, p. 293.

23. Ibid.

24. Ibid., pp. 293–94.

25. See Descartes, *Discours de la méthode*, in *Oeuvres*, ed. Victor Cousin, I, 136. Weber states that Cyrano follows Descartes "dans son principe de la table rase" (in his principle of the tabula rasa) in the *Estats de la lune*. Weber, "L'Imagination au service du rationalisme," p. 276. Such a principle is, however, much more in evidence in the *Fragment* than in the moon voyage.

26. Cyrano, *Fragment de physique*, in *Oeuvres*, ed. P. L. Jacobs, p. 294.

27. Ibid.

28. Ibid., pp. 294–98.

29. Ibid., p. 298.

30. Cf. Popkin, *History of Scepticism*, pp. 186-88.

31. Rohault, *Traité de physique*, p. 4.

32. Ibid.

33. Spink, *French Free-Thought*, p. 62.

34. See Spink, *French Free-Thought*, p. 63.

35. Cyrano, *Fragment de physique*, in *Oeuvres*, ed. P. L. Jacobs, p. 286.

36. Rohault also professed a willingness to be satisfied with verisimilitude. "Ainsi, nous nous contenterons pour l'ordinaire de rechercher comment les choses peuvent estre, sans prétendre d'aller jusqu'à connoistre et determiner ce qu'elles sont en effet." (Thus, we will ordinarily be content to inquire as to how things could be, without claiming to go so far as to know and determine what they are in effect.) *Traité de physique*, p. 21. But Rohault's treatise is eclectic and at times paradoxical to the point of great confusion. There are chapters, for instance, entirely Aristotelian in inspiration. Cf. Paul Mouy, *Le Développement de la physique cartésienne*, p. 116. Armand Gautier sees Rohault as a proponent of the experimental method. See A. Gautier, "Un Précurseur français de la science expérimentale moderne: Jacques Rohault," *Revue générale des sciences pures et appliquées*, 26 (1915), 267–72.

37. Cyrano, *Fragment de physique*, in *Oeuvres*, ed. P. L. Jacob, pp. 299–300.

38. Ibid., p. 301 (italics not mine).

39. See the *Apologie*, in *Essais*, I, 562. According to Busson, Montaigne's scepticism serves but as a preparation for the faith. "Le pyrrhonisme s'accorde très bien chez Montaigne avec foi chrétienne . . . même la faiblesse de la raison lui paraît un préparatif à la foi." (Pyrrhonism is quite consistent with Christian faith in Montaigne . . . he considers even the weakness of reason a preparation for faith.) Busson, *Pensée religieuse*, p. 203. For a somewhat different interpretation of the scepticism of the *Apologie*, and for a full discussion of the problems raised by this essay, see Donald M. Frame, *Montaigne: A Biography*, pp. 162–80. See also Frame's article, "Did Montaigne Betray Sebond?" *Romanic Review*, XXXVIII (Dec. 1947), 297–329.

40. Popkin remarks that the sceptical crisis seems to have bypassed Descartes (as well as Campanella and Galileo), who did believe that certainty could be attained. See Popkin, *History of Scepticism*, pp. 151–52.

41. Montaigne, *Apologie*, in *Essais*, I, 630.

42. Bernier, *Abrégé*, I, 3.

43. Popkin, *History of Scepticism*, p. 86. See also Pintard, *Le libertinage érudit*, p. 479.

44. Bernier, *Abrégé*, I, 10–11.

45. Ibid., p. 29.

46. Ibid., pp. 32–35.

47. Gassendi defines the roles of sense and reason thus in the *Syntagma*: "On peut distinguer en nous double Critérium, l'un par lequel nous percevons le signe, et c'est la sensation; l'autre par lequel nous saisissons par le raisonnement la réalité qui est elle-même cachée, et c'est l'esprit, l'intelligence, ou la raison." (A double Criterion can be distinguished in us, one by which we perceive the sign, and that is sensation; the other by which we grasp by reasoning the reality which itself is hidden, and that is mind, intelligence, or reason.) As quoted in Berr, *Du scepticisme de Gassendi*, p. 102.

48. Cf. George Boas, *Dominant Themes of Modern Philosophy*, p. 135.

49. Bernier, *Abrégé*, I, 180.

50. Gassendi's goal was therefore not truth, that is, knowledge of essences, but probability or knowledge of appearances. In a letter to F. Liceti (1640) he states his aims: "Aussi n'allez pas vous imaginer . . . que je tienne pour entièrement assuré tout ce que j'aurai à exposer en divers endroits, car partout où c'est moi qui parle, mon intention n'est pas d'aller au delà des limites de la probabilité. La vérité, comme disait Platon, je laisse aux Dieux et aux enfants des Dieux." (Also do not think . . . that I consider as entirely certain everything which I will set forth in various passages, for whenever I am the speaker my intention is not to go beyond the limits of probability. As for truth, as Plato said, I leave it to the Gods and to the children of the Gods.) As quoted by Berr, in *Du scepticisme de Gassendi*, p. 79. Cf. Pintard, *Le Libertinage érudit*, p. 479.

51. See Popkin, *History of Scepticism*, p. 146.

52. In the *Syntagma Philosophiae Epicuri* (1649), he states: Il nous semble qu'il faut suivre une voie moyenne entre les Dogmatiques et les Sceptiques." (It seems to us that you have to take the middle road between the Dogmatists and the Sceptics.) As quoted in Berr, *Du scepticisme de Gassendi*, p. 100. For another discussion of Gassendi's scepticism, see Gaston Sortais, *La Philosophie moderne depuis Bacon jusqu'à Leibniz*, II, 252–57. Sortais's conclusion that Gassendi occupied a middle place between the Sceptics and the Dogmatists agrees with Berr's. See Sortais, II, 256, n. 2.

53. Popkin, *History of Scepticism*, p. 107.

54. Ibid., p. 132.

55. Ibid., p. 143.

56. See ibid., pp. 148–49.

57. Ibid.

58. See Randall, *The Career of Philosophy*, I, 309; Lovejoy, *The Great Chain of Being*, pp. 101–2; Collingwood, *The Idea of Nature*, pp. 96–97.

59. See Collingwood, *The Idea of Nature*, pp. 97–98.

60. See Lovejoy, *The Great Chain of Being*, pp. 102–3. Marjorie Nicolson points out the theological difficulties, incurred by a

belief in the habitability of other globes: the "Special creation" and Christ's sacrifice are questioned. See Nicolson, *A World in the Moon*, pp. 61–62.

61. See Lavers, "La Croyance à l'unité de la science dans 'L'Autre Monde,'" pp. 411–12.

62. Weber, "L'Imagination au service du rationalisme," p. 277.

63. Ibid. An unpublished master's essay comparing the two works includes no detailed discussion of Cyrano's relativism. See Ruth Plaut, "Cyrano's l'Autre Monde and Voltaire's Micromégas: A Confrontation."

64. Busson remarks that Cyrano was one of the first to reject geocentrism and anthropocentrism. See his *Pensée religieuse*, p. 498.

65. Borel, *Discours nouveau*, p. 6.

66. Montaigne, *Apologie*, in *Essais*, I, 493.

67. See ibid., pp. 588–89, 594.

68. See ibid., p. 640.

69. See *Micromégas*, in Voltaire, *Romans et contes*, p. 122.

70. See Lachèvre, I, 71, n. 1. Other uses of this theme are cited by Weber in his edition of Cyrano's *Autre Monde*, p. 127, n. 2.

71. René Jasinski, "Sur les *deux infinis* de Pascal," *Revue d'histoire de la philosophie et d'histoire générale de la civilisation*, N.S. Fasc. 2 (April 1933), 134–59.

72. See Spink, *French Free-Thought*, p. 63. Rochot thinks that Cyrano was influenced by Gassendi's *Animadversiones* of 1649. See Rochot, *Les Travaux de Gassendi*, p. ix, n. a.

73. Jasinski, "Sur les *deux infinis* de Pascal," p. 152: "Rien n'empêche qu'il soit une telle infinité de mondes. . . . Aucune raison ne s'oppose à ce qu'il existe d'autres mondes, les uns semblables au nôtre, les autres différents: il en peut être d'égaux, de plus grands ou de plus petits; il en peut être qui aient les mêmes parties ou disposées dans le même ordre; il en peut être qui en aient d'autres, ou disposées dans un ordre différent. . . . " (Nothing prevents there existing such an infinity of worlds. . . . No reason can be brought to bear against the existence of other worlds, some similar to ours, others different; there can be ones of the same size, larger, or smaller; there

can be some which have the same particles, or arranged in the same order; there can be some which have others, or arranged in a different order. . . .) Quoted from the *Syntagma philosophiae Epicuri* (1649). The French translations quoted from this article are Jasinski's.

74. Ibid., p. 153.

75. Mersenne had used a Pascalian "disproportion" as a commentary on human ignorance. In his *Quaestiones in Genesim* (1623), the sceptic says: "Ce que nous voyons n'est que comme un point au respect de toute la terre, sur laquelle nous vivons comme de pauvres petits Vermisseaux." (What we see is like a mere point in comparison to the entire earth, on which we live like miserable little Earthworms.) As quoted in Berr, *Du scepticisme de Gassendi*, p. 42.

76. Jasinski, "Sur les *deux infinis* de Pascal," pp. 155–56. As quoted from the *Syntagma*, Preface to the *Physics.*

77. Ibid., pp. 143–44.

78. Petro Borello, *De vero telescopii inventore, cum brevi omnium conspiciliorum historia* (The Hague, 1655). *Observationum Microcospicarum centuria* (The Hague, 1656). Cf. Jasinski, "Sur les *deux infinis* de Pascal," pp. 142, 146. It is not unreasonable to assume that if Cyrano knew one work of Borel's, he could have known others. Although the treatise on the telescope was published in the year of Cyrano's death, and the one on the microscope a year later, the texts could have been available before, as in the case of the *Discours nouveau.*

79. Cyrano definitely knew and used the work of Sorel. Lachèvre cites Hortensius's speech in *Francion* on the world in the moon, which was unquestionably utilized by Cyrano. See Lachèvre, I, xlvii. Lachèvre also lists Sorel's romance among Cyrano's sources, p. L. Cyrano himself acknowledges his debt to Sorel's *Francion* in borrowing the idea of using poetry as money. See Lachèvre, I, 43. Other borrowings are listed both by Lachèvre in his footnotes passim and by Émile Roy in his *La Vie et les oeuvres de Charles Sorel*, pp. 386–87, n. 2.

80. Roy, *Charles Sorel*, pp. 378–85.

81. Ibid., pp. 384–85.

82. Ibid., p. 385. Ernest Jovy cites Cyrano's passage as an antecedent of the "infiniment petit" (infinitely small) in the *Pensées*. See Jovy, *Études pascaliennes*, VIII, 47–48.

83. Roy, *Charles Sorel*, p. 382.

84. Ibid., p. 385.

85. See the *Apologie*, in *Essais*, I, 504. Montaigne quotes Ecclesiastes to show man's equality with his fellow creatures. "Nous ne sommes ny au dessus, ny au dessoubs du reste: tout ce qui est sous le Ciel, dit le sage, court une loy et fortune pareille." (We are neither above nor below the rest: all that is under heaven, says the sage, incurs the same law and the same fortune.) (*Apology*, in *The Complete Essays of Montaigne*, trans. Frame, p. 336.)

86. Montaigne places the earth in the lowest part of the heavens, "au dernier estage du logis et le plus esloigné de la voûte céleste" (Apologie, p. 496) (on the lowest story of the house and the farthest from the vault of heaven) (*Apology*, p. 330). See also Lovejoy, *The Great Chain of Being*, p. 102.

87. See Lachèvre, I, p. 71, n. 1.

88. Mongrédien, *Cyrano de Bergerac*, p. 186.

89. Charles Sorel, *Histoire comique de Francion*, ed. Émile Roy, vol. 4, Bk. XI, p. 12.

90. Cf. Mongrédien, *Cyrano de Bergerac*, p. 188.

91. Blaise Pascal, *Pensées*, ed. Brunschvicg, No. 72, p. 88.

92. Mounin, "Cyrano de Bergerac et Pascal," p. 77.

93. See ibid., p. 76.

94. See ibid., p. 77.

95. Wilkins, *Discovery*, p. 50.

96. Ibid., pp. 104–5.

97. See Nicolson, *The Breaking of the Circle*, pp. 168–69.

98. See Popkin, *History of Scepticism*, pp. 87–88.

99. See ibid., pp. 64–66.

100. See ibid., p. 64. Camus's conclusion that if Copernicus can question the centuries-old Ptolemaic system then we must doubt the veracity of any principle is typical of this reaction. Montaigne's conclusion is similar. See the *Apologie*, in *Essais*, I, 640.

101. See the *Apologie*, in *Essais*, I, 568.

102. Albert Thibaudet, "Reflexions sur la littérature: le roman de l'aventure," *Nouvelle Revue française*, XIII (1919), 608–9. Cf. Lavers, "La Croyance à l'unité de la science dans 'L'Autre Monde,'" p. 409.

CHAPTER 4. SATIRICAL RELATIVISM: MAN AND SOCIETY

1. A passage in Cyrano's letter "Contre le caresme" in which he satirizes Ash Wednesday also calls to mind the *Lettres persanes*: "Ce Turc qui racontoit au Grand Seigneur que tous les François devenoient foux à certain jour, et qu'un peu de certaine poudre appliquée sur le front les faisoit rentrer dans leur bon sens, n'estoit point de mon opinion; car je soûtiens qu'ils ne sont jamais plus sages que cette journée" (II, 161). (The Turk who related to the Lord that all Frenchmen went mad on a certain day, and that a smudge of a certain powder applied to their foreheads made them come to their senses, was not at all of my opinion; for I maintain that they are never wiser than on that day.) Leo Jordan is also reminded of the *Lettres persanes* in reflecting on Cyrano's aim of eliminating national prejudices. See Jordan, "Cyrano Bergerac und Montaigne," p. 388.

2. David Worcester, *The Art of Satire*, p. 80. Cyrano's use of this device is mentioned by Elsie Nolan in her study of satire in Cyrano's works. She discusses various ways in which the device is exploited by Cyrano but does not treat it in connection with relativism. See Elsie Nolan, "Satire and Related Ironical Devices in the Works of Cyrano de Bergerac," Master's Essay (New York: Columbia University, 1947).

3. Worcester, *The Art of Satire*, p. 80.

4. This device is noted by Brun, Mongrédien, and Weber, who do not attempt, however, to relate it to Cyrano's relativism. See Brun, *Cyrano* (1893), p. 280; Mongrédien, *Cyrano de Bergerac*, p. 178; Weber, "L'Imagination au service du rationalisme," p. 276. That the

device is representative of one of Cyrano's favorite ideas is attested to by a brief discussion in the *Pédant joué* (II, 18; Act I, scene ii) of a "monde renversé" (world in reverse).

5. The same idea appears in Cyrano's letter "A M. de Gerzan sur son *Triomphe des femmes.*" He praises women as bearers of life and suggests his disapproval of men as bearers of swords: "Que si, comme nous, elles ne vaquent pas au massacre des hommes; si elles ont horreur de porter au costé ce qui nous fait détester un Bourreau, c'est à cause qu'il seroit honteux que celles qui nous donnent à la lumière portassent de quoy nous la ravir; et par ce aussi qu'il est beaucoup plus honneste de suer à la construction qu'à la destruction de son espèce" (II, 219). (If they are not occupied with slaughtering men the way we are, if they have a horror of carrying at their side that which makes us hate the Executioner, it is because it would be disgraceful for those who have brought us into the light of day to carry the wherewithal to rob us of it; and also because it is much more decent to sweat over the construction rather than the destruction of one's species.)

6. Brun, *Cyrano* (1893), p. 270. Jordan points to the influence of Montaigne here. See Jordan, "Cyrano Bergerac und Montaigne," p. 391.

7. See Béroalde de Verville, *Le Moyen de parvenir*, ed. Charles Royer, I, 39–40. John Dunlop finds here a satirical treatment of a passage in Charron's *De la Sagesse*. See John Dunlop, *The History of Fiction*, p. 396.

8. See Lachèvre, I, li–lvii. Cyrano was not, however, displaced in the will by any elder brother, all three of whom had died young. Cyrano's father left practically everything he had to a servant.

9. George Boas, *The Happy Beast*, p. 64. The term is Boas's. See also p. 141 for the use of theriophily by seventeenth-century satirists.

10. Lachèvre cites the remark of Jacques Denis that this passage is meant as a satire on the lines of Ovid: "Os homini sublime dedit, caelumque tueri/ Jussit, et erectos ad sidera tollere vultus."

(He gave man an uplifted face, and ordered him to gaze at the sky and to lift his face straight up to the stars.) Lachèvre also observes that Cyrano's dislike of final causes is obvious here. Lachèvre, I, 53, n. 1. Leo Jordan points out the similarity between these lines of the *Estats de la lune* and a passage from Montaigne's *Apologie*. See Jordan, "Cyrano Bergerac und Montaigne," p. 393. The spirit of Cyrano's passage is in direct contradiction to the passage in Borel's *Discours nouveau* in which the author compares men who will not accept the plurality of worlds to beasts. They are like "bestes brutes, qui mangent les fruits des arbres sans jamais regarder de quel costé ils leur viennent, car les hommes ont esté logez au monde pour contempler les merveilles que Dieu leur met devant les yeux, et à laquelle fin il leur a donné la face en haut pour regarder vers le Ciel, mais ils ne veulent point se servir de leurs dons ny esplucher le lieu de leur habitation" (brute beasts, who eat the fruit of the trees without ever looking to see from what direction they fall, for men have been placed in the world to contemplate the wonders which God puts before their eyes, and to which end he has turned their faces upward to look at the sky, but they do not wish to use their gifts nor examine their dwelling place). Borel, *Discours nouveau*, p. 6. Cyrano could well have had this comparison in mind when composing his satire by inversion.

11. Leonora Cohen Rosenfield, *From Beast-Machine to Man-Machine*, pp. 114–15.

12. Ibid., p. 117.

13. See Boas, *The Happy Beast*, pp. 9–11.

14. Rosenfield, *From Beast-Machine to Man-Machine*, p. 7.

15. See ibid., p. 49. For a detailed discussion of this problem in Cartesian thought, see Albert G. A. Balz, "Cartesian Doctrine and the Animal Soul: An Incident in the Formation of the Modern Philosophical Tradition," in his *Cartesian Studies*, pp. 142–46.

16. Cf. Rosenfield, *From Beast-Machine to Man-Machine*, p. 47. For the argument of the *fils de l'hôte*, see Lachèvre, I, 93–94.

17. Boas, *The Happy Beast*, pp. 84–85. Boas quotes (in English) the following passage from the fifth part of the *Discours de*

la méthode: Après l'erreur de ceux qui nient Dieu . . . il n'y en a point qui éloigne plutôt les esprits foibles du droit chemin de la vertu, que d'imaginer que l'âme des bêtes soit de même nature que la nôtre, et que par conséquent nous n'avons rien à craindre ni à espérer après cette vie, non plus que les mouches et les fourmis; au lieu que lorsqu'on sait combien elles diffèrent, on comprend beaucoup mieux les raisons qui prouvent que la nôtre est d'une nature entièrement indépendante du corps, et par conséquent qu'elle n'est point sujette à mourir avec lui; puis, d'autant qu'on ne voit point d'autres causes qui la détruisent, on est naturellement porté à juger de là qu'elle est immortelle." (After the error of those who deny the existence of God . . . there is none that is more powerful in leading feeble minds astray from the straight path of virtue than the supposition that the soul of the brutes is of the same nature with our own; and consequently that after this life, we have nothing to hope for or fear, more than flies or ants; in place of which, when we know how far they differ we much better comprehend the reasons which establish that the soul is of a nature wholly independent of the body, and that consequently it is not liable to die with the latter, and, finally, because no other causes are observed capable of destroying it, we are naturally led thence to judge that it is immortal.) Descartes, *Oeuvres,* I, 189–90. Cf. Boas, *The Happy Beast,* pp. 84–85.

18. See Rosenfield, *From Beast-Machine to Man-Machine,* p. 112.

19. Mrs. Rosenfield also notes that in his satire Cyrano is following freethinking tradition. See ibid., p. 117.

20. There is perhaps a reference here to the decree published in 1624 by the *parlement* of Paris forbidding teachings contesting those of Aristotle. Cf. Dunlop, *The History of Fiction,* p. 395, and Rochot, *Les Travaux de Gassendi,* p. 9.

21. Descartes, *Discours de la méthode,* p. 187.

22. "Mais, de bonne foi, est-il possible que les perroquets ou les pies pussent imiter nos sons, s'ils n'entendaient et s'ils n'apercevaient par leurs organes ce que nous disons . . . pourquoi ne voulez-vous pas qu'ils prononcent ce qu'ils désirent, savoir leur nourriture

qu'ils viennent à bout d'obtenir de leur maître par ce moyen." (But, in good faith, is it possible that parrots or magpies could imitate our sounds, if they did not understand and perceive through their organs what we say ... why do you not allow that they speak their desires, to wit their food which they succeed in obtaining from their master by this means.) Henry More, Letter to Descartes of 11 December 1648, in Descartes, *Correspondance*, ed. Charles Adam and Gérard Milhaud, VIII, 103. Montaigne had also thought that the ability of parrots and magpies, among other birds, to imitate human speech was evidence that they possess some kind of reason. See the *Apologie*, in *Essais*, I, 510.

23. Descartes, *Discours de la méthode*, p. 186.

24. Ibid., p. 188.

25. Balz points out, however, that instinct is often conceived of in the same way by both opponents and advocates of Cartesian automatism. Balz, "Cartesian Doctrine and the Animal Soul," in his *Cartesian Studies*, p. 140.

26. Boas, *The Happy Beast*, p. 25.

27. Montaigne, *Apologie*, in *Essais*, I, 497. *Apology*, in *The Complete Essays of Montaigne*, trans. Frame, p. 331.

28. *Apologie*, p. 594. *Apology*, p. 397.

29. *Apologie*, p. 514. *Apology*, p. 343.

30. *Apologie*, p. 545. *Apology*, p. 363.

31. Pierre Villey, *Les Sources et l'évolution des essais de Montaigne*, II, 163–209. Cf. Montaigne, *Apologie*, in *Essais*, I, 678.

32. Villey, *Essais de Montaigne*, p. 204. See the *Apologie*, p. 678. *Apology*, p. 455.

33. Villey, *Essais de Montaigne*, p. 209.

34. Cf. Weber, "L'Imagination au service du rationalisme," p. 277.

35. Weber remarks that intellectual freedom is one of the causes championed by Cyrano: "C'est bien cette liberté de pensée que Cyrano proclame, comme une condition indispensable à l'exercice de toute philosophie." (It is freedom of thought which Cyrano proclaims as an indispensable condition for the practice of any philosophy.) Ibid., p. 276.

36. Eddy, *Gulliver's Travels*, p. 42.

37. Ibid., p. 187.

38. Lavers, "La Croyance à l'unité de la science dans 'L'Autre Monde,'" p. 411.

39. See Lachèvre, I, 52, variant f.

40. It is noteworthy that the bird explaining the "langue matrice" to Dyrcona is a phoenix (I, 148), who could very naturally represent the principle of the continuity of matter.

41. Francisque Bouillier notes that Descartes had a "moral" reason, as well as metaphysical, physiological, and theological ones, for advocating animal automatism, which was that with his theory man could kill animals with a clear conscience. See Bouillier, *Histoire de la philosophie cartésienne*, I, 140. The cruelty of Cartesians to animals is satirized by Father Daniel in the fourth part of his *Voyage au monde de Descartes* (1690). See Bouillier, *Histoire de la philosophie cartesienne*, p. 146.

42. The implications are in effect quite pointed, since it is the high priest himself who uses the trumpet.

43. Montaigne, *Apologie*, in *Essais*, I, 668. *Apology*, in *The Complete Essays of Montaigne*, trans. Frame, p. 448.

44. Brun considers this idea an imitation of Seneca and his school. See Brun, *Cyrano* (1893), p. 273.

45. Weber notes the effectiveness of the device in this passage. See Cyrano de Bergerac, *L'Autre Monde*, ed. Weber, p. 243, n. 1.

46. See Bouillier, *Histoire de la philosophie cartésienne*, p. 153.

47. Balz states that none of the parties to the beast-machine controversy went so far as to deny a human soul, and that the whole dispute preceded the concept of a universal materialism. Balz, "Cartesian Doctrine and the Animal Soul," in his *Cartesian Studies*, pp. 118–19. By these facts may be measured the audacity of the *Autre Monde* of Cyrano, who did not bluntly deny humans a soul, but who in refuting immortality and expounding the unity of matter came very close to the eighteenth-century materialists' philosophical outlook.

48. Spink, *French Free-Thought*, p. 64.

49. See Brun, *Cyrano* (1893), p. 343; Henri Weber, "L'Imagination au service du rationalisme," p. 278.

50. Mongrédien, *Cyrano de Bergerac*, p. 195.

51. Leonard Marsak remarks that Fontenelle's notion of the plurality of worlds "served admirably well" to express his attitudes of scepticism and relativism in the *Entretiens sur la pluralité des mondes*. See Marsak, *Bernard de Fontenelle: The Idea of Science in the French Enlightenment, Transactions of the American Philosophical Society*, N.S. Vol. 49, Part 7 (1959), 19.

52. Cyrano de Bergerac, *L'Autre Monde*, ed. Weber, p. 235, n. 1.

53. Howard G. Harvey, "Cyrano de Bergerac and the Question of Human Liberties," *Symposium*, IV (May and Nov. 1950), 127.

54. Ibid., pp. 127–28.

55. Eddy, *Gulliver's Travels*, pp. 20–21.

56. Ibid., p. 181.

57. Toldo, "Voyages merveilleux," p. 305.

58. Rosenfield, *From Beast-Machine to Man-Machine*, p. 114.

59. See Cyrano de Bergerac, *L'Autre Monde*, ed. Weber, p. 32. Bridenne concurs in this judgment, although he feels that the *Estats du soleil* is a representation of "une démocratie complète ayant nominalement à sa tête un roi élu" (a complete democracy having as its nominal head an *elected* king). Bridenne, "A la Recherche du vrai Cyrano de Bergerac," pp. 170, 172 (italics not mine).

60. Cyrano de Bergerac, *L'Autre Monde*, ed Weber, p. 34.

61. Cyrano de Bergerac, *Voyages*, ed. Richard Aldington, p. 35.

62. Mongrédien, *Cyrano de Bergerac*, p. 178.

63. Ibid.

64. As Lachèvre has pointed out, this is a contemporary allusion to the *droit de chasse,* an aristocratic privilege especially burdensome to the peasants who were thereby denied the right to kill game even on their own ground. See Lachèvre, I, 159, n. 2, and John Lough, *An Introduction to Seventeeth Century France*, pp. 8–9.

65. Cyrano also protests against war in his "Lettre contre l'automne." See Cyrano de Bergerac, *Oeuvres diverses*, ed. Lachèvre, p. 19.

66. In his letter "Sur le faux Bruit qui courut de la mort de Monsieur le Prince," Cyrano, à la Rochefoucauld, declares that For-

tune plays the leading role in government, and then again stresses the presence of servitude: "Et puis, tous les Royaumes ont des intelligences qui les gouvernent? Non, non, le Hasard jouë nos entreprises, le Sort entraisne aveuglement tout ce qui vit sous les Estoilles; et les Monarques qui comptent leurs Esclaves en comptant leurs Sujets, sont eux-mesmes les plus gourmandez Esclaves de la Fortune" (II, 222). (And then, do all Kingdoms have intelligences governing them? No, no, Chance maneuvers all our undertakings; Fate sweeps along blindly everything living under the Stars; and Monarchs who count all their Subjects as so many Slaves are themselves the most glutted Slaves of Fortune.)

67. Denis, "Sceptiques ou libertins," pp. 245 ff.

68. See Brun, *Cyrano* (1893), p. 143. Cf. Lachèvre, II, 278.

69. Brun, *Cyrano* (1893), p. 143.

70. See, for example, Ernest Lavisse, *Histoire de France depuis les origines jusqu'à la révolution*, 27–29, 59–60. See also Lough, *Seventeenth Century France*, pp. 1–26. The question of taxes was one of the major preoccupations of the public during the Fronde. See Henri Sée, "Les Idées politiques à l'époque de la Fronde," *Revue d'histoire moderne et contemporaine*, 3 (1901–1902), 733.

71. For a serious comment on the style of the letters, as well as a conscientious discussion of the various editions, see Cyrano de Bergerac, *Lettres*, ed. Luciano Erba, pp. ix–xlix.

72. François Davenne in his treatise *De la puissance qu'ont les rois sur les peuples et du pouvoir des peuples sur les rois* (1650) makes a similar statement of the people's rights: "Les rois n'ont pas fait les peuples, mais les peuples, les rois; les princes ne sont que ce que les hommes veulent qu'ils soient." (Kings have not made peoples, but peoples, kings; princes are only what men want them to be.) As quoted in Sée, "Les Idées politiques de la Fronde," p. 720.

73. One of the principal complaints of the *Frondeurs*, aimed at Mazarin, was the authority of the royal favorites. See Henri Sée, "Les Idées politiques de la Fronde," pp. 726–27.

74. Scarron's poem was in fact a rather shocking lampoon on the cardinal, outdoing even Cyrano's "Ministre d'état flambé" in its harshness. See Scarron, *Oeuvres*, I, 283–96.

75. For a clear presentation of the events of the Fronde, see Lavisse, *Histoire de France*, VII, 42–65.

76. On the other hand, Sée points out that there began a revival of promonarchist sentiment around 1651, especially after the proclamation of the young Louis XIV's majority on Sept. 7, 1651. The Cardinal de Retz, for instance, who prior to this time had been hostile to the court, now defended royal power. See Henri Sée, "Les Idées politiques de la Fronde," pp. 724–25. Nevertheless, it is doubtful that Cyrano was eager to have it bruited about at this time that such vehement diatribes against the people as are found in the "Lettre contre les frondeurs" represented his true feelings.

77. Mongrédien, *Cyrano de Bergerac*, p. 199.

78. For a slightly different interpretation of these lines, see Ramos, *Cyrano, Auteur tragique*, p. 36.

79. Sée, "Les Idées politiques de la Fronde," p. 714.

80. Ibid., pp. 716–28.

81. Ibid., pp. 737–38.

82. Lavisse, *Histoire de France*, VII, 40.

83. Ibid., p. 64.

CONCLUSION

1. Lachèvre defines seventeenth-century libertinism as: "l'esprit d'indépendance et d'hostilité à la tradition et aussi le refus de s'assujettir aux croyances et aux pratiques de la religion." (the spirit of independence and hostility to tradition and also the refusal to subject oneself to the beliefs and practices of religion). Lachèvre, *Les Successeurs de Cyrano de Bergerac*, p. vi.

2. Ibid., p. vii.

3. Fellows, "Cyrano de Bergerac," p. 286.

4. For the history of the different editions of Cyrano's works see Lachèvre, I, xcvii–cxii.

5. See ibid., pp. cvii–cviii.

6. Cf. Lachèvre, *Les Successeurs de Cyrano de Bergerac*, p. vii: "Cyrano de Bergerac . . . n'a pas eu de disciples" (. . . had no disciples).

7. See ibid.

8. See Brun, *Cyrano* (1893), pp. 284–85.

SELECTIVE BIBLIOGRAPHY

Adam, Antoine. *Histoire de la littérature française au XVIIe siècle.* 5 vols. Paris: Éditions Domat, 1948–1956.

Armitage, Angus. *The World of Copernicus.* New York: New American Library, 1947.

Atkinson, Geoffroy. *The Extraordinary Voyage in French Literature before 1700.* New York: Columbia University Press, 1920.

Bacon, Francis. *New Atlantis,* in *Ideal Empires and Republics,* ed. Charles M. Andrews. New York: Aladdin Book Co., 1901.

Balz, Albert G. A. "Cartesian Doctrine and the Animal Soul: An Incident in the Formation of the Modern Philosophical Tradition," in his *Cartesian Studies.* New York: Columbia University Press, 1951.

Bernardin, Napoléon Maurice. "Cyrano de Bergerac," in his *Hommes et moeurs au dix-septième siècle.* Paris: Société française d'Imprimerie et de Librairie, 1900.

Bernier, François. *Abrégé de la philosophie de Gassendi.* 2d ed., 7 vols. Lyons: Anisson, Posuel & Rigaud, 1684.

Béroalde de Verville. *Le Moyen de parvenir,* ed. Charles Royer. 2 vols. Paris: Alphonse Lemerre, 1896.

SELECTIVE BIBLIOGRAPHY

Berr, Henri. *Du scepticisme de Gassendi,* trans. Bernard Rochot, Paris: Centre international de synthèse, Albin Michel, 1960.

Blanchet, Léon. *Campanella.* New York: Burt Franklin, [1963?].

Blanchot, Maurice. "L'Homme noir du XVIIᵉ siècle," *Saisons,* No. 2 (1946), 69–80.

Boas, George. *Dominant Themes of Modern Philosophy.* New York: Ronald Press, 1957.

————. *The Happy Beast.* New York: Octagon Books, 1966.

Boase, Alan M. *The Fortunes of Montaigne, A History of the Essays in France (1580–1669).* London: Methuen, 1935.

Borel, Pierre. *Discours nouveau prouvant la pluralité des mondes.* Geneva, 1657.

Bouillier, Francisque. *Histoire de la philosophie cartésienne.* 2 vols. Paris: Durand; Lyons: Brun, 1854.

Brandwajn, Rachmiel. *Cyrano de Bergerac.* Warsaw: Państwowe Wydawnictwo Naukowe, 1960.

Brett, George Sidney. *The Philosophy of Gassendi.* London: Macmillan, 1908.

Bridenne, Jean-Jacques. "A la Recherche du vrai Cyrano de Bergerac," *Information littéraire,* Vᵉ année (1953), 169–76.

————. "Cyrano de Bergerac et la science aéronautique," *Revue des sciences humaines,* N.S. Fasc. 75 (July–Sept. 1954), 241–58.

Brun, Pierre. *Savinien de Cyrano Bergerac, gentilhomme parisien.* Paris: H. Daragon, 1909.

————. *Savinien de Cyrano Bergerac, sa vie et ses oeuvres.* Paris: Armand Colin, 1893.

Bury, John B. *The Idea of Progress.* New ed. New York: Dover, 1955.

Busson, Henri. *La Pensée religieuse française de Charron à Pascal.* Paris: J. Vrin, 1933.

————. *Les Sources et le développement du rationalisme dans la littérature française de la renaissance (1533–1601).* Paris: Letouzey et Ané, 1922.

Campanella, Tommaso. *The City of the Sun,* in *Ideal Empires and Republics,* ed. Charles M. Andrews. New York: Aladdin Book Co., 1901.

————. *The Defense of Galileo*, trans. and ed. Grant McColley. *Smith College Studies in History*, XXII, nos. 3–4 (April–July 1937).

————. *Oeuvres choisies*, ed. Louise Colet. Paris: Lavigne, 1844.

Chinard, Gilbert. *L'Amérique et le rêve exotique dans la littérature française au XVIIe et au XVIIIe siècle*. Paris: Librairie Hachette, 1913.

Collingwood, Robin G. *The Idea of Nature*. Oxford: Clarendon Press, 1945.

Cusanus, Nicholas. *Of Learned Ignorance*, trans. Fr. Germain Heron. London: Routledge & Kegan Paul, 1954.

Cyrano de Bergerac, Savinien. *L'Autre Monde, ou Les États et empires de la lune*, ed. Leo Jordan. *Gesellschaft für Romanische Literatur*, 23 (Dresden, 1910).

————. *L'Autre Monde: Les États et empires de la lune, Les États et empires du soleil*, ed. Henri Weber. Paris: Éditions sociales, 1959.

————. *The Comical History of the States and Empires of the Worlds of the Moon and Sun*, trans. A. Lovell. London: Printed for Henry Rhodes, 1687.

————. *Histoire comique des État et Empire* [sic] *de la lune et du soleil*, eds. Claude Mettra, Jean Suyeux. Paris: Jean-Jacques Pauvert, 1962.

————. *Lettres*, ed. Luciano Erba. Milan: Edizioni di Vanni Scheiwiller, 1965.

————. *Oeuvres*, ed. P. L. Jacob [Paul Lacroix]. New ed. Paris: Adolphe Delahays, 1858.

————. *Oeuvres*, ed. Le Blanc. Paris: Victor Lecou; Toulouse: Librairie centrale, 1855.

————. *Oeuvres comiques, galantes et littéraires*, ed. P. L. Jacob [Paul Lacroix]. New ed. Paris: Garnier, 1900.

————. *Oeuvres diverses*, ed. Frédéric Lachèvre. New ed. Paris: Garnier, 193[?].

————. *Oeuvres libertines*, ed. Frédéric Lachèvre. 2 vols. Paris: Édouard Champion, 1921.

SELECTIVE BIBLIOGRAPHY

————. *Le Pédant joué*, ed. M. C. H. L. N. Bernard. Boston: Jean de Peiffer, 1899.

————. *Voyages to the Moon and the Sun*, ed. and trans. Richard Aldington. New York: Orion Press, 1962.

Dassoucy, Charles Coypeau. *Les Pensées dans le Saint-Office de Rome*, in his *Aventures burlesques*, ed. Émile Colombey. New ed. Paris: Garnier, 1876.

Delvaille, Jules. *Essai sur l'histoire de l'idée de progrès jusqu'à la fin du XVIIIᵉ siècle*. Paris: Félix Alcan, 1910.

Denis, Jacques. "Sceptiques ou libertins de la première moitié du XVIIᵉ siècle," in *Mémoires de l'Académie nationale des sciences, arts et belles-lettres de Caen*. Caen: F. Le Blanc-Hardel, 1884.

Descartes, René. *Correspondance*, eds. Charles Adam, Gérard Milhaud. 8 vols. Paris: Presses Universitaires de France, 1963.

————. *Oeuvres*, ed. Victor Cousin. 11 vols. *Discours de la méthode* and *Méditations* in Vol. I; *Les Principes de la philosophie* in Vol. III; *Le Monde, ou Traité de la lumière* in Vol. IV. Paris: F. G. Levrault, 1824.

Dictionnaire de l'Académie française. Paris: Jean Baptiste Coignard, 1694.

Dunlop, John. *The History of Fiction*. 3d ed. London: Longman, Brown, Green, and Longmans, 1845.

Eddy, William. *Gulliver's Travels, A Critical Study*. Princeton: Princeton University Press, 1923.

Erba, Luciano. "L'Incidenza della magia nell'opera di Cyrano de Bergerac," *Pubblicazioni*. Università Cattolica del sacro cuore (Milan). *Contributi del Seminario de Filologia Moderna*, I (1959), 1–74.

Febvre, Lucien. *Le Problème de l'incroyance au XVIᵉ siècle: la religion de Rabelais*. Rev. ed. Paris: Albin Michel, 1962.

Fellows, Otis E. "Cyrano de Bergerac," in *Encyclopedia of Philosophy*, editor-in-chief Paul Edwards, II, 285–86. 8 vols. New York, Macmillan and The Free Press; London: Collier-Macmillan, 1967.

Flammarion, Camille. *Les Mondes imaginaires et les mondes réels*. 17th ed. Paris: Didier, 1880.

————. *La Pluralité des mondes habités.* Paris: Didier, 1872.

Fournel, Victor. *La Littérature indépendante et les écrivains oubliés.* Paris: Didier, 1862.

Frame, Donald M. "Did Montaigne Betray Sebond?" *Romanic Review,* XXXVIII (Dec. 1947), 297–329.

————. *Montaigne: A Biography.* New York: Harcourt, Brace & World, 1965.

————. *Montaigne's Discovery of Man: The Humanization of a Humanist.* New York: Columbia University Press, 1955.

Gautier, Armand. "Un Précurseur français de la science expérimentale moderne: Jacques Rohault," *Revue générale des sciences pures et appliquées,* 26 (1915), 267–72.

Gautier, Théophile. "Cyrano de Bergerac," in his *Les Grotesques.* New ed. Paris: Michel Lévy Frères, 1856.

Geymonat, Ludovico. *Galileo Galilei,* trans. Stillman Drake. New York: McGraw-Hill, 1965.

Gillot, Hubert. *La Querelle des anciens et des modernes en France.* Paris: Champion, 1914.

Godwin, Bishop Francis. *The Man in the Moone* and *Nuncius Inanimatus,* ed. Grant McColley. *Smith College Studies in Modern Languages,* XIX (Oct. 1937–July 1938).

Gourmont, Rémy de. "Le Vrai Cyrano de Bergerac," in his *Promenades littéraires.* 3d series, 5th ed. Paris: Mercure de France, 1916.

Gove, Philip B. *The Imaginary Voyage in Prose Fiction.* New York: Columbia University Press, 1941.

Guéret, Gabriel. *La Guerre des autheurs anciens et modernes.* La Haye: Arnout Leers, le fils, 1671.

Haber, Francis C. *The Age of the World, Moses to Darwin.* Baltimore. Johns Hopkins Press, 1959.

Hadzsits, George Depue. *Lucretius and His Influence.* New York: Longmans, Green and Co., 1935.

Harvey, Howard G. "Cyrano de Bergerac and the Question of Human Liberties," *Symposium,* IV (May and Nov. 1950), 120–30.

Jasinski, René. "Sur les *deux infinis* de Pascal," *Revue d'histoire de la philosophie et d'histoire générale de la civilisation*, N.S. Fasc. 2 (April 1933), 134–59.

Jones, Richard Foster. *Ancients and Moderns: A Study of the Background of the Battle of the Books. Washington Universty Studies*, N.S., No. 6 (St. Louis, 1936).

Jordan, Leo. "Cyrano Bergerac und Montaigne," *Archiv für das Studium der neuren Sprachen und Literaturen*, 8° Bd. 135, N.S. Bd. 35 (1916), 386–95.

Jovy, Ernest. *Études pascaliennes*, VIII. 9 vols. Paris: J. Vrin, 1932.

Juppont, A. "L'Oeuvre scientifique de Cyrano de Bergerac," *Mémoires de l'Académie des sciences, inscriptions et belles-lettres de Toulouse*, 10ᵉ série, tome VII. Toulouse: Imprimerie Douladoure-Privat, 1907.

Kepler, *Dream*, ed. John Lear; trans. Patricia F. Kirkwood. Berkeley: University of California Press, 1965.

Kernan, Alvin. *The Cankered Muse*. New Haven and London: Yale University Press, 1959.

Koyré, Alexandre. *From the Closed World to the Infinite Universe*. Baltimore: Johns Hopkins Press, 1957.

Lachèvre, Frédéric. "Paul Lacroix et Cyrano de Bergerac, l'édition originale du Voyage dans la lune (1657)," in his *Mélanges sur le libertinage au XVIIᵉ siècle*. Paris: Champion, 1920.

———. *Les Successeurs de Cyrano de Bergerac*. Paris: Champion, 1922.

La Mothe Le Vayer, François de. *La Physique du Prince*, in his *Oeuvres*, II. 7 vols. New ed. Dresden: Michel Groell, 1756–1759.

Lancaster, Henry Carrington. *A History of French Dramatic Literature in the Seventeenth Century*. 2 vols. Baltimore: Johns Hopkins Press, 1936.

Lange, Frederick Albert. *The History of Materialism*, trans. Ernest Chester Thomas. London: Kegan Paul, Trench, Trubner; New York: Harcourt, Brace, 1925.

Lanius, Edward W. *Cyrano de Bergerac and the Universe of the Imagination*. Geneva: Librairie Droz, 1967.

Lavers, A. "La Croyance à l'unité de la science dans 'L'Autre Monde' de Cyrano de Bergerac," *Cahiers du sud*, vol. 45, no. 349 (March 1959), 406–16.

Lavisse, Ernest. *Histoire de France depuis les origines jusqu'à la révolution*. 9 vols. Paris: Hachette, 1900–1911.

Lawton, Harold W. "Notes sur Jean Baudoin et sur ses traductions de l'anglais," *Revue de littérature comparée*, VI (1926), 673–81.

Lefèvre, Louis-Raymond. *La Vie de Cyrano de Bergerac*. Paris: Gallimard, 1927.

Loewenstein, A. W. "Die naturphilosophischen Ideen bei Cyrano de Bergerac," *Archiv für Geschichte der Philosophie*, Bd. XVI, N.F. (1903), 27–58.

Lough, John. *An Introduction to Seventeenth Century France*. New York: David McKay, 1954.

Lovejoy, Arthur O. *The Great Chain of Being*. Cambridge: Harvard University Press, 1961.

Lucretius. *On the Nature of Things*, ed. and trans. Cyril Bailey. Oxford: Clarendon Press, 1910.

Mabilleau, Léopold. *Histoire de la philosophie atomistique*. Paris: Félix Alcan, 1895.

Magnon, Jean. *Séjanus*. Paris: Antoine de Sommaville, 1647. (Modern Language Association, French Plays, 17th Century, vol. 115.)

Magy, Henriette. *Le Véritable Cyrano de Bergerac*. Le Rouge et le Noir, 1927.

Mansuy, Abel. "L'Aviation à Varsovie et à Reims au XVIIe siècle et Cyrano de Bergerac," in his *Le Monde slave et les classiques français*. Paris: Champion, 1912.

Marsak, Leonard M. *Bernard de Fontenelle: The Idea of Science in the French Enlightenment. Transactions of the American Philosophical Society*, N.S. Vol. 49, Part 7 (1959).

McColley, Grant. "The Seventeenth-Century Doctrine of a Plurality of Worlds," *Annals of Science*, I (1936), 385–430.

Michaut, Gustave. *La Jeunesse de Molière*. Paris: Hachette, 1923.

SELECTIVE BIBLIOGRAPHY

Mongrédien, Georges. *Cyrano de Bergerac*. Paris: Berger-Levrault, 1964.

Montaigne, Michel de. *The Complete Essays of Montaigne*, trans. Donald M. Frame. Stanford: Stanford University Press, 1965.

————. *Essais*. 2 vols. Paris: Garnier, 1962.

More, Sir Thomas. *Utopia*, in *Ideal Empires and Republics*, ed. Charles M. Andrews. New York: Aladdin Book Co., 1901.

Mounin, Georges. "Cyrano de Bergerac et Pascal," in *Le Préclassicisme français*, ed. Jean Tortel. Paris: Cahiers du sud, 1952.

Mouy, Paul. *Le Développement de la physique cartésienne 1646–1712*. Paris: J. Vrin, 1934.

Nicéron, le R. P. "Savinien Cyrano de Bergerac," in his *Mémoires pour servir à l'histoire des hommes illustres dans la république des lettres*, XXXVI. Paris: Briasson, 1736.

Nicolson, Marjorie Hope. *The Breaking of the Circle*. Rev. ed. New York: Columbia University Press, 1960.

————. *Voyages to the Moon*. New York: Macmillan, 1960.

————. *A World in the Moon*. *Smith College Studies in Modern Languages*, XVII, no. 2 (Jan. 1936).

Nodier, Charles. "Cyrano de Bergerac," *Bulletin du bibliophile*, No. 8, 3e série. Paris: Techener (Oct. 1838), 343–57.

Nolan, Elsie Lucille. "Satire and Related Ironical Devices in the Works of Cyrano de Bergerac." Master's Essay, Columbia University, 1947.

Normano, J. F. "A Neglected Utopian: Cyrano de Bergerac, 1619–1655," *American Journal of Sociology*, XXXVII, No. 3 (Nov. 1931), 454–57.

Nussbaum, Frederick L. *The Triumph of Science and Reason*. New York: Harper and Row, 1953.

Pascal, Blaise. *Pensées*, ed. Brunschvicg. Paris: Garnier, 1958.

Perrens, François Tommy. *Les Libertins en France au XVIIe siècle*. Paris: Léon Chailley, 1896.

Pintard, René. *Le Libertinage érudit dans la première moitié du XVIIe siècle*. 2 vols. Paris: Boivin, 1943.

Plattard, Jean. "Le Système de Copernic dans la littérature française au XVIᵉ siècle," *Revue du seizième siècle*, I (1913), 220–37.

Plaut, Ruth. "Cyrano's L'Autre Monde and Voltaire's Micromégas: A Confrontation." Master's Essay, Columbia University, 1960.

Pomponazzi, Pietro. *Les Causes des merveilles de la nature, ou Les Enchantements*, ed. and trans. Henri Busson. Paris: Éditions Rieder, 1930.

Popkin, Richard H. *The History of Scepticism from Erasmus to Descartes*. Rev. ed. New York: Humanities Press, 1964.

Pujos, Charles. *Le Double visage de Cyrano de Bergerac*. Agen: Éditions de l'Imprimerie Moderne, 1951.

Ramos, Vítor. *Cyrano, Auteur tragique*. São Paulo: Faculdade de Filosofia, Ciências e Letras, de Assis, 1966.

Randall, John H., Jr. *The Career of Philosophy*, Vols. 1 and 2. New York and London: Columbia University Press, 1962.

Rigault, Hippolyte. *Histoire de la Querelle des anciens et des modernes,* in his *Oeuvres complètes*, I. 4 vols. Paris: Hachette, 1859.

Rochot, Bernard. *Les Travaux de Gassendi sur Épicure et sur l'atomisme*. Paris: J. Vrin, 1944.

Rogers, Cameron. *Cyrano: Swordsman, Libertin, and Man of Letters*. New York: Doubleday, Doran & Co., 1929.

Rohault, Jacques. *Traité de physique*. Paris: Charles Savreux, 1671.

Rosenfield, Leonora Cohen. *From Beast-Machine to Man-Machine*. New York: Oxford University Press, 1941.

Roy, Émilie. *La Vie et les oeuvres de Charles Sorel*. Paris: Hachette, 1891.

Sage, Pierre. *Le Préclassicisme,* in *Histoire de la littérature française,* vols. 1 to 10, ed. J. Calvet, III. Paris: del Duca, 1962.

Satyre Ménippée de la vertu du catholicon d'Espagne et de la tenuë des estats de Paris durant la Ligue en l'an 1593. Nouvelles Régions de la lune. [By P. LeRoy, J. Gillot, J. Passerat, N. Rapin, F. Chrestien, and P. Pithon.] Paris, 1593–1595.

Scarron, Paul. *La Mazarinade,* in his *Oeuvres*, I. 7 vols. New ed. Paris: Jean-François Bastien, 1786.

Sée, Henri. "Les Idées politiques à l'époque de la Fronde," *Revue d'histoire moderne et contemporaine*, 3 (1901–1902), 713–38.

Singer, Dorothy W. *Giordano Bruno: His Life and Thought*. New York: Henry Schuman, 1950.

Sorel, Charles. *Bibliothèque françoise*. 2d ed. Paris: Compagnie des Libraires du Palais, 1667.

———. *Histoire comique de Francion*, ed. Émile Roy. 4 vols. Paris: Hachette, 1924–1931.

Sortais, Gaston. *La Philosophie moderne depuis Bacon jusqu'à Leibniz*. 2 vols. Paris: P. Lethielleux, 1920.

Spink, John Stephenson. "Form and Structure: Cyrano de Bergerac's Atomistic Conception of Metamorphosis," in *Literature and Science* (Proceedings of the Sixth Triennial Congress of the International Federation for Modern Languages and Literatures, Oxford, 1954). Oxford: Basil Blackwell, 1955.

———. *French Free-Thought from Gassendi to Voltaire*. London: Athlone Press, 1960.

Stimson, Dorothy. *The Gradual Acceptance of the Copernican Theory of the Universe*. Hanover, New Hampshire, 1917.

Tacitus. *Annals*, in his *Complete Works*, trans. Alfred John Church and William Jackson Brodribb. New York: Random House, 1942.

Thibaudet, Albert. "Réflexions sur la littérature; le roman de l'aventure," *Nouvelle Revue française*, XIII (1919), 597–611.

Thorndike, Lynn. *A History of Magic and Experimental Science*. 8 vols. New York: Columbia University Press, 1958.

Toldo, Pietro. "Les Voyages merveilleux de Cyrano de Bergerac et de Swift et leurs rapports avec l'oeuvre de Rabelais," *Revue des études rabelaisiennes*, IV (1906), 295–334; V (1907), 24–44.

Tristan l'Hermite. *La Mort de Sénèque*, ed. Jacques Madeleine. Paris: Hachette, 1919.

———. *Le Page disgracié*. Paris: Stock, Delamain et Boutelleau, 1946.

Vartanian, Aram. *Diderot and Descartes, A Study of Scientific Naturalism in the Enlightenment*. Princeton: Princeton University Press, 1953.

Villey, Pierre. *Les Sources et l'évolution des essais de Montaigne.* 2 vols. Paris: Hachette, 1908.

Voltaire. *Romans et contes.* Dijon: Librairie Gallimard, 1954.

Weber, Henri. "L'Imagination au service du rationalisme: 'Le Voyage de Cyrano dans la lune,'" *Les Cahiers rationalistes*, no. 167 (Dec. 1957), 270–82.

Whitehead, Alfred North. *Science and the Modern World.* New York and Toronto: New American Library; London: New English Library, 1925.

Wilkins, John. *The Discovery of a New World*, in his *Mathematical and Philosophical Works.* London: Printed for John Nichols, 1708.

Wolf, Abraham. *A History of Science, Technology and Philosophy in the 16th and 17th Centuries.* 2d ed., 2 vols. New York: Harper & Bros., 1950.

Worcester, David. *The Art of Satire.* New York: Russell and Russell, 1940.

INDEX

C

INDEX

Creation, theory of, (*Continued*)
concept of fire, 62, 230n11;
Campanella's view of, 48; La
Mothe Le Vayer's treatment
of, 106–7
Cyrano, Abel de (father), 5, 159
Cyrano de Bergerac, Savinien de,
his place in Quarrel, 1–5, 112–
13, 210–13; as *libertin*, 3–5, 21,
25, 52–54, 106–6, 118–19, 210–
13; his relativism, 3, 37–44, 148–
49, 151, 155–57, 170–71, 189–
90; attacks religion, 3, 13, 26,
31–38, 40–41, 164–67, 185–
86, 197; influenced by Epicu-
rus, 4, 59, 65; his heliocentrism,
4, 55, 72 ff., 97–98, 103–4, 111,
122–23, 211; his materialism, 4,
17–18, 21–23, 31, 47, 55, 71,
79–80, 95–96, 98, 100, 107,
110–11, 181–84, 189, 232n35,
234n46; evaluation of his work,
4–5, 66, 108, 113, 130, 133,
210–13, 216n13; his use of satire, 4–5, 9–13, 45, 48, 52;
biographical notes on, 5–7,
216n21; influences Molière, 6;
influenced by Gassendi, 6, 56,
62, 79, 99–101, 107, 133, 145,
147, 164, 233n40; publishers
of, 7–8; his treatment of Creation theory, 10–11, 13, 20–21,
56, 104–6; his naturalism, 12,
16–17, 20, 47, 111; his rationalism, 12, 14–17, 26, 31, 104,
114–16, 127–32, 155, 172, 179–
84, 197; influenced by Descartes, 14, 67, 77, 79, 103,

106–8, 133–34, 211; his power
of imagination theory, 15–19;
influenced by Pomponazzi, 17–
20; influenced by Montaigne,
17, 118–19, 129; his rejection
of occult powers (demons, sorcery, and witchcraft) and superstition, 19, 31–41, 43, 46–
47, 54; his atheism, 20–21, 24–
27, 29–32, 52–53; his atomism,
21, 24, 47, 56 ff., 99–102, 122,
175–76, 183–84, 189, 255n47;
his rejection of immortality and
resurrection, 21–24, 32, 62–63,
164, 178, 181–83, 187, 233n38,
255n47; his theory of the
senses, 21–23, 67–70, 82–83,
102, 121–26, 132, 179–80, 184,
187–89; his stoicism, 23–25,
31, 181; influenced by Lucretius, 24, 56–59, 67–69, 77, 79,
95, 99–102; his Machiavellianism, 25–26, 51, 116–17; influenced by Kepler, 39–40; influenced by Godwin, 42–43;
compared to Wilkins, 43–45,
88–90; influenced by Campanella, 45, 76, 143; his panpsychism, 47; his rejection of anthropocentrism, 48–49, 139–42,
157, 161, 163–65, 169–70,
176–77, 185, 193, 196; his
theory of Providence, 57–58;
his concept of fire, 59–62, 230-
n11; his spontaneous generation concept, 59, 79; his monism, 71, 80, 110, 184; his
microcosm concept, 71, 75–77,

D

INDEX

INDEX